Leadership in the Public Sector

In view of the approaching age of austerity for the public sector, leadership is likely to continue to become a key theme. This edited volume brings together a host of material from the public sector to analyze the issue internationally.

Teelken, Ferlie and Dent lead a team of contributors in examining three key aspects of this increasingly important theme:

- The meaning of public sector leadership, and how this changes in different contexts.
- The implications for leadership style given the growing role of the private sector.
- The response to the leadership issue from professionals moving into senior management roles.

With contributions from respected academics such as Jean-Louis Denis, Mike Reed and Mirko Noordegraaf, this book will be an invaluable supplementary resource for those undertaking studies across public sector management and administration.

Christine Teelken is Associate Professor of Organization Science at VU Amsterdam, the Netherlands.

Ewan Ferlie is Professor of Public Services Management at King's College London, UK.

Mike Dent is Professor of Health Care Organization at Staffordshire University, UK.

'This edited book on leadership in the public sector will undoubtedly be well-thumbed, rather than sit on my book shelf, for both research and teaching purposes. It covers a wide expanse of theoretical and empirical ground, and remains academically rigorous and practically relevant in so doing. It offers: comparison across domains of the public sector, and internationally; encompasses individual, group, organizational and system level analysis; integrates policy and management concerns; is inter-disciplinary in its orientation. I, for one, will be citing its contents in my research publications.'

Graeme Currie, *Professor of Public Management,*
Warwick Business School, UK

'Everyone involved in this wonderful book takes the idea and practice of leadership seriously, developing useful theory through close observation of what people do in organizations. The public sector context is important but not defining, enabling the contributions to speak to all involved in leading. Above all it challenges those who cry "we need more leadership" whenever there is a public sector organizational problem. I'm sure it will become a key text in universities and in government departments around the world.'

Dr Scott Taylor, *Reader in Organizational Behaviour, School*
of Business and Economics, Loughborough University, UK

Leadership in the Public Sector

Promises and pitfalls

Edited by
Christine Teelken, Ewan Ferlie
and Mike Dent

 Routledge
Taylor & Francis Group

LONDON AND NEW YORK

First published 2012
by Routledge
2 Park Square, Milton Park, Abingdon, Oxon OX14 4RN

Simultaneously published in the USA and Canada
by Routledge
711 Third Avenue, New York, NY 10017

Routledge is an imprint of the Taylor & Francis Group, an informa business

© 2012 Christine Teelken, Ewan Ferlie and Mike Dent

British Library Cataloguing in Publication Data
A catalogue record for this book is available from the British Library

Library of Congress Cataloging in Publication Data
Leadership in the public sector: promise and pitfalls/edited by
    Christine Teelken, Ewan Ferlie and Mike Dent.
    p. cm.
    Includes bibliographical references and index.
    1. Leadership. 2. Public administration. I. Teelken, Christine.
    II. Ferlie, Ewan, 1956– III. Dent, Mike, 1944–
    JF1525.L4L43 2012
    352.23'6–dc23   2011046202

ISBN: 978-0-415-59174-4 (hbk)
ISBN: 978-0-203-11976-1 (ebk)

Typeset in Times New Roman
by Florence Production Ltd, Stoodleigh, Devon

MIX
Paper from
responsible sources
FSC
www.fsc.org   FSC® C004839

Printed and bound in Great Britain by the MPG Books Group

For Peter Kragh Jespersen
1946–2010

In memory of his kind and great personality,
his academic leadership and his support for
our EGOS stream – and everything else.

Contents

Tables

Contributors

David Buchanan BA Ph.D. FRSA FCIPD FBAM is Professor of Organizational Behaviour at Cranfield University School of Management. He has a doctorate in Organizational Behaviour from Edinburgh University and is author/co-author of over two dozen books, including *The Sage handbook of organizational research methods* (with Alan Bryman, Sage 2009), and numerous book chapters and articles on organizational behaviour and change. Current projects include a study of changing management roles in health care, and managing change in extreme contexts.

Damien Contandriopoulos Ph.D. is Associate Professor at the Faculty of Nursing, University of Montreal. He is also a member of the FERASI multi-university centre for training and expertise in nursing administration research and co-manager of the policy and ethics axis of the University of Montreal Public Health Research Institute (IRSPUM). His research programme deals with the reciprocal relationships between public policies and organizations in the health field.

Rosemary Deem is Vice Principal (Education) and Professor of Higher Education Management at Royal Holloway, University of London. She is also Visiting Professor of Education at Bristol University and Visiting Professor of Management at Leicester University. From 2001–2009 she was Professor of Education and from 2007–2009 Research Director for the Faculty of Social Sciences and Law, both at the University of Bristol. An Academician of the UK Academy of Social Sciences, Rosemary is a sociologist who has also worked at Loughborough, York, Lancaster, The Open University and the former North Staffordshire Polytechnic. She was a UK Education Research Assessment Exercise panellist in 1996, 2001 and 2008, has twice chaired the British Sociological Association and was Vice-Chair of the Society for Research into Higher Education from 2007–2009. From 2001–2005 she was joint editor of the Blackwells international journal *The Sociological Review* and is currently on the Editorial Board of *Studies in Higher Education, Equal Opportunities International, Higher Education* and *Higher Education Quarterly*.

Jean-Louis Denis Ph.D. is Full Professor at École nationale d'administration publique (ENAP) and holds the Canada Research Chair in Governance and Transformation of Health Organizations and Systems. His current research looks at the integration of care and services, the role of physician leadership in health care improvement, the dynamic of health system reform, and the role of scientific evidence in clinical and managerial innovations. He is a member of the Royal Society of Canada, fellow of the Canadian Academy of Health Sciences and Visiting Professor at Euromed Management (Marseille).

Mike Dent is Professor of Health Care Organisation in the Faculty of Health, Staffordshire University. His main research interests currently are: the comparative study of medical and nursing professions and the management and organization of health care; and the organizational and sociological aspects of health care computing and information systems. His publications include: *Remodelling hospitals and health professions in Europe* (Palgrave Macmillan 2003); *Managing professional identities* (edited with Stephen Whitehead, Routledge 2002); *Gender and the public sector* (edited with Jim Barry and Maggie O'Neill, Routledge 2003); *Questioning the New Public Management* (co-edited with John Chandler and Jim Barry, Avebury 2004); *New Public Management and the new governance* (co-edited with Jim Radcliffe, a special guest section in *Policy and Politics*, 33(4), 2005); and *Changing modes of governance in public sector organizations* (a symposium co-edited with Nicolette van Gestel and Christine Teelken in *Public Administration*, 85(1), 2007).

Jürgen Enders is Professor at the School of Management and Governance and Research Director of CHEPS at the University of Twente, the Netherlands, and a leader in the Institute of Innovation and Governance Studies. His research interests are in the political sociology of higher education and science, organisational change and the academic profession, and higher education and work. He is a member of the Academia Europaea and the German Academe of Science and Engineering, and is also a member of the editorial boards of the book series 'Higher Education Dynamics' and the journal *Higher Education*. He has written and (co-)edited 14 books and published more than 100 articles in books and journals.

Ewan Ferlie is currently Professor of Public Services Management at King's College London. He has published widely on aspects of public service organizations and reorganizing, particularly in relation to health care and universities. He has also been a non-executive member of an English Health Authority.

Louise Fitzgerald is Visiting Professor at Manchester Business School and Emeritus Professor at De Montfort University. She has previously held management posts in the private sector and academic university posts at Warwick, City and De Montfort universities. She is currently working on an SDO-funded project on health care managers' utilization of research evidence. She was, until recently, Academic Lead in the Greater Manchester Collaboration for Leadership in Applied Health Research and Care (CLAHRC). Her research focuses on the implementation of organizational change and innovations in complex organizations, and on issues in knowledge exchange.

Ian Kirkpatrick is Professor in Work and Organisation at Leeds University Business School and Director of the Leeds Social Sciences Institute. His research interests include: management of change in professional organizations, restructuring of public services, flexible employment and comparative developments in human resource management (HRM). He has published widely in a range of leading academic journals including *Public Administration, Organization, British Journal of Management* and *Work, Employment and Society*. Ian is also co-author of two recent books: *The new managerialism and public service professions* (Palgrave Macmillan 2004) and *Managing residential child care* (Palgrave Macmillan 2004). He has been involved in a number of large research projects, including studies funded by the Department of Health, the Economic and Social Research Council and Framework Seven. Currently he is a member of the executive editorial team of the British Sociological Association journal, *Work, Employment and Society*.

Peter Kragh Jespersen was Professor of Public Organization and Administration at Aalborg University. His main research interests included the sociology of professions and public management reforms in health and local government, and he published widely on these subjects. Peter also contributed regularly to the EGOS standing working group on Public Sector Management. He was research manager on the first Danish research programme for organization and management in Danish health care (FLOS) and, most recently, served as vice chair of COST Action ISO903, focusing on the changing relationship between medicine and management in the European context. Sadly, Peter passed away in 2010.

Gerry McGivern is a Lecturer in the Department of Management, King's College London and an Associate Fellow at the Said Business School, University of Oxford. He received a Ph.D. in Organisational Behaviour from Imperial College Business School. His research, which focuses on how health care regulation and organization affect professionals' knowledge and practice, has been published in leading journals including *Organization Studies, Human Relations, Social Science and Medicine*, the *British Journal of Management* and *Public Administration*. Gerry is Organisation and Systems Editor for the *London Journal of Primary Care*.

Indranath Neogy MBA FRSA is a business consultant specializing in organizational culture and innovation issues. He was a researcher and associate of the CIHM at the University of Leeds from 2005–2009. He has worked in the public and private sectors, across a number of industries, including health care, energy and financial services. He is an accredited culture analysis consultant using the Hofstede Model and recently co-founded Kiln Ideas, an innovation catalyst company.

Mirko Noordegraaf is a Full Professor of Public Management at the Utrecht School of Governance (USG), Utrecht University, the Netherlands. He studies public management, the work and behaviour of public managers, managerial professionalism, public professionals and connections between professionalism and organizations. He has published in journals such as *Organization Studies, Public Administration, Public Management Review, Administration and Society, Journal of Management Studies, Current Sociology, Comparative Sociology* and the *International Journal of Public Sector Management*. With R.A.W. Rhodes and Paul 't Hart he published *Observing government elites: up close and personal* (Palgrave Macmillan, 2007). In 2012 he will publish *Perspectives on public management: how professional public managers get things done* (Palgrave Macmillan).

Dermot O'Reilly is a Lecturer in Lancaster University Management School, Lancaster University. His research interests focus around the re-construction, coordination and evaluation of forms of work and social organization, and are informed by critical theory and critical realism.

Mike Reed is Professor of Organizational Analysis at Cardiff Business School, Cardiff University. His research interests are focused around the control of expert labour in complex organizations and the role of organizational elites in shaping control regimes. Recently, he has published a number of papers and chapters on realist organizational analysis. He is a founder editor of the journal *Organization*.

Christine Teelken works as Associate Professor at the VU University of Amsterdam, Faculty of Social Sciences. She specializes in research in higher education, particularly from a comparative perspective. Her publications have appeared in *Studies in Higher Education, Research in Higher Education, International Review of Administrative Sciences, Public Administration* and many other journals. Currently she is working on a longitudinal study in three countries, involving more than 100 interviews.

Nicolette van Gestel is Professor of New Modes of Governance in Social Security and Employment Services at Tilburg University and Associate Professor in Business Administration at Radboud University, both the Netherlands. Her research interests focus on the institutional dynamics of public governance and their effects on organizations. In particular, she is interested in how public and private managers cope with multiple, often competing, logics in organizations and networks. Nicolette has published seven books and volumes, numerous book chapters and articles in journals such as *Public Administration, Public Money and Management, Organization Studies* and *Personnel Review*. She is a convener of the EGOS standing working group 'Organizing the Public Sector: Public Governance and Management' and Chair of the National Association for Industrial Relations, as well as a national representative of the International Labour and Employment Relations Association.

Glossary of abbreviations and acronyms

ABD	General Governing Service (the Netherlands)
ANT	Actor Network Theory
BMA	British Medical Association
CAP	Change Agent Project (UK)
DfE	Department for Education (UK)
DfES	Department for Education and Skills (UK)
DMA	Danish Medical Association
DoH	Department of Health (UK)
EGOS	European Group for Organizational Studies
EHMA	European Health Care Management Association
HEFCE	Higher Education Funding Council for England
HMO	Health Maintenance Organization (USA)
HQS	Health Quality Services (UK)
HRM	Human Resource Management
HSSCs	Health and Social Services Centres (Denmark)
ICMA	International City/County Management Association
ICP	The International Confederation of School Principals
IKAS	Institute for Quality and Accreditation in Health Services (Institut for Kvalitet og Akkreditering i Sundhedsvæsenet) (Denmark)
ISTC	Independent Sector Treatment Centre (UK)
JCIA	Joint Commission International Accreditation (Denmark)
LFHE	Leadership Foundation for Higher Education (UK)
LIT	Local Implementation Team (UK)
NCSL	National College for School Leadership (UK)
NHS	National Health Service (UK)
NHSIII	NHS Institute for Innovation and Improvement (UK)
NIP	National Indicator Project (Det nationale indikatorprojekt) (Denmark)
NLDBs	National Leadership Development Bodies
NPG	New Public Governance
NPM	New Public Management
OECD	Organization for Economic Co-operation and Development

OFSTED	Office for Standards in Education (UK)
ONS	Office for National Statistics (UK)
OPSR	Office of Public Service Reform (UK)
PCT	Public Care Trust (UK)
PEC	Professional Executive Committee – within a PCT (UK)
PIU	Performance and Innovation Unit (UK)
PSA	Public Service Agreement (UK)
PVC	Pro-Vice Chancellor of a university (UK)
RAE	Research Assessment Exercise (now superseded by the REF) (UK)
REF	Research Excellence Framework (UK)
SES	Senior Executive Service (the Netherlands)
SIOO	Inter-University Institute (the Netherlands)
TMP	Top Management Programme (UK)
UDITE	European Municipal Secretary Association
VC	Vice Chancellor of a university (UK)
VGS	Association of Municipal Secretaries (the Netherlands)

Acknowledgements

The idea for writing a book on leadership within the public sector based on the EGOS subtheme 'Organizing the Public Sector' in Amsterdam, 2008, came originally from a number of participants within our standing working group. We the editors were very happy to learn that all our contributors were immediately enthusiastic about our idea and willing and able to keep to our various deadlines. We are greatly indebted to them, and thankful for their patience and energy when going through the various rounds of revisions and editing. It is thanks to their high standards that we were able to compose this book.

Fortunately for all of us, Routledge was very supportive of our idea and the input of their reviewers was very helpful, as was the whole process of turning the manuscript into the finished book.

We dedicate this book to the memory of Peter Kragh Jespersen, who, sadly, died in September 2010. He was a colleague and friend of many of us within the EGOS community. For his obituary, written by Ian Kirkpatrick, please refer to the July 2011 issue of *Current Sociology*, at http://csi.sagepub.com/content/59/4.toc.

1   Introduction

An overview and conceptualization

Christine Teelken

Purpose of the book

Currently, we cannot come up with a more accurate illustration of the title of our book than the positioning and discussions around the leadership of US President Barack Obama. After being elected in the autumn of 2008 with much fanfare, his Inaugural Speech was given on 20 January 2009, promising change and providing inspiration and hope for US citizens and the rest of the world. However, two and a half years later, the media, which were first so enthusiastic about his presidency and leadership, play a very different tune and sound increasingly disappointed and disillusioned. As Drew Weston commented in the *New York Times* of 6 August 2011:

> The public was desperate for a leader who would speak with confidence, and they were ready to follow wherever the president led. Yet instead of indicting the economic policies and principles that had just eliminated eight million jobs, in the most damaging of the tic-like gestures of compromise that have become the hallmark of his presidency – and against the advice of multiple Nobel-Prize-winning economists – he backed away from his advisers who proposed a big stimulus, and then diluted it with tax cuts that had already been shown to be inert. The result, as predicted in advance, was a half-stimulus that half-stimulated the economy. That, in turn, led the White House to feel rightly unappreciated for having saved the country from another Great Depression but in the unenviable position of having to argue a counterfactual – that something terrible might have happened had it not half-acted.

After a promising start and a revival of his popularity in spring 2011 (e.g., through the elimination of Osama bin Laden), Obama's presidency seemed to develop into a nightmare in the summer 2011, as this quote shows. In the middle of worldwide financial turmoil and a serious economic crisis, he is increasingly accused of a paralyzing lack of decision-making capacity and strength to act. His failure to settle the issue of the escalating national debt resulted in decreased US financial credibility, consequently leading to chaos at the stock exchange and speculation that there might be a new recession. Westen (2011) particularly emphasizes Obama's avoidance of expressing a clear point of view in political and philosophical debates, while instead showing a postmodern duplicity by considering the various sides of such discussions. An additional explanation of the current state of his presidency is that voters place too much faith in individual leaders and that structural factors – such as a divided Congress – constrain Obama's ability to realize promised change. Voters move from excessive hope to excessive disillusion across the electoral cycle. In other words, despite his promising election campaign and very high popularity in the beginning of his term, Obama has failed to act as a political leader who is able to stand up to the current economic, financial and social problems in the USA and abroad.

Although, as editors writing and compiling this book, we cannot pretend that we are able to solve any of the serious problems of current worldwide politics and economics immediately, we do, however, believe that our book will contribute to the leadership debates within the broader contexts of narratives of public service reform. By combining a variety of empirical studies carried out in the field of public sector leadership in diverse sectors and countries, we attempt to explain why and how leadership, as one among other policy instruments, can play a crucial role in pursuing successful public management reform. However, next to investigating the opportunities of leadership, we also want to explore the limitations of leadership in relation to its political and organizational context.

The composition of the book is based on a number of EGOS papers that were presented at the meeting of our standing working group 'Organizing the Public Sector' in Amsterdam in July 2008.

Quite deliberately, we have not requested that the authors use a certain theoretical framework – we have simply left it up to them to decide what suited their empirical situation best. However, we did compose a more general review of the various academic literatures and debates on the broad theme of leadership in public services organizations in advance. This review usefully served to solidify the theoretical basis of the book, enabling all chapter authors to place their empirical material within a more theoretical perspective.

The purpose of this introductory chapter is threefold. First, we will provide a review of the relevant literature currently available on public sector leadership, and after defining the major theme of this book, explain our standpoint in this context with reference to the debate about the 'promises and pitfalls' of public sector leadership. This standpoint will be used for the second purpose, the presentation of the key concepts and the new leadership approach, as the chapter provides a general interpretative framework for taking an overview across the various empirical studies presented in this book. Third, we will offer an overview of the content of the following eleven chapters and their relationship with the general theme of the book.

The leadership field in the public sector is highly contested with a number of different and, indeed, competing perspectives, which we will review here briefly, as this book intends to go beyond a mere definition of public sector leadership. We want to give a background on the various empirical settings of public sector leadership by relating them to the various discourses and theories seen as relevant for public sector leadership. The empirical settings vary per chapter, but are all related to the general theme of the book and use an institutional/organizational perspective. We will therefore sketch the various dominant discourses as they provide an overall framework in which the empirical studies on leadership, presented in this book, have been emplaced.

Defining leadership

Leadership was and still is one of the main themes in organizational studies and neighbouring fields for research, often influenced by more psychological perspectives. Leadership studies have greatly expanded over the last thirty years, along with the greater emphasis on the role of senior leaders in 'turning round' failing private or, indeed, public sector organizations and also the teaching demands of MBA programmes. Higgs (2003) states that we have been obsessed with (effective and ineffective) leaders for centuries. For example, in 1999 over two thousand books were published on the topic of leadership (Goffee and Jones, 2000, quoted in Higgs, 2003).

Bess and Goldman (2001) distinguished the situational, charismatic, transformational, path–goal, and leader–member exchange models as influential approaches to core leadership theories. The heroic individual leader model has been particularly influential in received private sector accounts, and there is a tendency to import such concepts into the public services. Examples of these are the use of 'superheads' to turn failing schools round (Currie *et al.*, 2005) and the charismatic leader who is expected to transform the culture of a health care organization and thereby substantially improve the quality of its services (Gray, 2009). There is always an underlying debate about the relative importance of structure against action within social science and this applies particularly to leadership theories that are often highly action orientated. We will explore these tensions further in the concluding discussion. These leadership theories often do not take underlying social structures or the institutional environment adequately into account, which is particularly relevant in public sector research, as it is here powerful groups (e.g. medicine) are well established and 'the state' tends to be very different institutionally from 'the firm'.

The leadership theme has played an important role in recent discussions concerning improvements of the public sector in the public policy domain (Newman, 2001; 2005; O'Reilly and Reed, 2010). Through this more specific focus evidence concerning leadership theories can be drawn from public sector research. In this light, particularly interesting questions involve: why has there been a growth of policy emphasis on the greater use of leadership-based approaches to securing major organizational change over the last decade (Newman, 2005)? What lies behind this? And how do we assess the literature in this field? While many ideas concerning leadership began in the private sector, it is remarkable that a critical investigation of public sector leadership followed at a comparatively leisured pace (Currie *et al.*, 2009).

The context of public sector leadership

Currently, public leadership finds itself under increasing scrutiny. Through the international financial crisis, but also through older, gradual but persistent developments such as the New Public Management (NPM) and now network governance reform narratives, public leaders have been under close communal scrutiny, not only by the media who meticulously follow certain incidents but also by the increased pressure for accountability towards their clients, employees or local authorities. With the decline in conventional vertical line management, new control modes are coming to the fore in the public services. There is an increased public hunger for effective leadership from elected politicians and, indeed, public service managers, as seen in the response in the USA to President Obama, whose leadership style we commented on earlier. Within the academic domain, there is a rapidly developing literature on public services leadership – which can be seen as a live and compelling theme internationally – and to which we are well placed to contribute.

Hogan *et al.* (1994) present a timeless and morally neutral description of leadership, in an attempt to make the concept more accessible for a larger public of researchers. This description can be applied to a variety of situations, for example, a Somali warlord trying to pursue a common goal of protecting communal food supplies versus a Chicago minister attempting to bring together a group of parishioners to help the homeless. Interestingly, they see persuasion as a major feature of leadership, as leadership only functions when others willingly adopt the goals of the group as their own and team performance plays a crucial role (1994: 493).

Denis *et al.* (2005: 450) summarized the central dilemma of public sector leadership in one central question: 'Can leaders intervene proactively or not in public organizations?' In order to answer this question, they distinguish between the entrepreneurial view and the stewardship view on leadership. While the entrepreneurial view refers to innovative behaviour, with emphasis on the demands of the environment and the preferences of stakeholders, stewardship leadership concerns a more conservative role, implying conformation to bureaucratic rules, focusing on continuation and negotiations with the various stakeholders. The entrepreneurial view should be considered in line with the so-called model of transformational leadership, while the stewardship view remains more closely connected to transactional leadership. Given high institutionalization, there may be obstacles to enacting entrepreneurial leadership in public sector contexts (Currie *et al.*, 2008). Denis *et al.* suggest that leadership in public organizations falls somewhere between those two poles. Transformational leadership may be more likely in simpler settings such as schools (Currie *et al.*, 2005). There is also the important question of whether leadership patterns in the public sector are individualized or involve a small team setting and are dispersed in nature (Denis *et al.*, 2001; Buchanan *et al.*, 2007).

Recent investigations by Ferlie *et al.* (forthcoming) in the British health and social policy sector show that a shift towards 'public policy networks' will also involve the displacement of vertical management by broader and lateral forms of leadership, with public sector leaders as active agents of government reform, demonstrating personal/individual characteristics such as charisma and vision, and developing into a more entrepreneurial style of leadership. There is also the question of how these leaders influence important constituencies of public services professionals (e.g. doctors, nurses).

The particular circumstances of public sector (or non-profit) organizations (Denis *et al.*, 2005) make a contextualized study on leadership even more important. The emphasis on values and norms plays a critical role in assessment of leaders, going beyond more straightforward criteria such as amount of profit or percentage of satisfied clients. Compared to the private sector, a different and more complex set of pressures and obligations plays a role, involving a focus on processes and skills that implies much more than formal leadership only. In addition, public organizations have to deal with a complex system of rules and programmes, which require a considerable amount of knowledge. More specifically, public sector leaders have to cope with a complexity and ambiguity of power that is dispersed throughout the whole political and administrative context (Denis *et al.*, 2005). Successful leaders, particularly in the sectors with larger organizations, should be able to bridge the gap between decisions at the top and the daily realities of professionals at the operational level (Coble Vinzant *et al.*, 1998).

Background: key concepts and debates

Before going on with an overview of the contents of this book, we will briefly go into the well-known debate of transformational versus transactional forms of leadership, and place this against the context of the public sector background. In brief, transactional leaders intend to preserve the status quo by rewarding subordinates' efforts and commitment and maintaining a task-focused attitude, clarifying their expectations, while transformational leaders intend to change this status quo by mobilizing and motivating their staff and being more responsive to the environment (Bass and Riggio, 2006; Burns, 1978). In addition, 'transformational . . . leaders emphasize emotions and values' (Yukl, 1999: 285) and 'motivate behaviour by changing their followers' attitudes and assumptions' (Wright and Pandey, 2009: 76). Transformational leadership can be considered 'one of the most prominent theories of organizational behaviour' (Wright and Pandey, 2009: 76).

Interestingly, Wright and Pandey suggest a discrepancy between mainstream leadership theoretical expectations and empirical investigations. On one hand, they state that 'transformational leaders are expected to be both less common and less effective in public sector organizations than private sector organizations because the former are thought to rely more on bureaucratic control mechanisms' (2009: 75–76). On the other, two meta-analyses showed that transformational leadership is actually common and effective in public organizations (Dumdum *et al.*, 2002, quoted in Wright and Pandey, 2009). Public sector organizations often have a societal mission (teach students, care for patients), which is potentially more motivating for employees than, say, selling hamburgers. This may add to the suitability of transformational leadership in such organizations.

An explanation for this discrepancy theoretical expectations and empirical investigations is that government organizations are less bureaucratic than assumed by mainstream leadership theorists, and only show moderate levels of bureaucratic control. An additional explanation may be that reliance on bureaucratic control mechanisms has no effect on transformational leadership. The recent work by Wright and Pandey, who investigated senior managers in US local government, shows that municipal chief administrative officers exhibit higher levels of transformational leadership than expected. They had assumed on the basis of mainstream leadership theory that due to relying on bureaucratic control mechanisms, leaders in public sector organizations would demonstrate less 'transformational' behaviour (Wright and Pandey, 2009). However, Currie *et al.* (2009) investigated the occurrence of transformational leadership within secondary schools in England and were unable to establish a statistically significant relationship between leadership style and a school's performance, showing rather that a contingency type of leadership style prevailed – in other words, principals combined a number of leadership styles, with overlaps between these various styles.

Yukl (1999) explains that charismatic and transformational leadership theories are useful and provide essential insights, but several conceptual weaknesses need to be corrected in an attempt to make the theories more useful. The situational variables are often specified insufficiently, while too much emphasis is laid on the universal applicability of the theories. Several variables are being suggested (e.g. unstable environment, organic structure, entrepreneurial culture, dominance of boundary-spanning units over technical core), but few have been tested, nor is there any evidence on moderator variables. Yukl argues that the dyadic (one-to-one) perspective should be replaced by a systemic one.

Between these two conventional leadership categories lie 'shaping' models of public sector leadership (Pettigrew *et al.*, 1992) where leaders operate within small teams, interact with the local context and use subtle and long-term tactics to build bases of influence. The relationship between public sector managers and professionals is particularly important. Pettigrew *et al.* (1992) suggest that there is sharp variation in the ability of local management teams to secure strategic change, going beyond a macro structural perspective.

Before continuing with an overview of the content of the eleven following chapters, we will briefly mention the major themes to be discussed:

1   The context of leadership.
2   The various leadership models.
3   Professionalism versus managerialism.

1 The context of leadership

The particular comparative focus of this book will be the analysis of leadership styles within various public services (health, higher education, local and central government). Its specific strength involves the different empirical settings both across and within various countries including the UK, Canada, the Netherlands and Scandinavia. It is within these various political and public policy domains that we will investigate the nature of public sector leadership. These policy domains are linked to the post-NPM models of public services management. Within the network governance model of public services management (Newman, 2001, 2005), there has been a shift of emphasis from formal structure or operations of incentives/contracts (NPM) to leadership as a directing force. Public sector managers are reconstituted as active agents of state modernization, and this raises the question of individual identity shifts (Deem *et al.*, 2007). Who benefits and who loses? How is it presented ideologically? Does the leadership discourse over-promise? Is this discourse UK specific and are other countries on different tracks?

It should be noted that leadership development is only one possible policy approach to public service improvement, and typical NPM examples of alternative policy instruments are the setting of central targets and performance management, accreditation, inspection and audits. A typical new public governance (NPG) example would involve the increase in user influence, constructing more user-orientated and less producer dominated public organizations.

So it is interesting to explore why 'leadership' has been emphasized as a policy instrument in at least some influential accounts (e.g. the network governance model) of public management reform (Newman, 2001; O'Reilly and Reed, 2010).

2 The various leadership models

This refers to the leadership characteristics such as distributed, charismatic and transformational versus transactional leadership. A more normative perspective is introduced by O'Reilly and Reed who discuss leadership versus 'leaderism'. There are, of course, critics of those who see leadership as a central factor in public services management (e.g. Reed) – the so-called 'leaderism' movement. O'Reilly and Reed (2010) consider leaderism as a complementary set of discourses, metaphors and practices to those of managerialism, and as being utilized in support of the evolution of NPM and NPG approaches. Leaderism should be able to challenge some of the normative doctrines and organizational practices of NPM.

3 Professionalism versus managerialism

When approaching public sector leadership from a behavioural perspective, the controversy between professionalism and managerialism becomes apparent. This book discusses various practices of public sector professionals who are moving into more managerial roles, often involving a senior professional moving into a part-time managerial role (see Chapter 11 by Noordegraaf, but also Chapter 9 by Teelken, Chapter 6 by Dent *et al.*, and Chapter 8 by Deem). This is known in the health sector as clinical leadership and as academic leadership in higher education, and is an exemplar of professional practice, delegating leadership to the main body of teachers.

There are many behavioural studies available on leadership, such as de Hoogh *et al.* (2005); however, studies that combine such perspective with a more managerial or organizational focus are much scarcer, and this is even more acute for studies that focus on the public sector.

Contents of the book and overview of the twelve chapters

This book consists of three parts, and twelve chapters. Part I concerns the meaning of public sector leadership and its changing forms – particularly how it is being interpreted and implemented in different sectors and countries. The general (dynamic) concepts of the public sector are discussed here in specific sectors (higher education, health, local authorities) and in a variety of countries.

Part I: The meaning of public sector leadership and its changing forms

The first chapter following this introduction is by O'Reilly and Reed, and it argues that the policy discourse of leadership is a development of managerialism that has been utilized and applied within the project of the reformation of the public services in the UK. The policy discourse of leadership draws upon the ideological metaphor of 'leaderism', which is evolved from the ideological metaphor of managerialism. While managerialism has been inflected in the policy technology of NPM over the past thirty years, leaderism and the policy discourse of leadership have been utilized in the evolution of 'post-NPM', 'post-bureaucratic' and 'new public governance' technologies in the attempted re-orientation of the public services towards the consumer-citizen. A critical discourse analysis on the basis of key policy texts of the articulation of the discourse of leadership across the public services in the UK highlights how leadership is intertwined with representations of change agency – a process that is embedded with especial significance in the reformation of UK public services. Furthermore, the discourse of leadership occludes the differential positional interests of managers, professionals and citizen-consumers, serving to legitimate governmental proposals for public service reformation. The leaders are seen as change agents within possible transformational change. The chapter concludes with some critical reflections on the rise of leaderism and the policy discourse of leadership.

The goal of Chapter 3, by Contandriopoulos and Denis, is to analyze the role of governance and leadership in ensuring a connection of policy objectives to managerial systems and organizational dynamics (Saltman, Busse and Mossialos, 2002) in so-called complex systems (Evans, 2005; Denis *et al.*, 2001) and by using a macro perspective. These systems are characterized by a high heterogeneity of participants, distributed capacities and power and non-hierarchical relationships among actors and organizations. Empirical data from the process of implementing health care reforms in Quebec have been used. The space created in this implementation process has been invested, expanded and used by both individual and organizational leaders to interpret and implement policies in a way tallying their beliefs and interests. We rely on the concept of political slack to define the conditions under which the implementation of the new governance models, as defined by Hatchuel (2000), become possible and analyze under which conditions they support the achievement of reform's policy objectives. The chapter provides further insights into how local leaders can use the political slack created by the health care reforms – for example, by creating more decentralized governance structures and using distributed leadership and empowerment.

Chapter 4, by Fitzgerald, Ferlie, McGivern and Buchanan, addresses several current issues debated in the academic literature concerning the roles of leaders and managers in public organizations. This typical, processual organizational study was carried out at a meso level. Within the UK, current government policy places considerable emphasis on the role of 'leaders' (as opposed to managers) and multiple policy initiatives envisage a major part of the leader's role as being to act as a change agent (O'Reilly and Reed, 2010). Yet there is limited current evidence of how change agency is practiced in complex intra- and inter-organizational settings. So this paper focuses on two interrelated themes:

1 How does change agency occur in complex and ambiguous intra- and inter-organizational settings? Do managers see themselves as 'leaders' and perceive their role as one of a change agent?
2 In such complex types of contexts, what tasks do change agents perform? To use a term from the literature, what are the processes adopted for 'intervening' in these organizations?

The chapter draws on a substantial body of empirical data relating to the implementation of service improvement in eleven sites across the UK health care system, including acute hospitals and primary care trusts. The data are based on a qualitative study, using comparative case studies of organizational changes carried out within the eleven sites. The context was an important component of the design and the authors carefully selected contexts in relation to key components of *The NHS Plan* (Department of Health, 2000). Here

Fitzgerald *et al.* demonstrate that within health care, change leadership has to incorporate credibility based on clinical skills and active practice; influence and persuasiveness, rather than positional credibility; and highly honed strategic/managerial and political skills. They consequently identify who the successful 'opinion leaders' are and provide examples of effective tasks and tactics and also illustrate how and why other approaches have failed, comparing these findings with previous research from the private sector (Lovelady, 1984). Change agency involves the widespread distribution of individuals with at least some change agency skills, across the organizations. For effective service improvements in complex settings, distributed change agency is required with individuals operating across functions and vertical levels, involving a key role for clinical managerial hybrids. An interesting micro piece of analysis is that individual skills clearly play a role, as 'contextual sensitivity including the potential need for personal credibility' was considered an essential attribute.

Part II: Leadership style in the public services

This second part discusses the implications for leadership style in current public services organizations, in view of the growth of private provisions. Chapter 5, by van Gestel, aims to understand the changes in roles and leadership style of public managers after the privatization of public services. Exploring the consequences of privatized services for public management in the Dutch employment services will contribute to a key theme of this volume, namely the implications of the growth in private provision of public services for the leadership style in current public service organizations (Dixon *et al.*, 2004; Brodkin, 2006).

Van Gestel employs principal–agent theory and institutional theory in evaluating the public management of private employment services in the Netherlands between 2002 and 2009. Drawing on a systematic review of secondary sources and three rounds of interviews with government officials and managers of private employment services, this study reveals that the major promises have turned into pitfalls. Public managers both at a national and local level struggle with three issues in particular:

1   Balancing public and private responsibilities, where the reduced role of the state paradoxically leads to increased government involvement, such as through closer control and monitoring.
2   Attempting to deliver public services and achieve political goals at the same time.
3   Determining the new roles required for public leaders in order to deliver privatized services.

Her study shows that public managers build up an extremely formal and hierarchical style, which does not sit easily with the divergent interests and values of actors from various institutional domains. The substantial changes in public services provision do not only require better public leadership but also different policies, enabling a significant combination of material resources, greater clarity of purpose and better alignment of different interests and values.

Chapter 6, by Dent, Kirkpatrick and Neogy, examines the variation in reform trajectories and the outcomes for the hospital physicians within three countries in Europe: Denmark, the Netherlands and the United Kingdom, while also considering Kaiser Permanente, a major health maintenance organization (HMO) in the USA. The four cases have been selected because they reflect hospital systems within different welfare regimes and consequently provide an interesting comparative angle. Drawing on a mix of primary and secondary sources Dent *et al.* define the main variations in medical–management relations, identify their implications for hospital organizations and suggest reasons for the differences, drawing on sociological as well as organizational analysis. Hospital doctors in the different countries have developed a range of responses to the managerial reforms in an attempt to preserve, even if in a modified way, their leadership role within the newer hospital management structures. This suggests distributed rather than transformational leadership, quite similar to the chapters by Deem and Teelken. The variation in the responses and the reconfiguration of medical–management relations is largely path dependent, shaped by the profession's historical relations with other key actors, including the state (Wilsford, 1994).

The chapter by Peter Kragh Jespersen – 'Quality development and professional autonomy in modern hospital fields' – focuses mainly on two topics. The first topic is the long-term impact of NPM inspired reforms undergoing transformation and interpretation as they meet a highly professionalized field such as the hospital field. The second is the importance of public sector professionals as participants in policy processes and as hybrid managers. The empirical part of the chapter addresses the quality development schemes in hospitals by comparing the situation in Denmark and Norway, by comparing managerial and professional roles. Empirical analyses are based on official documents from the respective ministries, public commissions, health care journals and material from the professional associations supplemented by interviews with key informants. The development and importance of the quality discussion and the role of the medical profession in the development of quality policies in the two countries are analyzed by incorporating the importance of formal institutional structures and traditions. In both countries the development of quality schemes in hospitals has been affected by NPM strategies but also mediated by the influence of the professions (Nigam, 2006).

The results show that different quality definitions and interpretations continue to exist side by side, while in both countries the medical professionals engage in discourses and policy formation, taking upon them an active role, which can be seen as a new way of preserving their professional autonomy. This may not be accidental since some of them serve to maintain professional boundaries and autonomy and to uphold professional values that declined, while others assisted management in intruding into professional discretion and relations with patients. Discourse, definition and interpretation of quality can be one effective way to defend professional interest in highly professionalized fields, while apparently coherent quality schemes at the same time can allow some kind of bureaucratic regulation as well. The essential question is whether such quality schemes will improve service quality.

Part III: Leadership and public sector professionals

The third and final part of this book examines the challenge of leadership by the public sector professionals themselves, against the discourse of managerialism and NPM. This is discussed in four comparative chapters in both local and central government and in the higher education sectors. In Chapter 8, 'Universities under New Labour', Rosemary Deem examines changing conceptions of leadership in the context of recent reforms to publicly financed UK higher education. The UK government has moved in just over three decades from a laissez faire attitude to universities, which as a consequence had great autonomy, to a state approach that is on occasions directly interventionist at the level of government or, more usually, has its desired interventions mediated through the higher education funding councils (Leisyte *et al.*, 2006; Leisyte, 2007).

Deem explores the extent to which leaders of six universities in England and their senior colleagues perceive themselves to be leading change in their institutions, which are autonomous both from government and the Higher Education Funding Council for England (the HEFCE, which funds and regulates public universities). The chapter draws on thirty interviews conducted in 2007 with senior leaders in six universities in England and a small number of interviews conducted with current and former higher education policy makers in 2008.

Much of the power of these interventions lies in the provision of significant public financial support to universities (both in the form of annual block grants and through competitive bidding processes for special initiatives) and operates via the financial protocols and reporting mechanisms of the Higher Education Funding Councils. At the same time some university leaders are questioning – as more of their funding comes from private sources – the extent to which universities are providing a public service. This chapter raises questions of how realistic are the perceptions of independence of many of our sample of university senior teams, and whether we should use the charismatic or distributed leadership models. It is apparent that the balance between government and universities is shifting as more unregulated income (research/consultancy projects and international students) and variable undergraduate fees begin to alter the public/private funding relationship. Deem concludes the chapter by discussing how far the process of rebalancing between government and universities is likely to go and assesses its potential to disrupt established higher education policies and practices and to alter dominant conceptions of leadership.

Universities all over Europe have adopted organizational strategies, structures, technologies, management instruments and values that are commonly found in the private business sector (Aucoin, 1990; Deem, 1998). The purpose of Chapter 9, by Teelken, is to investigate the impact of NPM on the university, and particularly how the respondents (forty-eight academics in three countries) perceive academic leadership at their university. In her comparative analysis, she focuses particularly at the micro level and addresses the meaning of academic leadership, the implications of a more managerial approach and the responses to the leadership discourse as experienced by the individual academics. Teelken explains that there is a shifting balance between leadership and managerialism, resulting in an increased managerialization and hierarchicalization of academic work, with a specific, administrative focus on efficiency and output measurements. However, this managerial focus on transactional leadership coincides with an increased broadness and variety of tasks, as seems to be required by the external environment. This is making the role of the academic leader less univocal and less a role or a function to be carried out. Despite this increasingly administrative focus, the requirements of academic leadership go beyond such measurable standards of quality, as informal, networking skills are still just as important. Being an academic leader in the current higher education system is very challenging, and few academics will be able to unite both the administrative as well as the collegial and professional practices on an equal basis, particularly in the current dynamics of financial cutbacks and staff redundancies, which is quite similar to the findings by Fitzgerald *et al.* in the health care sector. However, it should be noted that in academia much of what happens at managerial level occurs outside the scope of daily interest of the individual academic respondent, and they are often satisfied as long as they can carry out their own research, without too much interference from others.

Chapter 10, by Jürgen Enders, explains why the public–private division is much more blurred than it appears at first sight. He uses classical economic theory and bases his analysis on the higher education sector and comments on the papers authored by Deem and Teelken. The public–private divide is a distinction basic to higher education studies as one of the primary coordinates in the analysis of institutions, national systems and their political economy. In contemporary societies, higher education, as with other education sectors, was considered a public responsibility and perceived as contributing to the public good. It was heavily subsidized, publicly provided by employees of the state and/or closely regulated with regard to curriculum, teaching and research staff, physical facilities and achievement standards. This is a recent phenomenon in historical perspectives and higher education is currently undergoing multiple transformations. We observe that traditional boundaries have become blurred, not unlike those in other sectors of society previously under tight public control. This relates to the delegation of public policy to semi-public organizations, quasi non-governmental agencies, independent regulatory bodies or public–private policy networks. It also relates to a process by which elements of the higher education fabric are drawn out of the public sphere, but we can also observe just the opposite: the process of bringing elements of the private sphere into the public realm of higher education. The paper discusses these changing relationships and boundaries between the public and private spheres in higher education and academic research and its various manifestations. The paper finishes with some suggestions for further research, particularly concerning the impact of managerial change on organizational identities and leadership practices on the one hand and performance on the other hand, because here the link between organizational capacities for self-steering and the primary processes in teaching and research are at stake.

Chapter 11, by Noordegraaf, addresses the idea that most public and non-profit managers have started to portray and organize themselves as 'professional managers', especially since managerialism started to dominate public and non-profit organizations. Leadership models and programmes construct an appealing policy promise: 'they promise the rise of competent leaders'. This paper explores initiatives in central and local government to develop public leadership, and it will analyze two real-life projects in which policy administrators are turned into competent leaders (Dutch Permanent Secretaries and Municipal Secretaries). The paper uses a constructionist perspective in order to understand professionalization as setting-up and institutionalizing professional 'projects'. On the grounds of these projects, the paper concludes that the making of managers/leaders depends on institutional conditions and is heavily influenced by outside events. The making of leaders is not a matter of consciously formalizing work content and systematically building occupational structures; it is much more a matter of coping with the ambiguities of managerial work. The promises made by the leadership models and programmes should not be taken too literally as they are also symbolic and political vehicles and interact with different organizational contexts.

Ewan Ferlie provides the concluding discussion for the collection. This chapter frames the leadership debate within the broader context of the narratives of public services reform, the NPM and NPG paradigms. This chapter finishes with six major, general observations in the area of public sector leadership and warns us against too much leadership rhetoric.

The first observation involves, *Understanding leadership doctrines in their ideological, political and institutional contexts*, referring to the NPM and NPG paradigms of public services reform, such as the use of leaderism as a reform instrument by O'Reilly and Reed. The second observation concerns, *Leadership patterns found in practice are often mixed, messy and mundane rather than heroic or inspirational*, referring for example to distributed leadership (see Fitzgerald *et al.* and Dent) because of its 'mixed and messy' patterns. The third observation, *Leadership patterns are sensitive to (multiple) contexts*, is closely connected to the previous observation as several chapters suggest that leadership capacity is strongly context-dependent, referring to the sectional as well as national context. The fourth observation, *The distinctive nature of leadership in professionalized public services organizations*, refers particularly to the professionalized fields within the public sector, as professionals are likely to context the authority of general managers on behalf of their professional colleagues, if they accept any authority at all. The fifth observation, *The rhetorical (over) promise of leadership: more mundane and less inspirational?*, describes the idea that leadership promises are either taken too literally (Noordegraaf) or implicitly replace leadership by management (Teelken), consequently providing food for thought for the leaderism discourse, as has been discussed by O'Reilly and Reed. The sixth and final observation, *Bringing individual leaders back in: becoming a leader*, implies the (self-)construction of leadership as both Deem and Teelken attempt in their chapters on higher education – they both show that the capacities of leaders in achieving organizational change were quite limited.

This brings us back to the example of Barack Obama: his very promising start seemed to have turned into a pitfall, not only because of his own failure to achieve change as a political leader, but also through the complexity of the political, economic and governmental developments. The purpose of this book is to examine in what manner leadership, as one among other policy instruments, can play a crucial role in supporting public management reform. However, next to investigating the opportunities of leadership, we also want to explore the limitations of leadership in relation to its political and organizational context and suggest alternative approaches. We will discuss these dilemmas in the subsequent chapters, within the broader contexts of narratives in pubic sector reform and in various sectional and national settings. It is up to the reader to decide whether we succeeded in doing so.

References

Aucoin, P. (1990) Administrative reform in public management: Paradigms, principles, paradoxes and pendulums, *Governance: An International Journal of Policy and Administration*, 2, 115–137.

Bass, B.M. and Riggio, R.E. (2006) *Transformational leadership* (2nd edn), Mahway, NJ: Lawrence Erlbaum Associates.

Bess, J.L. and Goldman, P. (2001) Leadership ambiguity in universities and K–12 schools and the limits of contemporary leadership theory, *Leadership Quarterly*, 12, 419–450.

Brodkin, E.Z. (2006) Bureaucracy redux: Management reformism and the welfare state, *Journal of Public Administration Research and Theory*, 17: 1–17.

Buchanan, D., Addicott, R., Fitzgerald, L., Ferlie, E. and Baeza, J. (2007) No one in charge: Distributed change leadership in health care, *Human Relations*, 60, 7, 1065–1090.

Burns, J.M. (1978) *Leadership*, New York: Harper and Row.

Coble Vinzant, J., Crothers, L. and Vinzant Denhardt, J. (1998) *Street-level leadership, discretion and legitimacy in front-line public service*, Washington, DC: Georgetown University Press.

Currie, G., Boyett, I. and Suhomlinova, O. (2005) Transformational leadership within secondary schools in England: A panacea for organizational ills?, *Public Administration*, 83, 2, 265–296.

Currie, G., Humphreys, M., Ucbasaran, D. and MacManus, S. (2008) Entrepreneurial leadership in the English public sector: Paradox or possibility?, *Public Administration*, 86, 4, 987–1008.

Currie, G., Boyett, I. and Suhomlinova, O. (2009) Leadership and institutional change in the public sector: The case of secondary schools in England, *The Leadership Quarterly*, 20, 664–679.

Deem, R. (1998) 'New managerialism' and higher education: The management of performances and cultures in universities in the United Kingdom, *International Studies in Sociology of Education*, 8, 47–70.

Deem, R., Hillyard, S. and Reed, M. (2007) *Knowledge, higher education and the new managerialism: The changing management of UK universities*, Oxford: Oxford University Press.

de Hoogh, A.H.B., Den Hartog, D.N. and Koopman, P.L. (2005) Linking the five-factors of personality to charismatic and transactional leadership: Perceived dynamic work environment as a moderator, *Journal of Organizational Behavior*, 26, 839–865.

Denis, J.-L., Langley, A. and Cazale, P.L. (2001) The dynamics of collective leadership and strategic change in pluralistic organizations, *Academy of Management Journal*, 44, 4, 809–837.

Denis, J.-L., Langley, A. and Rouleau, L. (2005) Rethinking leadership in public organizations, in Ferlie, E., Lynn, L.E. and Pollitt, C. (eds) *The Oxford handbook of public management*, Oxford University Press (pp. 446–467).

Department of Health (2000) *The NHS Plan*, London: Department of Health.

Dixon, J., Dogan, R. and Kouzmin, A. (2004) The dilemma of privatized public services: Philosophical frames in understanding failure and managing partnership terminations, *Public Organization Review*, 4, 1, 25–46.

Dumdum, U.R., Lowe, K.B. and Avolio, B.J. (2002) Meta-analysis of transformational and transactional leadership correlates of effectiveness and satisfaction: An update and extension, in Avolio, B.J. and Yammarino, F.J. (eds) *Transformational and charismatic leadership: The road ahead*, New York: JAI Press (pp. 35–65).

Evans, R.G. (2005) Fellow travelers on a contested path: Power, purpose, and the evolution of European health care systems, *Journal of Health Politics, Policy and Law*, 30, 1–2, 277–293.

Ferlie, E., Fitzgerald, L., McGivern, G., Dopson, S. and Bennett, C. (2011) Public policy networks and 'wicked problems': A nascent solution? *Public Administration*, 89, 2, 307–324.

Goffee, R. and Jones, G. (2000) Why should anyone be led by you?, *Harvard Business Review*, September–October, 63–70.

Gray, M. (2009) Public health leadership: Creating the culture for the twenty-first century, *Journal of Public Health*, 31, 2, 208–209.

Hatchuel, A. (2000) Prospective et gouvernance: quelle théorie de l'action collective?, in Heurgon, E. and Landrieu, J. (eds) *Prospective pour une gouvernance démocratique*, La Tour d'Aigues: Éditions de l'Aube (pp. 29–42).

Higgs, M. (2003) How can we make sense of leadership in the 21st century?, *Leadership and Organization*, 24, 5, 273–284.

Hogan, R., Curphy, G.J. and Hogan, J. (1994) What we know about leadership, effectiveness and personality, *American Psychologist*, 49, 6, 493–504.

Leisyte, L. (2007) University governance and academic research (Ph.D. dissertation), Centre for Higher Education Policy Studies, University of Twente, Enschede, the Netherlands.

Leisyte, L., de Boer, H.F. and Enders, J. (2006) England: The prototype of the 'Evaluative State', in Kehm, B. and Lanzendorf, U. (eds) *Reforming university governance: Changing conditions for research in four European countries*, Bonn: Lemmens (pp. 21–58).

Lovelady, L. (1984) Change strategies and the use of OD consultants to facilitate change, *Leadership and OD Journal*, 5, 4, 2–12.

Newman, J. (2001) *Modernising governance*, London: Sage.

Newman, J. (2005) Enter the transformational leader: Network governance and the micro politics of modernisation, *Sociology*, 39, 4, 717–734.

Nigam, A. (2006) Transformation of professional controls: Changes in medical work in the shift to managed care, Working paper, Atlanta: Goizueta Business School, Emory University.

O'Reilly, D. and Reed, M. (2010) 'Leaderism': An evolution of managerialism in UK public service reform, *Public Administration*, 88, 4, 960–978.

Pettigrew, A., Ferlie, E. and McKee, L. (1992) *Shaping strategic change*, London: Sage.

Saltman, R.B., Busse, R. and Mossialos, E. (2002) *Regulating entrepreneurial behaviour in European health care systems*, Buckingham: Open University Press.

Westen, D. (2011) What happened to Obama?, *New York Times*, 6 August.

Wright, B.E. and Pandey, S.K. (2009) Transformational leadership in the public sector: Does structure matter?, *Journal of Public Administration Research and Theory*, 20, 75–89.

Yukl, G. (1999) An evaluation of conceptual weaknesses in transformational and charismatic leadership theories, *Leadership Quarterley*, 10, 2, 285–305.

Part I

The meaning of public sector leadership and its changing forms

2 'Leaderism' and the discourse of leadership in the reformation of UK public services

Dermot O'Reilly and Mike Reed

Introduction

The election of the Labour Party to government in May 1997 heralded the onset of a new stage in the organization of public services within the UK. This re-organization of public services entailed the utilization of the self-conscious labels of the 'reform', 'modernization' and 'transformation' of the public sector similar to many OECD and World Bank documents addressing the public services across the world (OECD, 2000; OECD, 2004; OECD, 2010; Webb, 2008; Wiesner, 1993). The UK government was at the forefront of this second wave of the international problematizing of the structure and operations of the public sector. As in the first wave of New Public Management (NPM) reforms, this second wave was evidenced in a swathe of public service programmes and policy initiatives in the UK (Dunleavy *et al.*, 2006; Pollitt, 2007), which were exceptional, at least in terms of the regularity and ambition of these programmes and initiatives, even if the necessary comparative analytical frameworks and evidence for evaluating the impact of these changes is not readily available (Pollitt and Bouckaert, 2004).

While the zeal of the Labour government for accelerating changes in public services was expressed by the party itself and by contributors in terms of the 'third way' (Blair, 1998; Giddens, 1998; Giddens, 2000), it has been interpreted as having messianic and religious connotations by commentators (Odone, 1999), while Tony Blair's links to communitarian thinking have long been discussed (Driver and Martell, 1998; Hale, 2002). These religious and communitarian undertones inflected the UK government's project of public service reform – throughout the Labour administration the reform of public services was displayed as a totemic signifier of the intent and seriousness of the party (see Labour Party, 2006) – and this concern with public sector reformation is also discernible in the early days of its successor Conservative-led coalition government. A number of indicators point to the importance placed on public service reform – the sheer number of government documents and bills addressing either generic reform or reform of specific services, and the regular announcement of new 'stages' or 'phases' of reform.

The focus of this chapter is upon one aspect of this zeal for the 'reformation' of public services – the stress on leadership (also evident in OECD documents, for example OECD, 2001). Chapter 8 by Rosemary Deem, for example, indicates how leadership is interpreted and enacted by organizational actors in the UK higher education sector. In order to investigate the role of the *discourse* of leadership – which we argue is based on an underlying ideological metaphor of leaderism – within the project of public service reform, we employ a critical discourse analysis methodology (Fairclough, 2003). This approach enables us to analyze official statements and prescriptions of reform in order to identify the role of the discourse of leadership within these documents. These documents are treated as artefacts of the practice of government – which thereby offer us a window into the phenomenon of governance. A key finding from our analysis is that leadership is intertwined with representations of change agency – a process that is embedded with especial significance in the reformation of UK public services (see Chapter 4 for a more involved discussion of the practice of change agency in the UK health service).

By arguing for the importance of the role of leaderism in the policy discourse of public service reformation, we are also asserting that leaderism is different from the ideological metaphor of managerialism, which has been character-ized as the motivating logic behind NPM changes in public services over the last three decades. We substantiate these arguments by recourse to the critical discourse analyses of documents, which we interpret to show that leaderism is an evolution of managerialism. This leads us to consider both the link between leaderism and the so-called 'post-NPM' or 'post-bureaucratic' config-urations of public services such as network governance (Osborne, 2006; Ferlie and Andresani, 2006; Ferlie and Fitzgerald, 2002; Pollitt, 2008); the ramifi-cations of leaderism for professionally-based services within these shifting contours of governance; and some of the contradictions and potentialities inherent in the emergence of leaderism in public service reformation.

To begin, we outline our research methods and then move on to our dis-cussion of the differences between managerialism and leaderism.

Research methods

Our study of leaderism in the field of UK public services was enabled through investigating the discourses and metaphors of leadership through critical discourse analysis. Critical discourse analysis is concerned with analyzing the content and modes of communication along the lines of structures and mechanisms, and investigating how social structures are reproduced and changed through the interaction between discourse and social practice (Fairclough, 2003; Fairclough, 2005).

We were particularly interested in the UK government's representations of leadership. We looked at representations since 'representations enter and shape social processes and practices' (Fairclough, 2003: 206). The government texts analyzed were from central government (used here to denote the Cabinet Office and the Treasury), the departments of health and education (the two largest disciplinary-based sets of departmental expenditure in the UK), and more general documents produced by other government departments and agencies that touched upon the themes of this paper. Our analysis is thus focused on studying the discursive products of government agents. We do not assume that these discursive products have a necessary causal effect on the operations of other parts of the public service system.

A number of methods of critical discourse analysis were utilized: in particular, lexical analysis of the use and prevalence of the lexicons, or particular words, used in the texts (Firth, 1968; Nelson, 2006), and comparative qualitative analysis of the narratives and metaphors utilized and drawn upon in the texts.

We were interested, first, in the lexicons, or 'wordparts', used by the government in relation to public service reform and leadership in its texts. Through an initial search of documents produced by central government and the spending departments of health and education between May 1997 and mid-2008 we surfaced a number of documents from each of these levels that included explicit formulations of public service reform, either of a generic cross-service kind (nine from central government) or of reform in the education and health services (seven from the education department and five from the health department respectively). These documents (listed in the 'List of documents analyzed' at the end of this chapter) were classed as 'versions of reform', and from these a list of key wordparts used by the government to describe generic cross-service reform, education reform and health reform, were identified (see O'Reilly and Reed, 2010).

This wordpart analysis was supplemented by the use of collocation analysis – investigating the regularity and meanings of words commonly located close to particular search words. Collocation analysis is useful because the words that regularly co-occur around a search word effect its meaning (Firth, 1968).

The second mode of critical discourse analysis focused on the narratives, or storylines, that are composed and utilized in the different texts. A narrative is a generative sort of storyline 'that allows actors to draw upon various discursive categories to give meaning to specific social phenomena' (Hajer, 1995: 56). Narratives can be composed partly through the use of particular lexical terms, phrases or slogans, but they also require a storyline that produces some degree of internal consistency and plausibility. Narratives are important for at least two reasons. First, they provide a resource for meaning-making, for enabling agents to interpret events and develop plans of action. Second, they are an essential part of the strategic use of discourse since they implicate agents that are narrated in relation to other social phenomena. The framing of relations between agents and particular social phenomena or processes via particular narratives can activate or passivate social agents in relation to them.

The third mode of critical discourse analysis focused on the assumptions conveyed, evident in and relied upon through the lexicons, meanings and narratives produced in the government's texts. Assumptions are the presuppositions that people make when they speak or write. The particular linguistic vehicles that carry assumptions that we investigated were metaphors. Metaphors are important because they are powerful shapers of perceived realities. According to Lakoff and Johnson (2003) metaphors are deeply entailed in the processes of perception and cognition. In particular, we are interested in the degree to which the metaphors of leadership in the public services in the UK are in the process of becoming 'deep' metaphors – metaphors that shape perception and action, but that are not generally recognized as such (O'Reilly and Reed, 2010).

Managerialism and leaderism – differences and continuities

As a doctrine of ideas and related practices, managerialism has been advocated in the private sector since at least the 1970s (Peters and Waterman, 1982; Reed, 2007b). Of particular concern to practitioners, politicians and academics has been the related and continued advocacy for the implementation of managerialist ideas and practices in the public sector since the 1980s (e.g. Osborne and Gaebler, 1992). Managerialism has been defined as 'the belief that all aspects of organizational life can and should be managed according to rational structures, procedures, and modes of accountability in the pursuit of goals defined by policymakers and senior managers' (Wallace and Pocklington, 2002: 68). In turn, this belief has been characterized as entailing a set of associated disciplines for achieving control (Boltanski and Chiapello, 2005).

In the public sector, the government's pursuit of managerialism has been viewed as an attempt to reconstruct or 'hollow out' the state by 'rolling out' state power between central government and organizations at the periphery – private sector organizations, arms-length bodies or third sector organizations (Pollitt et al., 2004). A number of commentators have pointed out the ensuing contradictory tensions between control and delegation contained within this trend (e.g. Wallace and Pocklington, 2002). It is precisely this nexus of control and delegation that is addressed by the rise of public service 'leaderism', a particular evolution of managerialism (O'Reilly and Reed, 2010). The contrast between managerialism and leaderism lies in the fact that whereas conventional NPM-style managing implies organizational rational planning and implementation via a principal–agent relationship, leadership is construed as involving the establishment of a passion for a common goal between leaders and led (Wallis and Dollery, 1997). Moreover, leaderism presupposes that these common goals entail a strategic adaptation to, and shaping of, the social environment, the negotiation and overcoming of risk, and a sustained focus on radical change. The primary difference, then, between the root metaphors of managerialism and leaderism, as evident in UK government documents, is that they imply different approaches to the issue of social coordination. Management assumes a principal–agent relationship – that is, how is A to get B to do something? – evidenced in regular concerns with the relationships between management and performance measurement and accountability mechanisms in the documents (see Chapter 5 for an example of the idea of the principal–agent relationship being integrated into the formal structures of public services in the Netherlands). Leadership, on the other hand, assumes a commonality between different agents – that is, how will A and B coordinate each other's actions? – evidenced in regular concerns with the relationships between leadership and partnerships, influence and cultural change in the documents.

From the critical discourse analysis, there is a clear relationship between the legitimating assumptions that underpin managerialism and those associated with leaderism. As such, we have argued that leaderism is best seen as an evolution of managerialism rather than as a completely separate ideological element. At the same time, however, we stress the difference of the root metaphors at play in the different ideologies. The differences that these root metaphors are associated with in practice are highlighted when we consider the different role relationships of ideal-typical managers and leaders as represented in the documents. The role relationships of ideal-typical managers include the classical features identified in the tradition of bureaucracy:

- they do not own, but control, organizational resources;
- posts are filled nominally on merit;
- positions are salaried and permanent (with the exception that contemporary managers in the public services do not enjoy the same degree of permanency they once did (Boltanski and Chiapello, 2005));
- the structure of roles is governed by written rules and procedures; and, conception is separated from execution.

(Weber, 1978)

In contrast, the representations of the ideal-typical role of leader encompasses not only formal leaders who are associated with organizational performance, but also informal leaders – those in organizations able to mobilize resources without formal authority. Both formal and informal leaders are equated with a particular role in the setting of organizational objectives or 'vision', which is in contrast to the separation of conception and execution in bureaucratic management. Leaders are also represented as having a crucial role in extra-organizational activities – mobilizing resources and networks. In this way, leaderism can be understood as a symptom of the broader trend towards so-called 'post-bureaucratic' organizations (Hecksher and Donnellon, 1994).

Despite these differences between leaderism and managerialism, we are arguing that leaderism is an evolution of aspects of managerialism and that they have been used together. Some evidence for this is that 'leadership' is one of the most common collocations of 'manag'; while 'management' is one of the most common collocations of 'leader' in government documents. Because both wordparts are often found in the company of each other they can be understood as a 'standardised relational pair'; that is, they are a set of two categories that are tied together so that the activation of one member of the pair in interaction – that is, in talk or in activity – also invokes the other (Collet, 2009: 459). Not only is leaderism an evolution of managerialism, therefore, but because of the differences between the representations of their ideal-types, the invocation of leaderism is tied to managerialism, and the evolution of leaderism implies a qualitative difference in the trajectory of managerialism.

Having specified the core differences and continuities between managerialism and leaderism, in the next section we move on to a more detailed examination of the utilization of the discourse of leadership in policy documents.

The discourse of leadership in the project of public service reform

A series of themes were surfaced through the analysis of the use of the discourse of leadership in government policy documents. These themes can be distinguished according to those that are 'internal' to the ideal-type of leaderism – that is, aspects of the discourse of leadership that are reflective of the meanings typically assigned to leadership; and those that are 'external' to the ideal-type of leaderism – that is, aspects of discourse that do not constitute part of the meanings typically assigned to leadership but that are nevertheless relatively frequently present in the same contexts as leadership. These 'external' themes evidence the adaptability of leadership as a discourse – they represent the contextual themes and elements of the broader project of public service reformation, which mutually reinforce the logic of leadership, while at the same time gaining legitimacy through their associations to leadership.

Core themes internal to the ideal-type of leaderism

The core themes internal to the ideal-type of leaderism include both ideological elements and technical elements. Ideologically, leadership is equated to the narratives that change is endemic; that leaders are change agents; and that everyone has the potential to be a leader. The core technical element is the representation that leadership is a social and organizational technology.

Leadership is associated with a number of recurring narratives of public service reform, most importantly that contemporary life is characterized by 'New Times' (Hale *et al.*, 2004) where change is endemic to modern society. This narrative of endemic change represents higher order changes such as globalization and changes in modern society as requiring shifts in the politics and organization of nation states, which in turn places new requirements on the public sector to change and modernize. This in turn presents the introduction of restructured public service organizations (with practices such as work standardization, cost cutting, outsourcing and a more competitive ethos) as inevitable requirements of the new contextual realities (see Clarke and Newman, 1997). For example:

> People are exercising choice and demanding higher quality. In the private sector, service standards and service delivery have improved as a result. People are now rightly demanding a better service not just from the private sector, but from the public sector too.
>   The Government is committed to public service. But that does not mean public services should stand still. Public servants must be the agents of the changes citizens and businesses want. We will build on the many strengths in the public sector to equip it with a culture of improvement, innovation and collaborative purpose. Public sector staff need to respond to these challenges, working in partnership to deliver this programme.
>
> (Cabinet Office, 1999: 10)

The 'endemic change' narrative is used to legitimate the need for public service reformation, and in this particular instance it is also used to create an onus on public servants as the agents of change by which these pressures are addressed and new services are developed. Public service leaders are thus implicated as key agents in meeting the expectations of consumers and other stakeholders.

Public service leaders are furthermore variously associated with reform or with crucial elements of the project of reform:

> The NHSU and Leadership Centre will pick up this challenge, designing their development interventions to help local leaders increase choice and offer more personalised care.
>
> (DoH, 2003: 56)

> Alongside encouraging the expansion of successful schools, we are encouraging the leaders and governors of successful schools to establish entirely new schools in response to parental demand.
>
> (DfES, 2004: 50)

In these instances leaders, and the process of leadership, are cast as the motive force for reformation. In this way, leaders are represented as being responsible for reform; it is on them especially that the obligation of instigating and implementing change falls. These instances involve representations of leaders as adaptively responding to a new environment, and taking on the issues of government and the public, which are implicitly represented, crucially, as being coterminous.

As noted above, leaderism suggests a degree of commonality between the leader and the led. This is evidenced in the representation and construal of a social bond between government, public services and the public. This is vitally important when public services are in a process of reformation. Not least, such attempts at creating a social bond are an endeavour to overcome tensions between conflicts of positional interest – whether they are principal/agent, hierarchical, professional, geographical, sectoral or class-based. One way in which the discourse of leadership is used to create a social bond is through its multifarious attribution to all parties that the UK government seeks to address. This is most stark when comparing the following attributions of leadership by the former UK Prime Minister – first to public service workers, and second to himself:

> I believe that in each public service, we can point to progress where the money is going in, where the reforms have taken root, where these four principles are being applied.
>
> But I know we have a lot more to do. Without your support, your advice and your leadership we won't be able to achieve it. We are all involved in delivering better public services. My colleagues and I can – and will – play our full part but, in the end, you are the people who will deliver. But I am convinced that these principles, record investment, your skills and our shared commitment will help deliver the high quality services that the British people rightly expect. We must not let them down.
>
> (Tony Blair foreword in OPSR, 2002: 3)

> Eight years ago, I offered new leadership – fresh, idealistic, energetic, but untested. You voted for change and gave me the chance to serve.
>
> (Tony Blair foreword in Labour Party, 2005: 6)

In the first extract Tony Blair is directly addressing public sector workers, and attributes to them the potential for leadership, simultaneously placing the burden of delivery upon them. In the second he casts himself in the role of servant leadership for the electorate at large. The following extracts indicate the government's extensive attribution of leadership to public servants, trade unions and members of the public, which are also variously represented as having the causal power to lead:

> For public services to be renewed, we will need more staff, properly rewarded. It is these frontline staff, operating in new ways, who will drive up standards in our key public services. We will decentralise power to make that possible. We will now deliver: 20,000 more nurses . . . 10,000 more doctors . . . 10,000 more teachers . . . 6,000 extra police recruits . . . with strong local leadership and proper rewards for those on the frontline.
>
> (Labour Party, 2001: 6–7)

> Forward-looking trade unions know that the future is about partnership, and are leading the way in a number of projects.
>
> (OPSR, 2002: 21)

Using trained non-medical leaders as educators, people with arthritis and other long-term conditions have been equipped with the skills to manage their own conditions.

(DoH, 2004: 36)

Leadership, therefore, is represented, on various occasions, as a processual feature of UK public services. These representations highlight the potential communality of leadership as a collective resource, in that they put an onus on various communal agents to display leadership. As noted above, the communitarian aspect of New Labour has been associated with a concern for responsibilities as well as rights – entailing leadership as a responsibility as well as a causal power. This communal responsibility, in turn, is related to the focus on collaborative or 'joined up' working, networks and partnerships – key institutional and cultural innovations of New Labour's tenure of government (2004: 6; Bovaird and Russell, 2007; Davies, 2009; Lee and Woodward, 2002).

Leadership as a technology for reformation

The focus on leadership in the public services, however, is not limited to the construal of the agency or the responsibility of leaders as being for reform. Leadership has been identified by government as a core catalytic ingredient, skill or technology in the reformation of public services, for example: 'Fundamental to improved leadership is a clearer shared understanding of what leadership behaviours work in delivering today's public services' (PIU, 2001: 5).

A focus on leadership as a social technology for coordinating reformation is evidenced in the creation or support by central government of a series of new bodies to provide and commission leadership development for publicly funded services in the UK since 1997 (see O'Reilly *et al.*, 2007). An indication of the importance placed on leadership development as a means for changing public services is evident in both of the two following lists of programmatic edicts for improvement and change, and of the importance of leadership within them, in the education and health services:

The following core principles of school improvement are helping inform developing strategies to strengthen and support school leadership.

Core principles of school improvement:

- create a dominant focus for improvement: select key priorities for improving teaching and learning to concentrate effort and build experience of success;
- agree clear and unifying goals: ground goals for teachers and students in evidence, including performance data and benchmarks;
- build collective ownership of the development work: engage staff across the school in a school improvement group;

- enhance knowledge and teaching skills through focused professional development: create time for staff to learn together;
- embed the development work: reinforce it to make the results part of normal school practice;
- collaborate with other schools: widen the vision and create opportunities for joint development . . .

The College's programmes . . . are designed to develop leaders' skills in three areas: leading teaching and learning, personal and interpersonal skills, and organizational and strategic management. These skills underpin the five stages of school leadership training provided by the College.

(DfES, 2003: 31–2)

Managing change

Cultural change of the order required will take time. Success will depend on every single member of the NHS demonstrating leadership in promoting the values and vision of the NHS.

People in senior positions must set the right tone and accelerate the change by:

- describing the vision clearly and avoiding 'technocratic' explanations of change
- making sure that all the processes and incentives in this system support the change
- giving patients and staff early opportunities to experience the change in reality – trying new approaches quickly and learning from them
- prioritising training and education to equip staff with the new skills they will need
- supporting the changes with constant listening and feedback

(DoH, 2005: 26)

Such programmatic edicts for service improvement and change are intrinsically bound up with the promotion of leadership as a technology of reformation. Leadership development programmes built around such programmatic formulations of public service reformation put a premium on the affective and symbolic aspects of leaders' identities and interpersonal relations. Leaders are charged with exercising their personal powers in order to 'nurture and direct' the individual strivings of both themselves and those over whom they have influence (Newman, 2005: 721). The discourse of leadership development, therefore, works not only as a programmatic technology indicating to potential leaders how they can lead and operationalize change, but also simultaneously as an invitational trope to potential leaders to narrate, imagine, and thus construe themselves as leaders.

In this regard, however, it is important to note that the actual term 'transformational leader' is not contained in any of the 'version of reform' documents. As seen in the previous extracts, however, there are many examples where leadership is attributed with a role in transforming the system. As such, the concept of 'transformational leadership', which puts a particular onus on senior public service managers as change agents, is not explicitly invoked but strongly implied in these documents. In contrast, the notion of 'distributed leadership', which disperses agency across the public services, is infrequently implied. This has ramifications for the narrative of leadership being promoted in policy documents – one that puts a premium on vision and radical change, with all their connotations of conversion, in preference over versions that presuppose negotiated and incremental change.

Contextual themes external to the ideal-type of leaderism

Of the elements of the broader project of reformation external to the ideal-type of leaderism but contextually associated with it, we highlight two associations of particular interest – the re-orientation of performance management towards social outcomes, and the stress on post-bureaucratic forms of organizing public services.

The recasting of performance in terms of outcomes

The wordpart 'performance' is a regular collocation of 'leader' in central government documents. This is a further indication that leaderism is not far removed from managerialism. One of the changes in emphasis in government discourse over Labour's time in government, however, has been an attempt to move away from micromanaged performance targets to what it terms 'social outcomes'. These outcomes are intended to articulate more generically the standards government wants services to observe in practice: 'Strategic Leadership in practice: Across Government Departments we will: focus on just 30 high level outcomes, rather than micromanagement' (Cabinet Office, 2009: 17).

Elsewhere, in a chapter on 'strategic leadership' (which is concerned with the role of government) a focus on outcomes is construed as combining a government concern with minimum standards, professional concerns with determining work, and public satisfaction, while enabling local involvement in services:

Measuring what matters
The Government's priorities for the next three years are now set out in a streamlined set of 30 Public Service Agreements (PSAs). There are now fewer national targets, fewer indicators and, instead of being constrained by the boundaries between Whitehall departments, the PSAs are focused on the outcomes that matter to citizens and public service professionals. This allows a greater role for local communities to set local priorities and more space to deliver personalised, flexible services.

(Cabinet Office, 2008: 37)

The development and use of these 'social outcomes' as a means for directing and evaluating public services is construed as an holistic evolution of government performance management techniques. A perusal of some of these thirty PSAs that relate to education and health, however, may lead one to wonder how these social outcomes will practically change the machinery of government:

- Raise the educational achievement of all children and young people
- Narrow the gap in educational achievement between children from low income and disadvantaged backgrounds and their peers
- Increase the number of children and young people on the path to success
- Improve the health and wellbeing of children and young people
- Tackle poverty and promote greater independence and wellbeing in later life
- Promote better health and wellbeing for all

(The Treasury, 2009: 1)

We point to the difficulties of interpreting what these social outcomes may mean in practice for public service organizations in order to highlight that public service managers are operating in a context where they need to be involved in the interpretation, negotiation and operationalization of these outcomes. Such general edicts create an opportunity for public service managers to redefine and evidence their organizational activities in ways that can be related to these edicts. Simultaneously, however, despite the general nature of these edicts, they still presuppose the exclusion and marginalization of activities that are more difficult to relate to these principles, which entails the demobilization or curtailing of particular social aims or management practices.

Partnership, collaboration, networks, joined-up government and innovation – striving for a new post-bureaucratic public governance

Evident within the move from performance to outcomes is an associated concern with less bureaucratic, more networked and more innovatory forms and processes of public administration. As argued above, leadership has been attributed to various differentially located actors in the public service system – to government, public service managers, staff, trade unions and members of the public. These attributions are conjoined with the construal of these various actors as being responsible for showing leadership in the reformation of public services. This emphasis on a communitarian responsibility is keenly evident in the stresses on partnership and collaboration/joined-up government, which occur as headline elements of reform thrice and once, respectively. In contrast, the frequency of wordparts associated with a move towards 'post-bureaucracy' in the headline elements of reform – freedom (of services) (six), innovation (five), flexibility, personalization and new/ diversity of providers (four each), devolution (three), independence (of services) (two), delegation, continuous learning and entrepreneurial (one each) – indicates a strong concern by government for a re-engineering of the machinery of public service administration.

The discourse of leadership has taken root in public administration circles at the same time as these discursive elements that point towards a nascent post-bureaucratic milieu, implying that there is an association, if not a co-relation, between these discursive developments. This is thrown into relief if we consider that managerialism as a discourse was associated with the 'machine bureaucracy' (Mintzberg, 1979) at the organizational level, and NPM (Hood, 1991; McLaughlin *et al.*, 2002; Dunleavy *et al.*, 2006) at the system level. Taking this into account, it would appear as if leaderism is associated with a nascent public governance paradigm of self-improving, responsive networked public service systems with concomitant organizational, local, regional and system loci for coordination, which is a hybrid of both NPM and the systemic archetype of Public Service Networks – where policies and programmes are 'evolved and delivered by more than one organization, linked in networks or partnerships' (Pollitt, 2008: 202).

In summary, we have outlined how the discourse of leadership in the reformation of UK public services has involved both internal elements – where leadership is correlated to the 'new times' of endemic change; leaders are construed as change agents for reform; leadership is represented as a communal responsibility; and leadership is constructed as a technology for reformation (with both programmatic and invitational elements) – and contextual associations, where leadership has been associated with a focus on generic 'social outcomes' and a nascent post-bureaucratic public governance paradigm.

As a component of public service reformation, therefore, leaderism has both ideological (change is endemic, leadership is a communal responsibility) and practical moments (Ruef and Harness, 2009) (leaders as change agents, leadership as a technology). The ideological moments are both evidence of the use of symbolic power, and a symptom of the need felt by those in power to legitimate themselves. On the other hand, the practical moments are evidence of an attempt to inculcate senior managers into practices of becoming 'active reformers' or 'continuous improvers' – a larger enterprise than simply engaging them in leading particular reforms.

Post-crisis reforms and the evolution of the policy discourse of leadership

Two significant events have occurred since the period of analysis outlined above – the global financial crisis and the accession of a Conservative-led coalition government in the UK. These have resulted in the announcement of a series of cuts to public expenditure, variously mirrored in other countries, and a move back towards a reduction of the size and responsibilities of the state with a greater role envisaged for both private and third sector providers.

Despite these dramatic changes to the context and nature of reforms, there are still important continuities with the previous moves towards a post-bureaucratic system of public governance – networks and partnerships have not yet been completely dismantled, 'outcomes' are still the focus of government publications (ONS, 2010) and the notion of a 'Big Society' retains a communitarian tone to government aspirations. More specifically, in relation to leadership, a number of bodies established by the previous government for providing leadership development, though changed, have continued (e.g. Gove, 2010) and leadership is still a frequent term in health and education department documents (DoH, 2010a; DfE, 2010). Indeed, the role of leadership in the implementation of these new reforms is prominent:

> it is important to emphasise that the legislation is only the starting point. Implementing and embedding reform requires effective local leadership, a focus on our common NHS values and core purpose, and the creation of stronger partnerships with other organisations such as local councils.
>
> (DoH, 2010b: 16)

While the Conservative-led government's enactment of this new stage of reform is in its early stages, it is clear that its reforms will involve a number of key continuities with the previous Labour government, and while the language of leadership will no doubt be subject to changes in application, it is still seen as an important factor in public services reformation.

Concluding discussion – the contextual constraints and potentialities of leaderism for public service reformation

Our analysis of leaderism evident in UK government documents enacting the public services has outlined its features as a framing metaphor and an emergent discourse that has its ideological and cultural roots in managerialism. Its relationship with its intellectual progenitor, however, contains a number of contradictions and tensions that provide it with certain dynamic potentialities. As a framing metaphor, managerialism conceptualizes 'leadership' as a specific form of technical expertise that is to be captured and directed by management – usually within a set of hierarchical power structures and the bureaucratic administrative systems through which it is supported and maintained (Deem *et al.*, 2007; Miller and Rose, 2008). Thus, Blackler's study (2006) of the role played by chief executives in the modernization of the NHS under the New Labour government's ten-year modernization programme suggests that the official drive for strategic change belied an organizational reality in which highly centralized and rigid hierarchies, 'driven by fear' rather than collective involvement and participation, became the norm. This meant that tightly controlled performance management became the *sine qua non* of 'leadership in practice'. Consequently, the reality of organizational leadership in the second phase of NHS modernization undertaken by New Labour between 2000 and 2002 was driven by a populist agenda in which 'quick win' performance improvements, usually measured by the achievement of short-term output targets, crowded out any residual concern with 'the advantages of collective learning in complex work systems' (Blackler, 2006: 19) that might be derived from more bottom-up and distributed forms of collective leadership, and which, as noted, is backgrounded in government documents.

Leaderism (both as a framing metaphor and as an emergent discourse), however, opens up other possibilities and potentialities insofar as it conceptualizes and promotes a notion of *'leadership' as a generic cultural resource and process to be mobilized and diffused by and through a multiplicity of stakeholder interest groups*. As a framing metaphor, leaderism prioritizes 'agency' over 'structure' in a way that is intended to combat the bureaucratic inertia and technocratic myopia symptomatic of the institutional structures and organizational practices legitimated by New Public Management. As an emergent discourse, leaderism integrates, indeed fuses, 'authority', 'control' and 'implementation' in relatively novel and innovative cultural forms and practices that contain the promise of new ways for shaping 'the conduct of persons' (Miller and Rose, 2008) – both as service producers and as service users, or rather 'consumers'. In this respect, leaderism contains within itself the potential to reconstitute legitimacy and relocate accountability within public services insofar as it is aligned, however indirectly and messily in practice, with the hybrid form of neo-liberal ideology and consumerist discourse that has driven public sector restructuring in the UK for most of the present decade (Deem *et al.*, 2007; Frank, 2000; Miller and Rose, 2008; Clarke *et al.*, 2007). The organizational changes associated with this neo-liberal/consumerist ideology may also prove to be sufficiently attractive to public service professionals, or at least certain segments and groups within the latter, who are offered the chance to become pro-active participants in the process of reform that such an ideology legitimates. Thus, McDonald *et al.*'s (2008) study suggests that some public service professionals may be more receptive to new initiatives that emphasize the cultural values and practices associated with 'entrepreneurialism' and 'enterprise' than is often realized. While new, micro-level mechanisms of bureaucratic surveillance and control may be enacted as a result of enhanced 'customization' and 'financialization', these also offer public service professionals the opportunity to reconstruct their occupational identities and strategies around post-bureaucratic cultural values associated with 'independence', 'innovation' and 'change'. In these respects their analysis echoes work on earlier phases of NPM-inspired organizational restructuring, which discovered that public service professions were much more adept at adapting to, even embracing, market-led reforms than the conventional models of professional work practices and identities had suggested (McNulty *et al.*, 1994; Kitchener, 1999).

By consistently emphasizing and promoting the transformative potential inherent in new forms of thinking about and practising 'leadership', leaderism offers the opportunity, at the very least, to public service professionals to become pro-active participants within a system-wide change process that will reconfigure service provision around the 'citizen-consumer' (Clarke *et al.*, 2007). It also holds out the possibility of redefining their occupational cultures and identities in terms that involve the reconstitution of core ideas, such as 'professional autonomy', in ways that are more consistent with an internal institutional world and organizational setting in which consumer, rather than producer, interests are the dominant cultural and political reality. Indeed, the set of core ideas tied to a consumerist ideology and discourse – such as 'choice', 'competition', 'personalization', 'flexibility' and 'decentralization' – generate a wider deliberative context in which established notions of professional autonomy and control may have to be radically reworked if they are to continue to carry substantive cultural meaning and political significance. Both the speed and trajectory that this process of 'professional re-identification' follows may be highly incremental, disjointed, negotiated and fragmented, but the underlying 'direction of travel' seems to be one in which market-based values, however simulated and diluted they become in actual organizational practice (Miller, 2005), are emerging as the dominant icons and norms around which professional restructuring and reconstitution are taking place (Reed, 2007a). As Clarke *et al.* (2007) summarize the current situation:

> The organizational complexity of systems of governance in public services – combining different layers or levels, different spatial formations, different sorts of organizations and different sorts of expertise – produces an institutional architecture in which 'levers' have a hard time connecting central government and front line staff. If anything the last three decades of public service reform have made this architecture more, rather than less, complex through processes of marketization, contracting and partnership that produce multiple organizations engaged in service delivery . . . all of these organizations [included in the study] were in the process of reviewing, rethinking and remaking their relationships with the public. None of them were wholly at ease with a conception of the public as 'consumers' of their service but all recognized that consumerism marked something more than just another government 'initiative'. Relationships with the public were in flux – uncertain and unsettled.
>
> (101–2)

Both as a framing metaphor and as an emergent discourse, leaderism is a key element of this process of cultural re-orientation and political resettlement in UK public services. It has a potentially strategic role to play in helping to align macro-level policy initiatives such as the move towards 'outcomes', meso-level institutional reform and micro-level organizational reframing and restructuring within a wider ideological and political context characterized by the increasing dominance of neo-liberal values but also by deep-seated uncertainty as to how these are to be delivered 'on the ground' and at what cost to the country's social fabric and its underlying moral foundations. As Clarke *et al.* (2007) also note, as the progeny of an ideological/political hybrid of neo-liberalism and social democracy that was, and still is, New Labour, and is still evident in the Conservative aspiration of a 'Big Society', the new paradigm of the 'citizen-consumer' contains profound and potentially destabilizing contradictions and tensions generated by the complex interplay between its dominant and subordinate strands or logics. While the dominant neo-liberal strand or logic prioritizes market-based solutions to public service problems and challenges – as well as the crucial micro-level transformations in organizational culture and occupational practice that they require if they are to have any realistic chance of success – the subordinate social democratic or communitarian strand or logic strives to moderate the longer-term impact of this market fundamentalism on the nexus of social and moral relationships that sustain the social capital through which 'communities' and 'organizations' reproduce themselves (Sayer, 2008). But even the latter is forced to defend subordinate values of collective organization and action in ways that can accommodate sufficient elements of the dominant neo-liberal strand or logic, in which market individualism and consumer choice are the prime discursive conduits for contemporary notions of citizenship and community, if they are to stand any realistic chance of being recognized, much less accepted, within mainstream political debate.

As an element of this wider ideological and political formation, leaderism carries and conveys many of the inherent contradictions and tensions endemic to the former. As a framing metaphor and an emergent discourse, it is used in an attempt to reconcile, if not unify, a broad and complex spectrum of cultural values and organizational practices that are responsive to 'new times' in which the re-imaging of service users as 'citizen-consumers' becomes the dominant ideological motif and policy driver. New forms of distributed and transformational leadership, widely promulgated and diffused throughout public services, become central to the translation of these, rather remote, abstract and complex ideas into organizational realities that symbolize and signify radical and system-wide change. Yet, leaderism cannot entirely throw-off and escape its past; as a generic framing metaphor and as an emerging discourse in which 'leadership', 'change', 'competition' and 'choice' are the recurring strategic themes and images, it cannot afford to cut its ideological and cultural umbilical cord with its managerialist forebear. Neither can it avoid the reality of a plethora of complex organizational settings or 'implementation habitats' (Pollitt *et al.*, 1998) in which ensconced professionals and managers have to interpret the practical meaning of these higher level abstractions and mediate their operational significance for organizational members and, even more crucially, service users (Salaman and Storey, 2008). Taken together, the shadow cast by its intellectual and institutional history combined with the complexities and realities of contemporary organizational life across the UK, public services are likely to dilute the deeper-level impact of leaderism. As the work of the 'governmentality school' (Dean, 1998; Rose, 1999; Miller and

Rose, 2008) on the relationship between 'programmes or rationalities of governance' (that is, generic discourses of reform and the policies emerging from them) on the one hand and 'technologies or practices of governance' (that is, specific techniques, tools and instruments mobilized around these generic discourses) on the other hand suggests, 'government' is a perpetually failing activity.

Nevertheless, we are suggesting that leaderism is likely to 'leave its mark' on the governance systems, processes and practices that are taking shape in contemporary UK public services as they struggle to come to terms with the stark organizational realities that the ideological convergence between neo-liberalism and market consumerism entails. Emerging out of the technocratic culture and rationalistic discourse in which NPM was intellectually constructed and ideologically legitimated, leaderism offers a new and dynamic prospectus for reform in which entrepreneurial vision and market realism, effectively linked to strategic leadership and professional revitalization, will facilitate the institutional environments and organizational locales in which the iconography of the 'citizen-consumer' can become an operational reality. But the ever-present temptation to get dragged back into the 'bad old days and ways' of either, on the one hand, intrusive micro-level surveillance, meso-level authoritarianism and macro-level centralism, or, on the other hand, 'slash and burn' cost-cutting and contracting-out market principles are never too far away. However exciting and liberating the promise of radical strategic and operational change offered by the co-partnership of market individualism/consumerism and institutional/organizational leaderism, the incessant 'top-down' political pressure from policy-making elites (as documented by Blackler, 2006, for example) and the pressing 'bottom-up' demands from a range of stakeholder user and employee representative groups (as documented by Clarke *et al.*, 2007) are likely to prove to be enduring and obdurate constraints on future change programmes and technologies.

Acknowledgements

The research reported in this chapter was funded by the Economic and Social Research Council (ESRC), Award No. R-000–23–1136 'Developing Organisation Leaders as Change Agents in the Public Services'. The views expressed in this chapter are those of the authors and do not represent the views of the ESRC.

References

6, P. (2004) 'Joined-up government in the western world in comparative perspective: A preliminary literature review and exploration', *Journal of Public Administration Research and Theory*, 14, 103–138.

Blackler, F. (2006) 'Chief executives and the modernization of the English National Health Service', *Leadership*, 2, 5–30.

Blair, T. (1998) *The third way: New politics for the new century*, London: Fabian Society.

Boltanski, L. and Chiapello, E. (2005) *The new spirit of capitalism*, London: Verso.

Bovaird, T. and Russell, K. (2007) 'Civil service reform in the UK, 1999–2005: Revolutionary failure or evolutionary success?', *Public Administration*, 85, 301–328.

Cabinet Office (1999) *Modernising government*, London: Cabinet Office.

—— (2008) *Excellence and fairness: Achieving world class public services*, London: Cabinet Office.

—— (2009) *Working together: Public services on your side*, London: Cabinet Office.

Clarke, J. and Newman, J. (1997) *The managerial state: Power, politics and ideology in the remaking of social welfare*, London: Sage.

Clarke, J., Newman, J., Smith, N., Vidler, E. and Westmarland, L. (2007) *Creating citizen-consumers: Changing publics and changing public services*, London: Sage.

Collet, T. (2009) 'Civilization and civilized in post-9/11 US presidential speeches', *Discourse and Society*, 20, 455–475.

Davies, J.S. (2009) 'The limits of joined-up government: Towards a political analysis', *Public Administration*, 87, 80–96.

Dean, M. (1998) *Governmentality: Power and rule in modern society*, London: Sage.

Deem, R., Hillyard, S. and Reed, M. (2007) *Knowledge, higher education, and the new managerialism: The changing management of UK universities*, Oxford: Oxford University Press.

Department for Education (DfE) (2010) *The importance of teaching: The schools white paper 2010*, London: Department for Education.

Department for Education and Skills (DfES) (2003) *A new specialist system: Transforming secondary education*, London: Department for Education and Skills.

—— (2004) *Department for education and skills: Five year strategy for children and learners: Putting people at the heart of public services*, London: Department for Education and Skills.

Department of Health (DoH) (2003) *Building on the best: Choice, responsiveness and equity in the NHS*, London: DoH.

—— (2004) *The NHS improvement plan: Putting people at the heart of public services*, London: DoH.

—— (2005) *Creating a patient-led NHS: Delivering the NHS improvement plan*, London: DoH.

—— (2010a) *Equity and excellence: Liberating the NHS*, London: DoH.

—— (2010b) *Liberating the NHS: Legislative framework and next steps*, London: DoH.

Driver, S. and Martell, L. (1998) *New labour: Politics after Thatcherism*, Cambridge: Polity Press.

Dunleavy, P., Margetts, H., Bastow, S. and Tinkler, J. (2006) 'New public management is dead – long live digital-era governance', *Journal of Public Administration Research and Theory*, 16, 467–494.

Fairclough, N. (2003) *Analysing discourse: Textual analysis for social research*, London: Routledge.

—— (2005) 'Peripheral vision: Discourse analysis in organization studies: The case for critical realism', *Organization Studies*, 26, 915–939.

Ferlie, E. and Andresani, G. (2006) 'Understanding current developments in public-sector management: New public management, governance or other theoretical perspectives?', *Public Management Review*, 8, 389–394.

Ferlie, E. and Fitzgerald, L. (2002) 'The sustainability of the new public management in the UK', in McLaughlin, K., Osborne, S. and Ferlie, E. (eds) *New public management: Current trends and future prospects*, London: Routledge.

Firth, J.R. (1968) 'A synopsis of linguistic theory, 1930–55', in Palmer, F.R. (ed.) *Selected papers of J.R. Firth 1952–59*, London/Harlow: Longmans.

Frank, T. (2000) *One market under god: Extreme capitalism, market populism and the end of economic democracy*, New York: Secker and Warburg.

Giddens, A. (1998) *The third way: The renewal of social democracy*, Cambridge: Polity Press.

—— (2000) *The third way and its critics*, Cambridge: Polity Press.

Gove, M. (2010) *Public bodies reform: Letter to the chair of the national college for leadership of schools and children's services*, available at www.nationalcollege. org.uk/download?id=141051 (accessed 23 March 2012).

Hajer, M. (1995) *The politics of environmental discourse*, Oxford: Oxford University Press.

Hale, S. (2002) 'Professor MacMurray and Mr Blair: The strange case of the communitarian guru that never was', *The Political Quarterly*, 73, 191–197.

Hale, S., Leggett, W. and Martell, L. (eds) (2004) *The third way and beyond: Criticisms, futures, alternatives*, Manchester: Manchester University Press.

Hecksher, C. and Donnellon, A. (eds) (1994) *The post-bureaucratic organization: New perspectives on organizational change*, London: Sage.

Hood, C. (1991) 'A public management for all seasons', *Public Administration*, 69, 3–20.

Kitchener, M. (1999) 'All fur coat and no knickers: Contemporary organizational change in UK hospitals', in Brock, D., Powell, M. and Hinings, C. (eds) *Restructuring the professional organization*, London: Routledge.

Labour Party (2001) *Ambitions for Britain: Labour's manifesto 2001*, London: Labour Party.

—— (2005) *The Labour Party manifesto 2005: Britain forward not back*, London: Labour Party.

—— (2006) *Let's talk: Public service reform*, London: Labour Party.

Lakoff, G. and Johnson, M. (2003) *Metaphors we live by*, Chicago: University of Chicago Press.

Lee, S. and Woodward, R. (2002) 'Implementing the third way: The delivery of public services under the Blair government', *Public Money and Management*, 22, 49–56.

McDonald, R., Harrison, S. and Checkland, K. (2008) 'Identity, contract and enterprise in a primary care setting: An English general practice case study', *Organization*, 15, 355–370.

McLaughlin, K., Osborne, S. and Ferlie, E. (eds) (2002) *New Public Management: Current trends and future prospects*, London: Routledge.

McNulty, T., Whittington, R., Whipp, R. and Kitchener, M. (1994) 'Implementing marketing in NHS hospitals', *Public Money and Management*, 14, 51–57.

Miller, D. (2005) 'What is best value?: Bureaucracy, virtualism and local governance', in Du Gay, P. (ed.) *The values of bureaucracy*, Oxford: Oxford University Press.

Miller, P. and Rose, N.S. (2008) 'Mobilizing the consumer: Assembling the subject of consumption', in Miller, P. and Rose, N.S. (eds) *Governing the present*, Cambridge: Polity Press.

Mintzberg, H. (1979) *The structuring of organizations: A synthesis of the research*, Upper Saddle River, NJ: Prentice-Hall.

Nelson, M. (2006) 'Semantic associations in business English: A corpus-based analysis', *English for Specific Purposes*, 25, 217–234.

Newman, J. (2005) 'Enter the transformational leader: Network governance and the micro-politics of modernization', *Sociology*, 39, 717–734.

O'Reilly, D. and Reed, M. (2010) '"Leaderism": An evolution of managerialism in UK public service reform', *Public Administration*, 88, 960–978.

O'Reilly, D., Wallace, M., Deem, R., Morris, J. and Reed, M. (2007) 'The managerial innovation of national leadership development bodies to acculturate change agents for public service reform in England', paper presented at the International Research Symposium on Public Management, Potsdam University, Germany.

Odone, C. (1999) 'Tony Blair is one of life's cardinals: Stand by for his emergence as our new lord protector', *New Statesman*, 26 April, available at www.new statesman.com/199904260019 (accessed 30 March 2012).

Organization for Economic Co-operation and Development (OECD) (2000) *Government of the future*, Paris: OECD.

―― (2001) *Public sector leadership for the 21st century*, Paris: OECD.

―― (2004) *Policy brief: Public sector modernisation: Governing for performance*, Paris: OECD.

―― (2010) *Making reform happen: Lessons from OECD countries*, Paris: OECD.

Office for National Statistics (ONS) (2010) *Measuring outcomes for public service users*, Newport: Office for National Statistics.

Office of Public Service Reform (OPSR) (2002) *Reforming our public services: Principles into practice*, London: Office of Public Service Reform.

Osborne, D. and Gaebler, T. (1992) *Reinventing government: How the entrepreneurial spirit is transforming the public sector*, Reading, MA: Addison-Wesley.

Osborne, S. (2006) 'The new public governance?', *Public Management Review*, 8, 377–387.

Performance and Innovation Unit (PIU) (2001) *Strengthening leadership in the public services*, London: Performance and Innovation Unit.

Peters, T.J. and Waterman, R.H. (1982) *In search of excellence: Lessons from America's best run companies*, London: Harper and Row.

Pollitt, C. (2007) 'New Labour's redisorganization: Hyper-modernism and the costs of reform – a cautionary tale', *Public Management Review*, 9, 529–543.

―― (2008) 'Bureaucracies remember, post-bureaucratic organizations forget?', *Public Administration*, 87, 198–218.

Pollitt, C. and Bouckaert, G. (2004) *Public management reform: A comparative analysis*, Oxford: Oxford University Press.

Pollitt, C., Birchall, J. and Putnam, K. (1998) *Decentralising public service management*, Basingstoke: Macmillan.

Pollitt, C., Talbot, C., Caulfield, J. and Smullen, A. (2004) *Agencies – how governments do things through semi-autonomous organizations*, Basingstoke: Palgrave Macmillan.

Reed, M. (2007a) 'Engineers of human souls, faceless technocrats or merchants of morality?: Changing professional forms and identities in the face of the neo-liberal challenge', in Pinnington, A., Macklin, R. and Campbell, T. (eds) *Human resource management: Ethics and employment*, Oxford: Oxford University Press.

―― (2007b) 'New managerialism and public service reform: From regulated autonomy to institutionalized distrust', in Deem, R., Hillyard, S. and Reed, M. (eds)

Knowledge, higher education, and the new managerialism: The changing management of UK universities, Oxford: Oxford University Press.

Rose, N. (1999) *Powers of freedom*, Cambridge: Cambridge University Press.

Ruef, M. and Harness, A. (2009) 'Agrarian origins of management ideology: The Roman and Antebellum cases', *Organization Studies*, 30, 589–607.

Salaman, G. and Storey, J. (2008) 'Understanding enterprise', *Organization*, 15, 315–324.

Sayer, A. (2008) 'Moral economic regulation in organizations: A university example', *Organization*, 15, 147–164.

The Treasury (2009) *Public service agreements 2008–2011*, London: The Treasury.

Wallace, M. and Pocklington, K. (2002) *Managing complex educational change: Large-scale reorganisation of schools*, London: Routledge.

Wallis, J. and Dollery, B. (1997) 'An evaluation of leadership as a response to agency failure in the public sector', *Public Administration*, 75, 247–265.

Webb, S.B. (ed.) (2008) *Public sector reform: What works and why? An IEG evaluation of World Bank support*, Washington DC: World Bank.

Weber, M. (1978) *Economy and society: An outline of interpretive sociology*, Berkeley: University of California Press.

Wiesner, E. (1993) *From macroeconomic correction to public sector reform: The critical role of evaluation*, Washington DC: World Bank.

List of documents analyzed

Cabinet Office (1999) *Modernising government*, London: Cabinet Office.

—— (2008) *Excellence and fairness: achieving world class public services*, London: Cabinet Office.

DfEE (1997) *Excellence in schools*, London: Department for Education and Employment.

—— (1998) *Teachers meeting the challenge of change*, London: Department for Education and Employment.

DfES (2001) *Schools achieving success*, London: Department for Education and Skills.

—— (2003) *A new specialist system: transforming secondary education*, London: Department for Education and Skills.

—— (2003) *The future of higher education*, London: Department for Education and Skills.

—— (2004) *Department for Education and Skills: five year strategy for children and learners: putting people at the heart of public services*, London: Department for Education and Skills.

—— (2005) *Higher standards, better schools for all. More choice for parents and pupils*, London: Department for Education and Skills.

DoH (1997) *The New NHS. Modern, dependable*, London: Department of Health.

—— (2002) *Delivering the NHS Plan: next steps on investment, next steps on reform*, London: Department of Health.

—— (2004) *The NHS improvement plan: putting people at the heart of public services*, London: Department of Health.

—— (2005) *Health reform in England: update and next steps*, London: Department of Health.

—— (2006) *The NHS in England: the operating framework for 2007/08*, London: Department of Health.

OPSR (2002) *Reforming our public services: principles into practice*, London: Office of Public Service Reform.

—— (2005) *Putting people at the heart of public services*, London: Office of Public Services Reform.

Strategy Unit (2006) *The UK government's approach to public service reform – a discussion paper*, London: Cabinet Office.

—— (2007) *Building on progress: public services*, London: Cabinet Office.

The Treasury (1998a) *Modern public services for Britain: investing in reform*, London: HM Treasury.

—— (1998b) *Public services for the future*, London: HM Treasury.

—— (2000) *Public services productivity: meeting the challenge. A joint report by the Public Services Productivity Panel*, London: HM Treasury.

3 Leading transformation in public delivery systems

A political perspective

Damien Contandriopoulos and Jean-Louis Denis

Introduction

What does leadership look like from a macrosystemic perspective? This is the core question this chapter addresses. The idea that leadership plays a central role in the governance and politics of public delivery systems and, ultimately, in the achievement of better services is plausible considering the challenges faced by these systems. While the literatures on leadership and on governance deal with similar issues, for a long time they remained on two parallel tracks (with some exceptions in the implementation literature, such as Nakamura and Smallwood, 1980). In line with perspectives on horizontal and collective leadership, the aim of this chapter is to integrate these two streams to reach a deeper understanding of the practice of leadership in public delivery systems. Our approach is anchored in a political reading of the implementation of reform and is based on empirical data from studies of health care reform in Quebec, a Canadian province.

In recent decades health care organizations and systems have been consistently described as under pressure to make major changes to rectify perceived dysfunctions and to ensure long-term adaptability and sustainability (Flood, 2000; Ham, 1997; Mechanic, 2008; Saltman, Busse and Mossialos, 2002; Sinclair, 2002; Tuohy, 1999, 2002; Watson, 2005). As such, health care systems have become major laboratories for attempting large-scale changes in complex systems (Evans, 2005; Denis, Lamothe, Langley and Guérard, 2008). Despite the significant shifts in resource utilization already accomplished (McKee and Healy, 2002; Reid and Schneider *et al.*, 2002), a deeper understanding is needed of the conditions and processes required to bring about significant and sustainable changes in health care delivery and services (Ferlie and Shortell, 2001; Ham, Kipping, and McLeod, 2003; McNulty and Ferlie, 2002). The ability to implement such deliberate and desirable transformations appears to depend fundamentally on health care systems' capacity to connect policy objectives to managerial systems and organizational dynamics (Saltman, Busse and Mossialos, 2002). Proposals for reforming public service delivery systems tend, however, to consist of multiple loosely defined and ambitious changes or innovation programmes that involve diffuse networks of actors and organizations (Rhodes, 1990; Wallace and Pocklington, 2002).

Successful implementation of reforms in health care systems will have to go beyond simple command-and-control models, toward a broader approach that takes into account the dynamics of political negotiation, sensemaking and organizational learning within target institutions (Nakamura and Smallwood, 1980). This, in turn, means that individual and organizational political influence and capacities will play a central role in reform processes.

Conceptual frameworks for understanding reform processes in complex systems should offer actionable normative advice on what models of policy network governance are most likely to bring about desirable changes. For this to happen, two opposing theoretical perspectives need to be reconciled. First, productive conceptual frameworks must provide a way to grasp the interdependency of the individual and collective levels of action. Linking the concepts of power and leadership with policy network governance requires conceiving of leadership as, at least partly, a fit between abilities, institutional pressures and the existing power equilibrium in a given system. Second, such a framework needs to provide a more decentralized approach to governance. Governance is usually defined as the orchestration of collective actions from a position of authority (Hatchuel, 2000). Governance entails mobilizing power and allocating resources to coordinate the actions of organizations and individuals with potentially conflicting interests in order to achieve collective goals (Davis, 2005; Davis and Donaldson, 1997; Eisenhardt, 1989; Harding and Preker, 2003; Saltman and Ferroussier-Davis, 2000). Governance is clearly central to policy reform processes. However, the concept of governance should probably evolve toward a more decentralized notion in which multiple and potentially discordant sources of influence play a determining role in policy implementation. In this chapter we develop the notion of 'political slack' to discuss the practice of leadership in complex policy and delivery systems. As suggested by Rhodes' (1997) provocative statement, 'Messy problems need messy solutions', in systems characterized by fragmentation and distributed capacities, it is unlikely that policies can be successfully implemented by relying strictly on a command-and-control governance model (Nakamura and Smallwood, 1980). As will be argued in detail in this chapter, such decentralization of the concept of governance has implications for the role and nature of leadership in public delivery systems. It somewhat legitimizes the practice of leadership by a much broader range of actors and locates the leadership phenomenon within organizational and policy-arena politics.

Empirically, this chapter draws on two complementary sources of data on the development of regional governance as an instrument for continuous reform implementation. The first consists of evidence derived from a long-standing body of work on regional governance in the Quebec health care system (Contandriopoulos and Denis, 2007; Contandriopoulos, Denis, Langley and Valette, 2004, 2005; Contandriopoulos, Hudon, Martin and Thompson,

2007; Denis, Contandriopoulos and Beaulieu, 2004; Denis, Contandriopoulos, Langley and Valette, 1998; Denis, Contandriopoulos, Langley, Valette and Rodriguez, 2000; Denis *et al.*, 2008). The second source is a study of a Quebec health care system reform launched in 2004. Structurally, this reform created ninety-five local health networks across the province's publicly-funded health care system. At the heart of these networks were the new health and social services centres (HSSCs) created through the structural integration (merger) of community health clinics, long-term care institutions and, in a majority of cases, community hospitals in a defined geographical territory. Each HSSC was mandated to create local health networks through contractual arrangements and alliances (virtual integration) with physicians in private practices, teaching hospitals and non-governmental community organizations in their territory. These local health networks were aimed at improving the integration of care and services and ultimately the health of the population. The implementation of this reform required the active participation of agents who were distributed across the different organizations and levels of governance. The implementation of the reform requires, *de facto*, a concerted effort among a multiplicity of agents with various sources of expertise and legitimacy. Consequently, leadership cannot be approached from an individual perspective, but must instead be analyzed more systemically.

Conceptual background

Policy initiatives and political slack

Different perspectives have been adopted to analyze the evolution of governance practices in contemporary public delivery systems. One such perspective is the policy network tradition initially developed by Rhodes (1990, 1997, 2007), which recognizes the heterogeneity of participants, in situations of distributed capacities and power and of non-hierarchical relationships among actors and organizations. Public delivery systems, by their very nature, require that the state develop new roles and forms of control that depart from traditional hierarchical bureaucratic control. In other words, from a policy network perspective, governance practices must be transformed because delivery systems have become more complex and direct authority over all the system components required to adapt and improve services has consequently been diminished (Rhodes, 2007; Kickert, Kliijn and Koppenjan, 1997).

One alternative way of conceiving of governance would be to 'decentralize' it to take into account situations in which multiple and discordant sources of influence are the norm. In other words, rather than conceiving of governance as the exclusive prerogative of a central government, a more appropriate approach might be to focus on governance as a collective enterprise in which various actors try to influence organizational behaviours, resource allocation and ultimately service delivery. In decentralized governance, actors' leadership, abilities and power would play a key role in defining the governance system as well as its effects.

This conception does not negate the instrumental view, in which a given actor's action is seen as an effort to modify the governance system's rules or processes in order to achieve specific outcomes. For example, for a central government whose ambition is to reform public delivery systems, the instrumental question will be to identify the governance models that are most likely to bring about significant and desirable changes in line with policy objectives. However, in a context where power is diffused and goals at best partially convergent, achieving desired outcomes will require a much more dynamic conception of directivity that includes granting enough autonomy to local actors to allow for policies to be adapted to different organizational and social contexts. To accomplish this, it would be crucial to include a diversity of actors in open decision-making and learning processes. In other words, policy implementation can be conceived as the result of adopting a more flexible approach to steering a system, combined with intense bottom-up dynamics.

Reforms – conceived as significant, deliberate modifications in the governance of public systems – usually involve legislative or regulatory documents that state the goal of the policy initiative and link this goal with modifications to organizational structure, resource allocation, accountability lines or rules, structures and procedures. Such prescriptions are the result of the long and tortuous process known as policy-making. However, the literature on public policy implementation shows that every policy initiative leaves room for interpretation, negotiation and sensemaking (Cline, 2000; Matland, 1995; Sabatier, 1986). As Nakamura and Smallwood put it, 'Experience shows that these instructions can range from precise "blueprints" to rather vague exhortations. The degree of specificity in policy instructions defines the amount of discretion enjoyed by implementers and evaluators' (1980: 31). Sensemaking processes (Weick, 2001), power relations, and environmental and contingent influences (Schofield, 2004; Sabatier and Jenkins-Smith, 1993, 1999) across the system also play a central role in the implementation of reforms. This view suggests that policy implementation processes both continue and mimic the dynamics of policy-making (Barrett and Hill, 1984; Matland, 1995; Bardach, 1977).

In this chapter, we use the term 'political slack' to refer to the room left for processes of negotiation and interpretation in policy implementation. We coined this term by analogy with the concept of organizational slack within the behavioural theory of the firm (Cyert and March, 1963; Cohen *et al.*, 1972). Organizational slack is defined as organizational resources or capabilities in excess of the basic demands of the environment. Slack allows organizations to react to unexpected circumstances without disruptions in operations and output. It provides extra information treatment capacity outside the formal structure and enhances innovation capacities (Bourgeois, 1981). Organizational slack allows organizations to adapt to disruptions caused by policy changes.

The political and organizational levels are thus linked, since the capacity of target institutions to take advantage of political slack within a given policy arena will depend on their level of organizational slack.

While organizational slack is a characteristic of a single organization in relation to its capacity to buffer itself from the environment, political slack is almost the opposite. Political slack is a characteristic of the external environment's malleability and of the capacity of organizations to shape that environment. In the context of a given policy initiative, political slack refers to the extent to which individual targeted institutions have the capacity and opportunity to appropriate the policy, interpret it and shape its application. What makes political slack truly an environmental rather than an organizational characteristic is that, in any policy system, organizations will influence each other in the interpretation and implementation process. The more successful an organization is in taking advantage of political slack, the more it contributes to actually re-drafting the parameters of the original policy and modifying its impact on other organizations within the system. Through a feedback process, this would affect the policy environment and the level of political slack. One possible consequence of this dynamic is that it could set a precedent and be used by others to increase the level of political slack within the system. Alternatively, it could limit the possibility for others to offer or implement alternative interpretations of the policy and thus reduce the level of political slack. The leadership of policy processes is thus closely associated with actors' and organizations' involvement in promoting specific interpretations of a policy and strategies to adapt new policies to their contexts.

We also suggest that, in a given policy environment, the amount of political slack will be determined by structural characteristics (i.e., number of actors, interdependence, power equilibrium), individual characteristics (i.e., abilities, resources, leadership) and the characteristics of the policy itself (i.e., measurability of the policy goals, directivity of the implementation model, congruence between the policy's value base and actors' values). Obviously the levels are quite interdependent. For example, a system targeted by a policy initiative can have structural characteristics that allow organizations with sufficient legitimacy and diversified sources of power to set the conditions under which they will play the game and take the policy seriously. However, the decision to play the game or not will depend not only on an organization's capacity to act but also on the convergence between its own goals and the policy's underlying values and objectives. Conversely, an organization's capacity to control the policy environment will depend on the policy's degree of convergence with social values, the measurability of outcomes and the extent to which achieving outcomes depends on coordinated action.

Even if fundamentally different from organizational slack, political slack replicates some of its key features. For example, a high level of slack makes it possible to adapt policy to local context and unanticipated circumstances. Slack leaves room for adaptability and limits the information and standardized processes that have to accompany a given policy to secure implementation, thereby reducing the need for vertical information processing in target institutions. This suggests a potential for central government to employ political slack deliberately, much in the same way that top management can use organizational slack as a resource to enhance innovation (Bourgeois, 1981). Thus, in contrast to the hierarchical view of policy implementation, we do not see political slack as a problem to be circumvented, but rather as an inherent characteristic of systems that in some circumstances may generate learning and adaptation. As we discuss later on, we also suggest that efficient leaders can not only take advantage of the level of political slack, but also aim to influence the level of slack in accordance with their strategic goals and preferences.

However, as in organizational theory, slack is not a panacea. Political slack within a policy system will relieve the vertical information flow but will conversely create the need for an effective and powerful horizontal information system among local actors targeted by the policy, to support negotiation, dialogue and consensus. From a top-down perspective, political slack also introduces unpredictability into the final output. It could be hypothesized that, as in organizational slack, the optimal amount of political slack will adopt a curvilinear form, in which both too much and not enough will translate into suboptimal implementation. A policy initiative without enough slack would probably be unimplementable when confronted with an unexpected situation, whereas excessive slack would produce such large variations in implementation that the original policy objectives could be lost in the process.

We suggest that political slack will inevitably be an issue in health care reforms because of the size and complexity of the systems involved. Its relative importance and impact will vary greatly depending on how the policy imperatives and the strategies for implementation are designed, the number of actors concerned, the nature of those actors and the stakes for them and, finally, the policy domain.

The optimal level of political slack is thus contingent on many factors that are often outside the control of any single actor within the system. However, we contend that this concept can be helpful in understanding how an astute and powerful actor could exploit and influence the level of political slack within a governance system to achieve significant transformations. For example, we hypothesize that allowing a high level of slack at the beginning of a policy implementation process will promote variability in the policy's interpretation and implementation and the development of innovative solutions to practical challenges. Then, in a second step, squeezing out the slack and becoming more directive in diffusing promising models and weeding out the not-so-promising ones would maximize the probability of achieving policy goals. One informant in Quebec described such tactical control of political slack by the regional health authority as 'the python-swallowing approach'.

In the next section we use the concept of collective leadership to discuss how actors can exploit political slack in ways that are more or less aligned with initial policy objectives. This can be seen as an asset or an obstacle, depending on the policy's perceived desirability and intrinsic value. As such, the political slack framework developed in this chapter is both a theory of implementation and a theory of policy adaptation.

Collective leadership: abilities and power

Recent studies on collective, collaborative and distributive leadership in contemporary organizations suggest that effective forms of leadership are those that are aligned with the complexity of organizational and institutional contexts. To characterize more specifically the complexity of the organizational and institutional arrangements described in the previous section, we turn now to the concept of pluralistic contexts developed in earlier studies (Denis, Lamothe and Langley, 2001; Denis, Langley and Rouleau, 2007). Pluralistic contexts are characterized by distributed expertise, diffuse patterns of power and influence, and uncertainties about the relations between means and ends. In line with our discussion in the previous section, any reform policy undertaken in such contexts will be developed and implemented in a somewhat unpredictable pattern because of the multiple processes of interpretation and negotiation that will occur among a large set of actors and organizations (Denis, Lamothe, Langley *et al.*, 2009; Morrell and Hartley, 2006).

Two issues are central to the analysis of leadership dynamics in pluralistic contexts. The first relates to the social arrangements that enable the emergence of leadership capacity in a context where formal authority plays a marginal role. In previous research on leadership dynamics in health care organizations, we observed that leadership capacity is based on the ability to constitute a group of leaders who together have access to various sources of legitimacy and influence (Denis, Lamothe and Langley, 2001; Denis, Kisfalvi, Langley and Rouleau, 2010). In pluralistic contexts, the challenge of developing leadership calls for a collective capacity to incorporate the different institutional logics underlying the organization's structuration. Institutional logics are rooted in professionalization, bureaucracies and social norms and strongly influence the evolution of any given system (Lounsbury and Crumley, 2007). While institutional logics refer to broad principles that guide social action (Greenwood, Diaz, Li and Lorente, 2010), groups and organizations also promote specific interests that significantly influence the system's evolution (Alford, 1975). An analysis of the phenomenon of leadership in the health care reform context must necessarily focus on strategies used by aspiring leaders to take into account the wide range of potentially divergent norms and interests held by a variety of groups and organizations. As noted briefly above, legitimacy gained through effective mobilization of underlying norms and values is a key asset in the capacity to exploit available political slack to one's advantage. However, because of conflicting logics and interests, leadership capacity in major transformation processes will be highly unstable. The second issue in the analysis of leadership dynamics relates to the relative alignment with reformative templates. Leaders can be very effective in influencing the evolution of a system, although not always in line with policy objectives. In other words, we should not discount leaders' capacity to mobilize political slack in order to orient policy implementation in their own favoured direction. This could have very different implications depending on how convergent this favoured direction is with the original policy objectives. In one scenario, it could produce an ingenious adaptation of policy tools to achieve the original objective, while in another, it could provide the capacity to maintain the status quo in practice notwithstanding the policy's goal. As such, the mobilization of collective leadership in politically slack systems is a central determinant of the capacity to deliberately achieve significant reforms. Institutional theorists have recently paid much attention to the question of agency in highly institutionalized environment. As suggested by Lawrence and Suddaby (2006), actors may invest energy to impede or stimulate institutional transformation. In addition, the nature of any given system, even one with a loosely coupled structure, partly predefines the agency of different individuals, groups or organizations within it (Hallett and Ventresca, 2006). For example, in health care systems, the structural position of certain groups such as the medical profession will determine their ability to shape reforms (Contandriopoulos and Brousselle, 2010; Tuohy, 1999). While the practice of leadership implies the ability to take disconnected courses of action and to depart somewhat from the dominant institutional discipline (see, for example, Zietsma and Lawrence, 2010), the system's structure distributes the relative capacity for action among multiple agents.

In this chapter, we suggest that it is important to look beyond individuals' abilities to exert influence, and to focus instead on leadership as a collective phenomenon embedded in organizational and institutional contexts. Agents develop strategies to become influential in their own organizational and institutional contexts, and are both constrained and enabled by this context. This approach to the study of leadership provides a basis to understand the role of actors in policy networks that are driven by processes that depart from the hierarchical model of policy implementation. This approach is also in line with a more dynamic, decentralized and fluid notion of governance as described earlier.

The case of Quebec's health care reform

In this section, we describe our research context. We then provide a brief overview of the dynamic between political slack and the renewal of governance practices within the Quebec health care system. Finally, we look at strategies for getting the most out of political slack to implement significant changes.

Research context

Health care reforms can be conceived as attempts to effect multi-component changes in complex systems. Within health care systems, the pursuit of greater integration and better coordination of care, the resurgence of interest in a population health approach to health care delivery, and the reliance on networks in many reforms all underscore the need to analyze implementation dynamics and the conditions associated with increased capacities to govern such processes. In this chapter we use the case of the broad reform of Quebec's health care system initiated in 2004 to illustrate the potential of the approaches to governance discussed above.

As mentioned earlier, the reform created ninety-five local health networks across the province. The health and social services centres created from mergers of community health clinics, long-term care institutions, and most often community hospitals, were at the heart of the reform. HSSCs were mandated to develop local health networks through alliances with physicians, teaching hospitals and community organizations. These networks were aimed at improving the integration of care and services, and ultimately the population's health. In practice, these broad objectives left much room for interpretation in the conceptualization of the linkage between the reform's principles and the operational service delivery arrangements. Throughout the stages of policy elaboration, adoption and implementation, the level of available political slack was rather high, although, as we will discuss, it varied considerably depending on specific policy objectives.

Empirical illustration: variations in political slack and in leadership capacity

The dynamics of Quebec's implementation of a major health care reform illustrate the role of political slack in leadership capacity to carry out large-scale transformation. Quebec's health care system is structured around three main levels of governance: the Ministry of Health, the regional health authorities (RHA) and the HSSCs. In addition to the governance exercised at each of these levels, some health care organizations such as teaching hospitals also exert considerable influence. As mentioned earlier, Quebec's health care reform was based on a broad policy initiative with multiple, more or less integrated, objectives. To pursue these objectives, the government relied on different policy instruments with very different levels of political slack.

Some parts of the reform, such as performance contracts, were designed and implemented with tight controls and very limited political slack. Other parts, however, depended on embedded slack to allow a continuation of the policy-making process locally at the implementation stage. For example, crucial decisions such as defining the boundaries of HSSC territories, selecting the entities (community health centres, nursing homes, community hospitals) that would be part of each HSSC, determining the number of HSSCs for each health region, etc., were explicitly delegated by the Ministry of Health to the RHAs. The policy itself left, by design, a significant amount of political slack that could be used by actors locally and regionally to shape important aspects of the reform and consequently its potential and results. The negotiation process involved in determining the form and nature of the HSSCs has been analyzed elsewhere (Contandriopoulos *et al.*, 2007). That analysis suggested that political slack allowed rapid implementation of some components of what was a very ambitious reform (merging hundreds of hospitals, community clinics and long-term care centres into ninety-five new entities without disrupting service delivery) at the expense of some significant modifications to the model that had been originally planned (for example, many institutions were able to escape forced merger and maintain their autonomy). The reform also left significant political slack in other important policy areas. For example, HSSCs were expected (Bill 25, article 99.5) to adopt a broad population health perspective in their planning and delivery model, but the definition of what constituted population needs, population health or appropriate strategies to achieve such a perspective were left almost totally open. This prompted a great deal of interpretative and sensemaking activities during the reform implementation process (Denis, Lamothe, Langley *et al.*, 2009). It also meant that local organizations paid more or less attention (definitely less at the operational level) to this mandate.

From the perspective of the reform leaders in central government, leaving more slack produced results that were in line with the theoretical hypotheses discussed earlier. On one hand, it increased the amount of inter-organizational and inter-regional variation as well as overall variability in the implemented practices. On the other hand, it enabled the rapid and locally contextualized implementation of ambitious changes. Rapid implementation was possible in large part because opposition was channelled into local political struggles rather than into macro policy debates. Such local political struggles in politically slack policy implementation will weed out the weak and allow the strong to make sure their preferences and interests are well taken into account in the implemented policy. This in turn has a lot to do with leadership capabilities and the mobilization of sources of legitimacy. As such, political slack ensures rapid implementation of politically easy targets by local leaders and organizations, while politically tough targets are taken out of the implementation game, at least for the moment. As an example, local leaders in the first phase of the reform focused on consolidating the newly merged HSSCs as unified organizations and less on integrating care across networks with other providers, and much less on developing innovative interventions to improve the health of the population. There were exceptions, because some local leaders' capabilities were based not only on their political weight but also on their skill in using the broader policy context to induce more significant changes. Leaders who were able to develop policy discourses in line with dominant values and official policy goals gained influence over others and had more impact on the policy's implementation. From the perspective of the central government, allowing a significant level of political slack was a way to tap into such local leadership capabilities. It might be difficult (or impossible) to set out the implementation details definitively from the central level, but to the extent that local variability can be tolerated, political slack is a way to capitalize on distributed leadership across the policy system.

However, as mentioned, not all facets of this reform were characterized by a large amount of political slack. On the contrary, some aspects were deliberately drafted to limit political slack and maintain top-down implementation. For example, the HSSCs' and RHAs' financial accountability to the Ministry of Health was significantly tightened during this period. Modalities to achieve this were explicit and were implemented in a tight command-and-control mode that left little room for locally initiated adjustments. In addition, the Ministry of Health began signing contracts with each RHA that specified levels of activity, mainly volumes for certain types of procedures. RHAs then signed contracts with each HSSC that translated regional objectives into local contractual objectives. These contracts were initially seen as very top-down, and in some cases they were at variance with regional or local priorities. Some adjustments were made to the contract approach following a provincial tour by the Ministry of Health in each region to discuss the potential and limitations of contract-based management. However, local organizations complained that these contracts were only one aspect of the accountability dynamic within the system. Besides embedding objectives in contracts, the Ministry of Health also imposed additional mandates or priorities, such as the development of specific services or the resolution of long-standing problems (e.g. overcrowded emergency rooms), that added to their existing contractual obligations. These additional demands on RHAs and local organizations, often drafted in response to pressures that the government was under, operated within a strong top-down dynamic without much space for negotiation and interpretation. Local leaders could not protect themselves and their organizations from these pressures and had to respond to them and achieve the targets.

Finally, there is considerable variation in the length of time during which a reform process allows significant levels of political slack. Some components of Quebec's reform implementation showed very high initial levels of slack, which then rapidly evaporated. For example, we observed very high levels of political slack during the determination of the number and structure of HSSCs. However, once these elements were formally decided they became almost irreversible and political slack at that level disappeared. Yet for other components of the same reform, a significant level of political slack persisted years after their official adoption. For example, the practical operationalization of the HSSCs' population health mandate is still the object of negotiation, sensemaking and political activity today. In this case, a significant level of political slack should be considered a property of this specific reform component. This seems to be the fate of some reform components that a central government either cannot or does not want to control strictly but still wants to include formally in a larger reform project. From the perspective we have developed here, embedding such broad policy objectives in a reform proposal without linking them to any precise operational blueprint can be seen as a way to capitalize on leadership at the local level. Those objectives being formally and explicitly part of the reform bundle, local leaders whose interests or preferences converge with these objectives can mobilize them through sensemaking and sensegiving processes and create local momentum for change (Denis, Lamothe, Langley *et al.*, 2009). As such, these objectives are assets that leaders can mobilize in politically slack systems.

Finally, the reform was also based on the incorporation of new actors into local networks, for which HSSCs were in a position to design their own strategy for mobilizing the resources available on their territory. In fact, HSSCs were specifically mandated to negotiate the collaborative agreements among resources to create local health networks. Initially, they focused more on consolidating their own merged organization as a unified body. However, after four years of existence, HSSCs became more active in building relationships with their partners locally. The reform thus stimulated investments in developing collective leadership at the territorial level to plan and deliver care and services. As an example, the creation of local health networks depended on strategic alliances with non-governmental community organizations and private medical clinics. Again, the types of relationships and the policy objectives to be pursued through these alliances were relatively vague and left room for plenty of negotiations and interpretative activities. The strategies used by regional bodies to push HSSCs to develop local networks, and then by HSSCs to encourage clinics, community organizations and other institutions from non-health sectors to commit to such networks, varied dramatically from region to region and between HSSCs. Such variation of practice within a single reform and under the same provincial constraints suggests a significant level of political slack. In this case, the lack of formal hierarchical levers for structuring network participation, combined with a high level of political slack, rendered the achievement of functional networks dependent on the presence of just a few leaders who were able to mobilize non-hierarchical governance tools.

Conclusion

Our argument in this chapter is based on the assumption that varying levels of political slack associated with different policy instruments used to implement large-scale transformation strongly influence the implementation of reforms in public delivery systems. In turn, the level of political slack associated with given policy instruments will leave more or less room for the emergence of leaders and for the expression of leadership in reform implementation processes. Leadership has often been analyzed as a strictly individual property in which talented people gain influence in complex policy settings. Yet, in the Quebec health care reform, some individuals (certain CEOs and clinical leaders, for example) were clearly able to operate more strategically with the degree of freedom left in the policy system. It is also clear that leadership capacities are highly contingent on the political architecture of a reform. At first sight, this may suggest a limited role of agency in organizational and institutional transformation. Alternatively, we argue that large-scale reform will always incorporate a complex set of policy instruments with their own levels of constraints. In other words, there will always be room for the manifestation of agency. We suggest that this political perspective on reform is a basis from which leadership can be analyzed and deployed. By identifying pockets of political slack in the system, aspiring leaders can invest in these strategic zones to gain influence and shape the implementation of policies. Despite the recent inclination toward political centralization in many OECD countries, we argue that central governments will, intentionally or not, leave room for local leadership due to their limited capacity to fully programme reforms.

Our analysis suggests that central governments may see immediate benefits from leaving a high level of political slack because it enables a rapid pace of reform implementation by leveraging the capabilities of local leaders. However, it also suggests that such rapid implementation leads to greater variability in the implementation of reform. This may raise problems in terms of the overall policy coherence of reforms in public delivery systems. In other words, rapid uptake may dilute policy intent. Previous studies on organizational forms concluded that coherence and simultaneity of changes were key ingredients of successful major transformation (Pettigrew and Fenton, 2000; Pettigrew and Whittington, 2003; Whittington, Pettigrew *et al.*, 1999). To foster successful implementation of health care reforms, governance practices need to be coherent when initiating and implementing such a multidimensional process of change. The above-mentioned studies were mainly concerned with large private firms, but policy systems may face additional challenges in achieving the required level of coherence across the different components of reform, since reforms are by nature complex sets of propositions with variable levels of precision in terms of objectives and implementation strategies. Our analysis suggests that public delivery systems will deal with reform components in a much more chaotic way and will have difficulty in achieving a coordinated approach to implementation. The concept of political slack helps to show that reforms do not contend with only one implementation challenge, but rather with multiple implementation pathways along which leaders exploit this slack, with their own limitations and capacities, to shape implementation in various areas of concern.

Some implications for leading large-scale reforms in public delivery systems can be derived from our analysis. First there is an inherent tension between, on the one hand, the increased ability to exert control through sophisticated information systems and budgetary instruments for resource allocation and, on the other hand, the need for credible mechanisms to stimulate the commitment and participation of a large set of interdependent actors. Sophisticated instruments may help to get a clearer understanding of actors' and organizations' activities and use of resources. However, this 'new knowledge' does not by itself produce changes in the way organizations operate or in professionals' practices (Marshall, Shekelle, Davies and Smith, 2003). It can serve accountability purposes and send signals about the need for improvement, but it does not guarantee the implementation of complex policy objectives or the involvement of key powerful actors. Second, our analysis suggests that aspiring leaders of reforms need to attend not only to the technical dimensions of policy instruments, but also to their inherent political dimensions. To make sense of the inherent political nature of policy instruments, we apply the concept of political slack. When a reformative template leaves a high level of political slack, whether by design or unintentionally, it provides a more fertile ground for the emergence and activation of collective and distributed leadership. Plural forms of leadership appear to be more in line with the adaptive nature of policy implementation in complex delivery systems. Leading reforms thus means paying careful attention to the design of policy instruments and to opportunities for capitalizing on potential leadership capacity across the system. It also requires constant adjustment of instruments to respond to dynamics and orientations induced by collective and distributed leadership capacity.

In addition, as we saw in Quebec's health care reform process, the design of the reform left plenty of room for interpretation and negotiation around two particular types of policy areas. The first is when a given policy is peripheral to the type of control the government wants to reinforce in the system; an example of this in Quebec was the population health objective, which was not considered critical for the central government's 'realpolitik' agenda, compared to pressures for proper health care delivery. The second is any situation in which the central government cannot be too affirmative; an example of this was the cooptation of physicians within the Quebec reform. In these two situations, political slack is an indispensable resource and may help in implementing governance practices that are more aligned with the complexity of the system. That being said, political slack is no magical solution. If a high level of slack is an inherent characteristic of objectives that the government considers peripheral, as in the example given above (population health), then it is fairly clear that only marginal results can be expected. We might hypothesize that, from the government's perspective, having politically slack objectives can be a way of delegating responsibilities when there is no corresponding delegation of serious levers for change at stake, or in situations where the central government has only very weak levers for acting upon certain policy objectives. A cynic might say that overly slack policies provide inexpensive lip service for policy makers but do not significantly influence practices. We do not share this view, as our data suggest that even very slack policies will have an effect on practices. The problem lies not so much with the existence of an effect as with its unpredictability. After all, whether individual or collective, leadership is the ability to trace new paths and lead the way. We argue in this chapter that political slack can be instrumentalized as a way to tap into leadership capacities in reform implementation systems in order to stimulate innovations and experimentation, and that this can have desirable effects. It would nevertheless be foolish to expect leaders to passively follow reform objectives indiscriminately. Implementation is an ongoing, dynamic political game. The higher the level of political slack left open to bottom-up dynamics, the greater the need for strong leadership abilities at the central level.

References

Alford, R. (1975). *Health Care Politics: Ideological and Interest Group Barriers to Reform*. Chicago: The University of Chicago Press.

Bardach, E. (1977) *The Implementation Game*, Cambridge: MIT Press.

Barrett, S. and Hill, M. (1984) Policy, bargaining and structure in implementation theory: towards an integrated perspective, *Policy and Politics*, 12(3): 219–240.

Bourgeois, L.J., III (1981) On the measurement of organizational slack, *The Academy of Management Review*, 6(1), 29–39.

Cline, K.D. (2000) Defining the implementation problem: organizational management versus cooperation, *Journal of Public Administration Research and Theory*, 10(3): 551–571.

Cohen, M.D., March, J.G. and Olsen, J.P. (1972) A garbage can model of organizational choice, *Administrative Science Quarterly*, 17(1): 1–25.

Contandriopoulos, D. and Brousselle, A. (2010). Reliable in their failure: an analysis of healthcare reform policies in public systems. *Health Policy*, 95(2–3): 144–152.

Contandriopoulos, D. and Denis, J.-L. (2007). Réforme du système sociosanitaire québécois: promesses et défis d'une nouvelle gouverne. *Le Point en Administration de la Santé*, 3(2): 6–9.

Contandriopoulos, D., Denis, J.-L., Langley, A. and Valette, A. (2004). Governance structures and political processes in a public system. *Public Administration*, 82(3): 627–655.

——— (2005). Régionaliser pour restructurer au Québec. In D. Contandriopoulos, J.-L. Denis, and A. Valette (eds). *L'hôpital en restructuration*. Montreal: Presses de l'Université de Montréal: 59–80.

Contandriopoulos, D., Hudon, R., Martin, E. and Thompson, D. (2007). Tensions entre rationalité technique et intérêts politiques: Étude de la mise en œuvre de la Loi 25. *Administration Publique du Canada/Canadian Public Administration*, 50(2): 219–243.

Cyert, R.M. and March, J.G. (1963) *A Behavioral Theory of the Firm*, Englewood Cliffs, NJ: Prentice-Hall.

Davis, G.F. (2005). New directions in corporate governance. *Annual Review of Sociology*, 31: 143–162.

Davis, J.H. and Donaldson, L. (1997). Toward a stewardship theory of management. *Academy of Management Review*, 22(1): 20–47.

Denis, J.-L., Contandriopoulos, D., Langley, A. and Valette, A. (1998). *Les modèles théoriques et empiriques de régionalisation du système socio-sanitaire* (Report no. R98–07). Montreal: GRIS.

Denis, J.-L., Contandriopoulos, D., Langley, A., Valette, A. and Rodriguez, R. (2000). *Théorie et pratique de la régulation des Régies régionales de la santé au Québec.* Montreal: Research report submitted to HEALNet.

Denis, J.-L., Lamothe, L. and Langley, A. (2001). The dynamic of collective leadership and strategic change in pluralistic organizations. *Academy of Management Journal*, 44(4): 809–837.

Denis, J.-L., Contandriopoulos, D. and Beaulieu, M.-D. (2004). Regionalization in Canada: a promising heritage to build on (Commentary). *HealthcarePapers*, 5(1): 40–46.

Denis, J.-L., Langley, A. and Rouleau, L. (2007). Strategizing in pluralistic contexts: rethinking theoretical frames. In Strategizing: the challenges of a practice perspective (special issue), *Human Relations*, 60: 179–215.

Denis, J.-L., Lamothe, L., Langley, A. and Guérard, S. (2008). Réforme et gouverne en santé: L'attrait pour une managérialisation de l'action publique. In P. Laborier, P. Noreau, M. Rioux and G. Rocher (eds). *Les réformes en santé et en justice.* Québec: Les presses de l'Université Laval: 51–68.

Denis, J.-L., Lamothe, L., Langley, A., Breton, M., Gervais, J., Trottier, L.-H., Contandriopoulos, D. and Dubois, C.-A. (2009). The reciprocal dynamics of organizing and sensemaking in the implementation of major public sector reforms. *Administration publique du Canada/Canadian Public Administration*, 52(2): 225–224.

Denis, J.-L., Kisfalvi, V., Langley, A. and Rouleau, L. (2010) Perspectives on strategic leadership. In D. Collinson, A. Bryman, B. Jackson, M. Uhl-Bien and K. Grint (eds). *Sage Handbook of Leadership*. London: Sage: 71–85.

Eisenhardt, K.M. (1989). Agency theory: an assessment and review. *The Academy of Management Review*, 14(1): 57–74.

Ferlie, E.B. and Shortell, S.M. (2001). Improving the quality of health care in the United Kingdom and the United States: a framework for change. *The Milbank Quarterly*, 79(2): 281–315.

Flood, C.M. (2000). *International Health Care Reform: A Legal, Economic and Political Analysis*. London: Routledge.

Greenwood, R., Diaz, A.M., Li, S.X. and Lorente, J.C. (2010) The multiplicity of institutional logics and the heterogeneity of organizational responses. *Organization Science*, 21(2): 521–539.

Hallett, T. and Ventresca, M.J. (2006). Inhabited institutions: social interactions and organizational forms in Gouldner's patterns of industrial bureaucracy. *Theory and Society*, 35: 213–236.

Ham, C., Kipping, R. and McLeod, H. (2003). Redesigning work processes in health care: lessons from the National Health Service. *The Milbank Quarterly*, 81(3): 415–439.

Ham, C.J. (ed.). (1997). *Health Care Reform: Learning from International Experience*. Birmingham: Open University Press.

Harding, A. and Preker, A.S. (2003). A conceptual framework for the organizational reforms of hospitals. In A.S. Preker and A. Harding (eds). *Innovations in Health Service Delivery: The Corporatization of Public Hospitals*. Washington, DC: World Bank.

Hatchuel, A. (2000). Prospective et gouvernance: quelle théorie de l'action collective? In E. Heurgon and J. Landrieu (eds). *Prospective pour une gouvernance démocratique*. La Tour d'Aigues: Éditions de l'Aube: 29–42.

Kickert, H., Kliijn, E.-H. and Koppenjan, J. (1997). *Managing Complex Networks: Strategies for the Public Sector*. London: Sage.

Lawrence, T.B. and Suddaby, R. (2006). Institutions and institutional work. In S. Clegg, C. Hardy, W.R. Nord and T.B. Lawrence (eds). *Handbook of Organization Studies*. Thousand Oaks, CA: Sage: 215–254.

Lounsbury, M. and Crumley, E. (2007). New practice creation: an institutional perspective on innovation. *Organization Studies*, 28: 993–1012.

McKee, M. and Healy, J. (eds). (2002). *Hospitals in a Changing Europe*. Buckingham, PA: Open University Press.

McNulty, T. and Ferlie, E.B. (2002). *Reengineering Health Care: The Complexities of Organizational Transformation*. Oxford: Oxford University Press.

Marshall, M.N., Shekelle, P.G., Davies, H.T.O. and Smith, P.C. (2003) Public reporting on quality in the United States and the United Kingdom. *Health Affairs*. May/June: 134–148.

Matland, R.E. (1995) Synthesizing the implementation literature: the ambiguity–conflict model of policy implementation. *Journal of Public Administration Research and Theory*, 5(2): 145–174.

Mechanic, D. (2008). *The Truth about Health Care: Why Reform Is Not Working in America (Critical Issues in Health and Medicine)*. Camden: Rutgers University Press.

Morell, K. and Hartley, J. (2006). A model of political leadership. *Human Relations*, 59(4): 483–504.

Nakamura, R.T. and Smallwood, F. (1980). *The Politics of Policy Implementation*. New York: St. Martin's Press.

Pettigrew, A.M. and Fenton, E.M. (2000). *The Innovating Organization*. Thousand Oaks, CA: Sage.

Pettigrew, A.M. and Whittington, R. (eds). (2003). *Innovative Forms of Organizing: International Perspectives*. Thousand Oaks, CA: Sage.

Reid, R., Schneider, D., Barer, M., Hanvelt, R., McGrail, K., Pagliacci, N. and Evans, R.G. (2002). The doctor is out: physician participation in the Rationed Access Day work stoppage in British Columbia, 1998/99. *Hospital Quarterly*, 6(2): suppl. 3–10; discussion suppl. 11.

Rhodes, R.A.W. (1990). Policy networks: a British perspective. *Journal of Theoretical Politics*, 2(3): 293–317.

—— (1997). *Understanding Governance*. Buckingham, PA: Open University Press.

—— (2007). Understanding governance: ten years on. *Organization Studies*, 28(8): 1243–1264.

Sabatier, P.A. (1986) Top-down and bottom-up approaches to implementation research: a critical analysis and suggested synthesis. *Journal of Public Policy*, 6(1): 21–48.

Sabatier, P.A. and Jenkins-Smith, H.C. (1993) *Policy Change and Learning: An Advocacy Coalition Approach*. Boulder, CO: Westview Press.

Sabatier, P.A. and Jenkins-Smith, H.C. (1999) Policy change and learning: an advocacy coalition approach. In P.A. Sabatier (ed.). *Theories of the Policy Process*. Boulder, CO: Westview Press.

Saltman, R.B. and Ferroussier-Davis, O. (2000). The concept of stewardship in health policy. *Bulletin of the World Health Organization*, 78(6): 732–739.

Saltman, R.B., Busse, R. and Mossialos, E. (2002). *Regulating Entrepreneurial Behaviour in European Health Care Systems*. Buckingham, PA: Open University Press.

Schofield, J. (2004) A model of learned implementation. *Public Administration*, 82(2): 283–308.

Sinclair, D. (2002). After Kirby and Romanow: where to from here? *Hosp Q*, 6(2): 42–43.

Tuohy, C.H. (1999). Dynamics of a changing health sphere: the United States, Britain, and Canada. *Health Affairs*, 18(3): 114–134.

—— (2002). The costs of constraint and prospects for health care reform in Canada. *Health Affairs*, 21(3): 32–46.

Wallace, M. and Pocklington, K. (2002). *Managing Complex Educational Change: Large-scale Reorganisation of Schools*. London: Routledge Falmer.

Watson, J. (ed.). (2005). *Health Care Systems: Major Themes in Health and Social Welfare*. London: Routledge.

Weick, K.E. (2001) *Making Sense of the Organization*. Malden, MA: Blackwell Publishing.

Whittington, R., Pettigrew, A., Peck, S., Fenton, E. and Conyon, M. (1999). Change and complementarities in the new competitive landscape: a European panel study, 1992–1996. *Organization Science*, 10(5): 583–600.

Zietsma, C. and Lawrence, T.B. (2010). Institutional work in the transformation of an organizational field: the interplay of boundary work and practice work. *Administrative Science Quarterly*, 55: 189–221.

4 Respond and deliver?

Change leadership in complex organizations

Louise Fitzgerald, Ewan Ferlie,
Gerry McGivern and David Buchanan

Introduction

In the introductory chapters of this text, several questions were raised concerning the nature of leadership in public organizations. In this chapter, we address two of these questions in particular. The first is summarized into one question by Denis *et al.* (2005: 450) as the central dilemma of public sector leadership: 'Can leaders intervene proactively or not in public organizations?' Our second focus relates to the important question of whether leadership patterns in the public sector are individualized or involve a small team or are dispersed in nature?

The focus of this chapter then is on the micro-processes of change and the roles of actors. Several authors have drawn attention to the need for further research on the roles of individuals. DiMaggio and Powell (1991) observe that there is a need for a distinct micro institutional perspective. To date, institutional theory has largely focused on the organizational and inter-organizational level of analysis, recording the conditions for stability and tracks of change (Greenwood and Hinings 1988; Cooper *et al.* 1996) while largely ignoring the detailed analysis of micro-processes. Other authors, such as McKinlay and Scherer (2000) and Balogun and Johnson (2004), plead for further examination of roles in change, focusing on the increasingly problematic role for middle managers attempting to lead change in complex settings.

In this chapter, we will draw on a substantial body of data relating to the implementation of service improvement in ten sites across the UK health care system, including acute hospitals and primary care trusts, to address aspects of the two questions mentioned in our introductory paragraph.

Our data suggest the need for an holistic view of change leadership as a process situated in an organizational context, rather than discrete interventions. Particularly in complex and inter-organizational settings, we perceive that change leaders assist other organizational members and external stakeholders to interpret and re-interpret how things are and how they can be done differently in order to progress improvements. In health care with multiple professional boundaries, our findings display that change leadership involves a certain amount of 'boundary spanning' based in a sophisticated understanding of local contexts and the development of customized approaches to the sharing of information. We demonstrate the distributed nature of change leadership, incorporating credibility based on clinical skills and active practice and highly honed influencing skills. Effective leaders frequently use the fluidity and ambiguity of their roles to innovate and generate novel means of service improvement.

Next, this chapter reviews selected literature and then in the section following offers empirical evidence from our research. This leads to the final section, which re-examines this literature in the light of our introductory questions:

- Are leadership patterns in the public sector individualized, small teams or dispersed in nature?
- What have we learned about whether leaders can intervene proactively in public organizations?

Literature review

Leadership of change

The introductory chapters of this book have laid out the main schools of thought on leaders and leadership; from transformational to transactional leaders (Bass 1990; Callan 2003) and from leadership incorporating followership (Fiedler 1967) and situational leadership (Hogg 2001) to the activities of leaders (Pettigrew 1985; Wallace and Pocklington 2002).

Here, we shall briefly examine selected ideas that are of relevance to the analysis in this chapter. We suggest that leadership of change may be perceived as a particular form of leadership. (If change leadership is conceptualized as driving and influencing the processes of change, then the literature on so-called change agents is also relevant to a discussion of change leadership since change agents are perceived as driving or facilitating change in organizations.) While there have been many texts on the leadership of change over the years (Kanter 1984; Anderson and Anderson 2010), there still remain many aspects that are relatively underdeveloped; in particular there is limited evidence of effectiveness of the roles within particular contexts (Hartley and Benington 2010). Increasingly, as we shall explore, there is evidence that change leadership may embrace a variety of roles with differing foci (Buchanan and Storey 1997; Locock *et al.* 2001) and in complex organizational contexts be perceived as an ambiguous and more interactive process (Fitzgerald *et al.* 2002; Grint 2005). So in this chapter, we shall examine these two under-developed areas – the dispersion or concentration of change leadership and the nature of these leadership roles in complex health care organizational contexts.

Selecting themes of relevance to our analysis, we start with a brief review of the concept of distributed leadership. Gronn (2000) set out the concept of 'distributed leadership' arguing that the single, charismatic leader is not the only or necessarily the most effective model of leadership. He then supported his conceptual ideas with empirical data (Gronn 2002; 2003), significantly for our comparisons, drawn from the public sector examining school leadership. This analysis identifies patterns of school leadership where significant numbers of staff held responsibility for 'leadership' within a specific arena. The studies also feature collective leadership diads and triads. More recently, Gronn (2009) has argued for hybridity as a focus of research, by which he means that empirical research suggests that there are varying combinations and degrees of concentrated and distributed leadership to be found in differing organizations. He further suggests that his original notion of distributed leadership underplayed the significance of the contribution of highly influential individuals.

A recent critique of distributed leadership by Grint (2010) raises some interesting and relevant points. He questions the thrust of recent analysis and asks – is everyone a leader? He argues that leadership has become almost sacred, meaning 'holy' or 'untouchable', something to be reverenced or set apart. Leadership, he says, embodies three elements of the 'sacred':

- separation between leaders and followers;
- the sacrifice of leaders and followers;
- the way leaders silence the anxiety and resistance of followers.

In making the first point about the 'sacred' nature of leadership, he argues that leaders need to be reverenced and respected and to maintain distance. He underlines that leadership may involve the sacrificing of organizational members; scapegoating; and the silencing of opposition. Intriguingly, he suggests that we may have shifted uncritically from heroic leadership to post-heroic collaborative leadership. Based on our data, we position ourselves at a mid point, suggesting that credible and legitimated leaders are crucial and therefore a degree of distance is necessary. We did not seek to argue in the past or currently (Buchanan *et al.* 2007a) as Grint suggests that leadership can be distributed equally among the collective, but rather that our empirical evidence presented here suggests that there are multiple players rather than one leader, who exercise a variety of forms of leadership.

Change leadership and individual capabilities

Change leadership roles in context

In considering the literature on individual roles, Ottaway's (1983) taxonomy makes a useful starting place. He identifies ten change agency roles in three broad categories:

- *change generators* (key agents, demonstrators, patrons and defenders);
- *change implementers* (external and internal);
- *change adopters* (early adopters, maintainers and users).

This categorization has resonance with the work of Rogers (1995) on the diffusion of innovation, in which he identifies early and late adopters, with differing characteristics. Stjernberg and Philips (1993) argue that change relies on a small number of committed individuals called 'souls-of-fire', from the Swedish *eldsjälar* meaning 'driven by burning enthusiasm'. Buchanan and Storey (1997) identify a broader range of change agency roles, including *initiators, sponsors, drivers* and *subversives*. They argue that these are not static positions, and that 'role taking and role switching' is an organizational political skill central to change management expertise. But, on the whole, these taxonomies tend to focus on a relatively narrow range of senior and middle managers. This focus is significant because research suggests that the change management role has become more widely dispersed, in public and private sector organizations, to involve staff from all organizational levels in substantive change design and implementation roles (Buchanan *et al.* 2007a; Baeza *et al.* 2008).

Clearly, in addressing the two foci set out in the introductory paragraph, a central issue is whether leadership patterns in the public sector are individualized or involve a small team or are dispersed in nature?

We are arguing that the context of change leadership has to be considered when exploring change leadership roles. Caldwell (2006) raises a challenge to the orthodoxy of change agency as an intentional and planned process. He argues that change agency can now be classified across four dimensions as rationalist, contextualist, dispersalist and constructionist, in relation to a wider array of theories of organizational change. Certainly, some evidence demonstrates that within the health care context, change agency is embedded in and affects and interacts with the organizational context (Fitzgerald *et al.* 2002). Adopting an embedded framing of change agency, Lovelady (1984) empirically identified the roles of change agents; the range of activities undertaken and the manner in which change approaches are selected, arguing that 'effective' change agency adapts to the scale and urgency of the required change and the past history of the organization. Delbridge and Edwards (2008) reinforce the notion of a range of roles for different actors, while simultaneously underlining the impact of context and particularly the organization's history.

These ideas accord with the growing body of evidence that proposes that effective change agency in health care depends on collective or even dispersed leadership (Pettigrew, Ferlie and McKee 1992; Denis, Langley and Cazale 1996; Denis, Lamothe and Langley 2001; Buchanan *et al.* 2007a). These authors interlink the literature on change leadership with that on change agency. This literature also discusses change leadership embedded within the specifics of current organizational contexts with team-based working, the growth of knowledge work and networked organizational forms (with the latter, as stated, increasingly common in health care). Thus, traditional leadership positions based on hierarchy and organizational symbolism are weakened. Research also offers some initial indicators of the roles change leaders play: clinical leaders are seen to play an influential part, both as the promoters of change *and* as the inhibitors of change (Pettigrew, Ferlie and McKee 1992; Fairhurst and Huby 1998; Locock *et al.* 2001); hence Locock *et al.* propose the term 'opinion leaders' to embrace the positive and negative influencing processes. Change agents play a variety of roles, both as instigators of change and as implementers depending on their position and personal skills (Fitzgerald *et al.* 2006; Buchanan *et al.* 2007b).

Individual capabilities

The individual capabilities perspective focuses on an individual's skills and capabilities. This literature must now address the fact that most managers combine change responsibilities with their regular duties, as well as identifying the skills required of specialist project managers and change consultants. Much of this literature adopts a competency-based approach (Howell and Higgins 1990; Beatty and Lee 1992). From research with senior project managers, Buchanan and Boddy (1992) identify fifteen competencies in five categories, which relate to goals; roles; communication; negotiation; and managing up. The majority of this literature, with the exception of individual case studies, is de-contextualized. As a result, this work produces a long list of commonly agreed competencies, but with virtually no evidence as to their relative utility in different organizational contexts.

We include here the extensive, empirical studies on leadership undertaken by Alimo-Metcalfe and Alban-Metcalfe (2005) because they are based on large samples from the UK public sector, while much prior research emanates from the USA. Additionally, the research samples include both male and female managers and both top managers and middle managers. Gender is a significant issue since many managers in health care are female and it has been noted that leadership styles differ between males and females. However, this research does not focus specifically on the leadership of change, but identifies the characteristics of leaders with the public sector (mainly health care and local government). The authors draw attention to the fact that much of the prior US research and some of the models were developed twenty years ago, while organizations themselves have changed. We note of particular relevance here, the growth of network forms of organization in the UK health care sector, placing greater demands on leaders for building inter-organizational relations and lateral links (Addicott *et al.* 2007; Ferlie *et al.* 2009).

Their research identifies six characteristics common to leaders in public sector organizations. These are:

* valuing individuals (genuine concern for other's wellbeing and development);

- networking and achieving (inspirational communicator, networker and achiever);
- enabling (empowers, delegates, develops potential);
- acting with integrity (consistent, honest, open);
- being accessible (approachable, in touch);
- being decisive (decisive, risk taking).

The authors underline the difference between these characteristics and those emerging from major US models of leadership. A central component of the US models is 'charisma/inspiration' (for example, Avolio and Yammarino 2002), whereas 'valuing others' was of overriding importance as a component in the UK study. The authors offer the explanation that US studies have been biased towards senior managers who have greater 'distance' from their followers.

The context of change: organizational characteristics

We have already argued that while the prime focus in this chapter is individual roles and skills, the context of change leadership has to be considered when exploring change leadership roles. However, due to space, we do not propose to review the literature on the organizational characteristics that may have an impact on change processes. Briefly, we note that a number of authors have made the point that charismatic leadership theories in particular underestimate the influence of contextual or situational variables. Yukl (1999) suggests that situational variables are frequently insufficiently specified and concludes by proposing a more systemic view of leadership. We would accord with this position. The notion of corporate capabilities that enable or facilitate change to occur has also been explored in a variety of ways, relating to ideas of organizational culture (Kanter 1990; Bate 1996) and to the idea of receptive contexts for change (Pettigrew and Whipp 1991; Pettigrew, Ferlie and McKee 1992).

In the next section, we set out the methods used in our study and, following this, we present our empirical data and then our analysis.

Methodology

The aim of this paper is to draw selectively on the results of a research project that explored the following question:

> How do mid-level leaders in health care interpret and enact their roles and use them to lead the implementation of service change?

Recognizing that 'effective' change management remains poorly understood, we utilized an exploratory approach, which enabled us to examine the enactment of these roles within given situations, and compare data. Because of our interest in the variable capacity of organizations, the context was an important component of the design and we carefully selected contexts where policy driven change was being enacted (Department of Health 2000a). This selection will be explained in further detail later.

Research approach: comparative case studies

The research approach employed was a qualitative one, comparing across multiple cases, because of the nature of the 'how' and 'why' questions under consideration and the need to thoroughly explore concepts in depth (Yin 2009). A comparative case study design was chosen because it enabled the purposeful selection of cases. Cases were all chosen within areas of care that had been nominated, nationally, as priority areas for improvement (Department of Health 2000a), and this design deliberately incorporates specialties in which the targets set nationally are creating pressures for change. Ten cases are utilized here, six from the acute hospital sector (focusing on cancer care and maternity services) and four from the primary care sector (focusing on diabetes care).

The principal investigators made contact with the sites and access was gradually negotiated. In two cases, members of the research team had had some prior contacts at the proposed sites. There were no case study sites that refused to participate. In one instance, a primary care organization approached the research team with an interest in participating as a case study site.

This study utilized an emergent and individualized approach to identifying specific tracer issues. Tracer issues were identified as significant service improvement initiatives enacted within the particular clinical area selected, driven by policy directives. For example, we examined policy-directed higher quality standards in cancer services; the re-configuration of services in maternity care; and service changes required to attain higher quality standards for diabetes care. Details of the specifics of the 'tracer' issues selected in each area of care are set out in Table 4.1. The tracer issues differed marginally for each site. Some detailed exemplars of the improvement initiatives under investigation in the study will be presented later in this chapter and all these changes were categorized nationally as high priorities.

Approach to data collection

We used multiple data sources or triangulation to strengthen the empirical grounding of our research. Three methods were employed to gather the data necessary for this analysis – semi-structured interviews, document analysis and observation at meetings. These multiple data sources addressed a range of issues and provided a more convincing and accurate contextual account. Multi-site ethical approval for this study was granted and all standards of confidentiality and anonymity were met.

Table 4.1 Focus of study – care groups and change issues

Cancer cases *3 acute hospital trusts*	*Maternity cases* *3 acute hospitals + community maternity units*	*Diabetes cases* *4 primary care organizations*
Change projects used as tracer issues:	Change projects used as tracer issues:	Change projects used as tracer issues:
The achievement locally of the Improved Outcomes Guidance on urological cancers (NHS Executive 2000) developed from the NHS Cancer Plan (DoH 2000b), which set standards for the care of patients with urological cancers, specifically prostrate cancer. These included the achievement of a maximum two week wait for care for urgent referrals and the implementation of care standards.	The continuing process of implementing the agenda of changes set out in 'Changing Childbirth' (DoH 1993). These included the provision of 'low tech', preferably community-based units for birth and the availability of choices for mothers in terms of where to give birth. Allied to these choices is development of midwife support for normal births. The National Service Framework for Women and Children's services (DoH 2004) reinforced these standards again.	The achievement locally of the National Service Framework standards (DoH 2001) for the care of diabetic patients in the community. These included setting up baseline records of diabetic patients; developing a local network between the acute and primary care sector; and regular monitoring of diagnosed patients.
Intended timescale of achievement: by 2004 (overall target to reduce mortality rates by 2010 by at least 20%).	Intended timescale of achievement: none set.	Intended timescale of achievement: 3–4 years.

Note: data collected mid-2002 through December 2005.

Semi-structured interviews

Semi-structured interviews were used as a means of allowing participants flexibility within pre-defined categories of investigation and to produce comparative data. In order to understand complex issues, it was important to be able to fully explore a topic with the participants. Semi-structured interviews formed a main source of data in this study and were conducted with 160 stakeholders across all the ten case studies. Table 4.2 provides a breakdown of the number of interviews by case study site and professional categorization. In some cases, there is variance between case studies in the number of interviewees and this reflects low representation within this site and negative responses from some of those who were approached. In two cases there were

Table 4.2 Interviewees by case study site and professional group

Case Study Site	Managerial	Clinical	Hybrid	Total
DIABETES				
Diabetes 1	6	4	6	16
Diabetes 2	8	0	9	17
Diabetes 3	9	7	4	20
Diabetes 4	4	0	8	12
MATERNITY				
Maternity 1	4	3	8	15
Maternity 2	6	5	5	16
Maternity 3	10	2	5	17
CANCER				
Cancer 1	9	1	6	16
Cancer 2	6	1	6	13
Cancer 3	11	2	5	18
TOTAL	73	25	62	160

a greater proportion of non-respondents (approximately 30 per cent). In these cases, the researchers relied more heavily on observational and documentary data sources. Overall, an average of 77 per cent of those who were approached agreed to be interviewed across the ten case study sites. Each interview lasted for approximately one hour and was recorded and transcribed. Interviews were conducted by four members of the six-member research team.

Documentary analysis

Key organizational documents, such as meeting minutes and terms of reference, strategic planning documents, discussion papers and job descriptions were analyzed to provide an historical narrative of organizational context and an archival description of the tracer issues and role interpretation.

Observation at meetings

Thirty-five meetings were attended across the ten case study sites to gain further insight into role enactment, relationships between professionals and the tracer issues, and to provide further support for the interview and documentary data collected. The variance in the number of meetings attended reflects the disparate focus at each of the sites. Meeting notes were taken regarding the content of the interactions, in conjunction with observations of group dynamics, decision-making, attendance and the time devoted to particular agenda items. Observation provided a more authentic image of group dynamics, compared to one-on-one interviews (Pettigrew *et al.* 1992).

Approach to data analysis

To familiarize all team members with the data, each case was initially written up as field case report. All of the primary data collected – interview transcripts and observational notes – were coded using the NVivo software package (QSR International). Analysis consisted of a two-stage process. The first stage of analysis was based on the spine of interview questions, and the research team collectively identified a range of codes, relating to the questions and the original research proposal, and these constituted the template for initial coding (Pettigrew *et al.* 1992). The findings from this phase were discussed. For the second stage, the coding framework was altered, expanded and elaborated collaboratively by the research team evolving from the data using an open, grounded approach with a continual, iterative discussion regarding the coding framework. The framework for this stage incorporated key aspects of the contexts that emerged from the data. Following the finalization of the codes and the coding process, the data were then organized and compressed to draw broad comparative conclusions regarding the research findings. Through an iterative process of data coding, final conclusions developed and became more explicit and a final report was produced (see www.sdo.nihr.ac.uk/change management) as required by the research commissioners.

Empirical data

In order to focus here on the positive facets of change leaders roles and activities, we first present three vignettes drawn from three of our ten cases. During the analysis, we broadly classified our cases in terms of their progress in service improvements into low, medium and substantial progress. In doing this, we sought to develop our analysis of aspects of change leadership and to contextualize these activities. The vignettes presented here illustrate the three cases making the most substantial progress in service improvement and also represent a range of organizational settings and care groups – Diabetes 3, Maternity 3 and Cancer 3. Later in the discussion, we will draw in illustrations from the remaining cases.

Diabetes 3

Diabetes 3 was the primary care organization that made the most progress towards improving the care of patients with diabetes. Table 4.1 sets out brief details of the improvement targets.

Background and characteristics

Diabetes 3 was formed as a primary care organization in 2002, serving an urban and rural population of 250,000 in the North West, and employed over 1,200 people. Its services included thirty general practitioner's surgeries, and a specialist mental health trust. The budget in 2003/04 was £225 million, and it anticipated being in surplus. Diabetes 3 received a one star rating from the Healthcare Commission in 2002/03 and two stars in 2003/04. (The star rating system is a national system of quality monitoring of all health care units in the UK based on standardized data and running from nil stars to three stars.) It scored in the top 20 per cent of similar organizations in its staff satisfaction survey. By 2004, all primary care organizations were under pressure and Diabetes 3 was focused on as it was struggling to respond to the organizational changes and performance targets imposed by central government, particularly given its dated technologies. Structurally, in the primary care sector the exercise of accountability and responsibility is difficult. The Board of the primary care organization, which includes the Chairman, Chief Executive Officer (CEO) and the Chair of the Professional Executive Committee (PEC), has formal accountability, but the cluster of individual general practices that form a primary care organization are independent businesses, run by general practitioners (GPs) who employ their own staff. Action is agreed through negotiation and the exercise of influence by clinicians and management. Structurally, the intervening level between the Board and the organization's members is a professional committee that contains many clinical representatives and retains considerable power.

The key players – the change leaders

This organization was led by a cohesive and experienced triumvirate made up of the CEO, the Chairman and the Chair of the professional committee, all experienced managers or clinical professionals. Generally, relationships within this triumvirate were perceived to be pivotal for effective functioning of the organization. This team was respected within Diabetes 3 for their leadership and for engaging with colleagues on equal terms. The CEO argued that he achieved change through creating 'the *vision*, hopefully a patient-centred *vision* of what we are actually trying to create', rather than hierarchy, and 'enabling people to go ahead and do that'. Influence was through debate, discussion and negotiation and the organization placed particular emphasis on communication and staff involvement; with all three senior executives perceiving themselves as change drivers. It was notable in Diabetes 3 that senior roles operated in a less overtly managerialist manner, compared to other primary care organizations.

The Chairperson of the professional committee in Diabetes 3 saw his role as strategic and was keen to lead and see that clinicians were at the heart of policy and decision-making. This role was heavily political; dealing with national and regional politics while mitigating conflict between the primary care organization and the local acute hospital. Another clinician with management responsibilities (a hybrid) in Diabetes 3 was a public health consultant, who saw the role as fluid and not managerial, but who wanted to engage everyone in working together towards a common vision, driven by a professional ethos.

There was an important group of general managers who were strategic leaders and change drivers, and this sub-group had two dominant role characteristics: they provided vision and leadership at strategic and operational levels within the organization; and they initiated and implemented change in collaboration with a vast network of external and internal stakeholders. In this group, we could place the Chair of the organization, the CEO, the Directors of Service Development and Corporate Development and two Service Development Managers. For example, the Director (Service Development) had a pivotal role in initiating and implementing change throughout the organization through service development. The department's role was to act as the interface between primary and secondary health care. In terms of commissioning, the role was clear, but in terms of service design this aspect was innovative and the Director stated:

> We tried to set off with a clear structure and my managers that work for me started to be very structured around what roles and which service areas they work on. What we found is that it is just not practical, you need to be able to move with the priorities as they come in.

The Director highlighted the radical changes that have hit the NHS and emphasized the massive change agenda. Their role was to establish strategic change priorities and translate these into specific projects and then to lead the implementation of them through a dedicated team of Service Development (project) Managers. The Director's own role was to guide, support, facilitate and manage this team.

As we shall illustrate in the narrative next, in terms of making progress in the delivery of service improvements in diabetes care, the Strategic Development Manager, Primary Care, was critical. She was one of the most energetic, enthusiastic and committed individuals interviewed. She can best be described as a competent and experienced change leader, working in the role of project manager with responsibility for some of the most challenging and high profile projects in the PCT, including the changes required to meet the standards in the National Service Framework (NSF) for diabetes. She displayed strong organizational and interpersonal skills reflecting her prior background in NHS leadership development. These skills were deployed extensively in her role in leading service development. She was ambitious and saw her current role as a career enhancing one. She relied heavily on her access and good relationships with senior management and her boss, the Director of Service Development, to achieve her goals and to deal with conflict.

In terms of relationship building, it was generally clear that professionals and managers had sympathy and empathy with their colleagues, and this individual illustrated this attitude:

> I think what I try to do is put myself in their shoes when I am doing whatever I am doing with them. So if I am talking to the practice managers

about a new whatever I think it is really important for them to know that I understand what the impact of that will be on them and their jobs and I do the same with the GPs.

The change narrative

Despite the capable, key players noted in the previous paragraph, the implementation of the new quality standards got off to a slow start. There were many competing priorities and the local acute hospital was reluctant to move diabetes services into the community or to accept any leadership from the general practitioners. A turning point came when the Board recognized that to make progress on improvements, dedicated resources would be required, and they appointed the Strategic Development Manager, Primary Care, in autumn of 2003. Despite her capabilities, she displayed early signs of initiative overload and fatigue – partly due to her enthusiasm to take on more work: 'In terms of the diabetes lead, I'd said foolishly before Xmas that I would take it on, and in my opinion diabetes should be a primary care led service.' This work overload was one of the reasons why there continued to be some delays in implementing the new standards as specified by policy during the first half of 2004.

Around the middle of 2004, there was a noticeable shift in priorities and the implementation of the new quality standards began to be placed on a sound organizational and management footing. A critical early initiative was the merging of the prior overseeing committee with the local implementation team (LIT), which then became the single body coordinating the changes. The LIT was a multi-functional group of specialists responsible for planning and delivering diabetes care (optometrist, diabetes specialist nurse, diabetologists, podiatrists, GPs, etc.). Most significantly, the LIT as the executive body responsible for implementing the new quality standards now came under the control of the primary care organization and not the acute hospital.

The re-energized LIT met every two months and brought together all the clinical functions, including patient representatives, and created sub-groups to progress work. Respondents stated that the new leadership enabled professionals to play an active role in delivering the higher standards. As a result, more progress was made in implementing a revised plan for improving standards in diabetes care. By July 2004, a self-assessment survey was carried out at the request of Dr Foster Ltd and the collated responses gave a positive impression of sound organization and management of the implementation. The Strategic Development Manager, Primary Care, displayed her change leadership expertise, including sound interpersonal and political skills. For instance, she was conscious of the need to manage the tensions between the acute and primary sectors and ensured that the Chair of the LIT was a clinical professional from the acute hospital. Further, she ensured that the LIT would report directly to the Professional Committee.

It is important to note the widespread involvement of others in change in this organization. Individual clinical professionals acted as important change agents/leaders, absorbing best practice and diffusing this among colleagues through networking and debate about how such changes could be integrated within the professions. There was strong evidence of the use of clinical information to influence and of the importance of data sharing:

> What ever you do to influence you've got to have done your homework and it's got to be sound. It's got to be evidence-based and credible . . . We have to be visionary and have charisma you know. Communication, that's the key thing. [Diabetes specialist nurse]

Several Allied Health Professionals saw their role more in terms of 'leadership' than management, and described the management style within the primary care organization as democratic rather than autocratic. Clinical professionals operated in a tight-knit world of like-minded and committed individuals united into a cohesive and supportive body, illustrated in diabetes care where one clinician described the 'diabetes mafia' who were not 'afraid to push when push is needed'.

Maternity 3

Table 4.1 sets out the changes required in maternity care and, as in many locations, in Maternity 3, this required the re-configuration of services, including new capital projects and buildings, as well as new ways of working.

Background and characteristics

This case centred on an acute hospital that offered a full suite of acute services, including emergency care and outpatients' services. The services extended to a local population of approximately 350,000 people, in a heavily populated urban area, covering approximately thirteen square miles. The trust had over 600 beds and employed over 3,500 staff. In 2003, the hospital provided services to 41,000 inpatients and 259,000 outpatients. The trust had an annual income of £248.365 million in 2003/04. While the trust performed well on most quality standards, it was held to have under-performed on financial targets. It served a population that is a mix of wealthy and deprived, with high and diverse levels of ethnic populations.

Within the overall organizational context of the acute hospital, improvements in maternity care were perceived to have fallen down the agenda, with higher priority going to improvements in areas such as cancer care and cardiac care. The CEO and the Board had major pre-occupations with a huge redevelopment of the whole hospital site, within which the provision of new capital buildings for maternity services was featured. Thus staff in the maternity function saw themselves as having to work hard to compete for resources, both of finance and senior management attention. The configuration of maternity services at Maternity 3 differed from the current norm, as all maternity services are provided from one site. On this site, there were only limited facilities for low risk, midwifery-led deliveries.

The key players

There were some unusual role configurations in this setting. As is normally the case, many management roles in this acute hospital are held by 'hybrids', who were practising clinicians who also had substantial management responsibilities. But the general manager post for the Directorate of Women's and Children's Services (which incorporated the role of Clinical Director in this hospital) was shared between two individuals – one with a clinical, the other with a management background. They each led on their area of respective expertise, which worked well, with complementary experience leading to effective outcomes. This, of course, was mediated by a good working relationship between the two:

> So given that I don't have a clinical background, I have a financial background, I lead on financial issues. In the same way, the other general manager who is from a clinical background, leads on more clinical issues [manager engaged in a job share with a clinical partner].

> *So are you suggesting that you and your job share partner complement one another?*

> We do very much. In fact she has a management, pure management background, and I have a clinical background, so I think we make a really good team in this sort of . . . like good value for money [her clinical counterpart].

These individuals defined their roles in terms of joint strategic leadership, with especial interest in quality improvement and a better patient experience. They also saw themselves as representing their service at the Board level.

A newly appointed consultant midwife with experience of this model of care acted as a clinical champion for the caseload model of midwifery. She played a peripheral but critical role and her credibility and evidence-based advocacy of the structure were instrumental in creating support for the change. In the background was the Director of Nursing, who provided strategic support and constantly offered public backing.

The change narrative

We specifically examined the introduction of community midwife 'caseload' teams. Traditionally, midwives have worked set hours either in a hospital or a community setting, however, within a caseload team, working arrangements are much more flexible as women can go into labour at any point. So, the job entails 'on call' work, and a different social pattern for the midwives themselves. One of the Joint General Managers of Women's and Children's indicated that the introduction of caseload teams was just part of an ongoing process within a five-year strategic plan. She planned to introduce five teams in total, so that women could choose between different models of care. This aligned with the recommendations of the 'Changing Childbirth' report and the new quality standards for Women and Children's services. The objectives of the changes were to offer choices to women by offering different models of care; and to improve the 'attractiveness' of the options to women locally.

These changes were introduced against a difficult background of financial constraints while the maternity service had faced a large and sustained increase in the demand for its service, which exacerbated the demands on an already tight establishment: 'So, we are delivering about 25% more babies this year than we did last year, and it's consistent and sustained. And we are doing that with the same funding . . . And everyone's very stressed.'

The pressure for change had emerged from a service review, but there had been no proactive proposals for change from the general practitioners. The review led to consideration of different ways of working, and how best to target deprived women with poor outcomes. The caseload midwifery model emerged from discussions as to the best available service model. The clinical Joint General Manager was broadly recognized as leading the change and acted in a strategic and supervisory capacity, as well as having direct involvement. She worked with the aid of the senior midwives, the other Joint General Manager and was supported by the Director of Nursing. The newly appointed consultant midwife was instrumental in creating acceptance of the caseload midwifery model among community midwives.

Interestingly, the senior midwife noted that the core team driving the changes differed between primary and acute care. Within primary care, the Joint General Manager/Head of Midwifery and the senior midwife for primary care services liaised with GPs and midwives via the steering group. In contrast, within acute care the trio was composed of the two Joint General Managers and the senior midwife for hospital services.

So there were two relatively small groups of individuals who were responsible for driving the changes in both acute and primary care. The core trio in both instances held managerial roles, although critically dispersed leadership was provided by hybrids and clinicians. Common to both groups was the clinical Joint General Manager, who had a role as a change leader, and as a bridge between primary and acute care. The consultant midwife filled a peripheral but critical role, acting as a clinical champion among hospital- and community-based midwives. Her credibility and evidence-based advocacy of the structure were identified as core in creating support for change.

Unlike our previous example of Diabetes 3, Maternity 3 had no one with a formal role with responsibility for generating change. In contrast, in this context the primary change generators and implementers took the form of duos and trios. They succeeded in generating and implementing changes against relatively unfavourable contextual conditions and in an area of care that was not a high organizational priority and had no additional investment.

Cancer 3

This case focuses on the improvement and development of urological cancer services, which were a major national priority, receiving extra funding. The main targets for improvement are set out in Table 4.1.

Background and characteristics

Cancer 3 was an acute district general hospital that provided a full range of elective and emergency services, with 440 beds, around 1,600 (whole time equivalent) staff, and an annual budget of around £80 million. In a typical year, the trust treated 23,000 inpatients and day cases, 130,000 outpatients, and 58,000 people attended the accident and emergency department. The hospital served a mix of urban and rural communities and a population of around 250,000. From 2002, the hospital worked closely with a national health care agency as a 'productivity laboratory', achieving significant performance improvements, for example, through the 'see and treat' process developed in the accident and emergency service. In 2003, the hospital established an Improvement Partnership for Health (IPH) initiative, to develop a 'No Wait Hospital' jointly with a local primary care organization.

In June 2002, the trust was carrying a historic deficit of just under £1 million. The financial position remained a cause for concern throughout and beyond the period of this study. By mid-2004, the trust was anticipating (in the absence of significant remedial action) a budget deficit in 2004/05 of around £4.5 million.

In terms of cancer care, Cancer 3 was part of the local cancer network. It was not the central 'hub' hospital, but a 'spoke' hospital with specific areas of specialism, including urological cancers.

The key players – the change leaders

Cancer 3 had a number of features of interest. During the period of study (three years from 2003–06) the hospital had five CEOs. Though senior managers do rotate through roles rapidly in the UK, this very high level of turnover of CEOs makes it an unusual outlier case.

A new, charismatic CEO took up his role in 1999 as part of a turnaround team and developed a strategy described as 'unashamed ambition'. This included active participation in a number of improvement projects. From the point of joining the cancer network in 1999, the senior management in this trust decided that this was an organization that could help them to achieve their aims. The CEO promoted the network, took an active role and encouraged other key staff to participate.

Assisting in implementing the improvements to urological cancer services, a cast of twenty-three people holding some twenty-six overlapping roles was identified. This complexity is increased when one remembers that different people played varying roles at different times. There was, however, general agreement that four particular roles were critical in implementing and sustaining improvements in prostate cancer services. These were: the consultant urologist/lead cancer clinician; the prostate project manager, cancer services collaborative; the lead cancer nurse; and the urology cancer nurse specialist.

At Cancer 3, the lead clinician for urology was also the lead cancer clinician and the Chair of the specialist tumour group in the Cancer Network, as well as the Chair of the Cancer Strategy Board for the Trust. He had a more strategic vision than the lead cancer clinicians from our other two cancer sites. He aspired to become the lead clinician or service improvement lead for the whole network in the future. He considered his managerial role was to work with the CEO to generate service improvement and reduce waiting lists.

Several respondents observed that no formal project management structures were evident. As one respondent explained, these changes were achieved mainly through, 'lead individuals being given an objective and getting on with it'. As a clinical director observed:

> I don't think there was any formal project management. This person just started to do some work, and then they said, we can do it this way, and the outpatient manager got involved with it, the cancer nurse, and that's the way it happened. But I don't think there was any formal structure.

In contrast, the paired roles of lead clinician and cancer nurse specialist were perceived to have been particularly influential. The core process was described as:

> [Our clinical nurse specialist], or any specialist nurse in cancer in our organization, was never put in as a project manager to change the way that you do cancer. It's just that, what we've always tried to do is, have lead clinician – lead nurse partnerships. They're the ones in charge of driving the change within their site. That then tends to be lead nurses, who end up doing it, because they're much more doers than the operational ones. So, no, not a conventional project management structure.

Beyond that key partnership, one respondent used the term 'snowballing' to indicate how the change agenda developed, and how various people became involved. Many respondents drew attention to the importance of relationships in helping to get things done, especially with key senior staff, as well as the disruption generated when people leave.

So, in Cancer 3, we can see a wide cast of involved and active characters, operating in a largely informal 'can do' style, but with a small core of respected and knowledgeable lead managers who coordinate and drive activities.

Another aspect of change agency observed in this site was that several people described their roles as lacking in clarity, and they claimed this was quite useful; as the network lead clinician stated: 'They are as defined, I think, as they can be under the circumstances. If they were any more defined than they are, they would lose the innovative uncertainty.'

The urology nurse specialist appeared unconcerned herself about role clarity but more concerned that others did not fully understand her role:

> It's very well defined to me what my role is, but I am not sure that generally people understand what my role is . . . My initial job description was very scanty, and brief because it was a developmental role and this job didn't exist before I had it.

The change narrative

We focused our researches on the central objective of achieving the 'two week wait' from referral by general practitioner to first outpatient clinic appointment with a specialist hospital consultant for persons with urological cancer. To achieve this, a package of related and interdependent changes was developed that involved substantial revisions to organization structures and processes, and to medical practice. While each of the individual components of this package of changes was relatively straightforward, together they accumulate to produce what may be described as systemic or 'deep change', reflecting entirely new ways of reconfiguring and providing the service.

The approach adopted used a range of influencing tactics to persuade people that the current systems needed to change. These tactics included presenting evidence-based cases, using clinical information and exercising this influence within regular forums such as monthly discussions and management meetings. In addition, there were more informal and one to one modes of influence used 'behind the scenes', especially by senior clinicians and managers. The nature of the actual changes developed gradually over time, but included, for example, difficult changes to referral processes so as to avoid queues of patients waiting to see one consultant, while another had available appointments.

Despite the instability in the senior management team, the hospital managed to make considerable progress in implementing improvements in cancer care. And this progress continued to be made, though with some setbacks, even with the changes of CEOs. In quantitative terms, in both 2002/03 and 2003/04, Cancer 3 achieved all of the nine 'key targets' contributing to the hospital's 'star rating'. This included the 'two week wait' target, and subsequent one month from that referral date for appropriate treatment to begin. The trust was also meeting the key standard in outpatient and elective (inpatient and day-case) booking, with respect to the pre-booking of first outpatient appointments, and elective inpatient and day-case admissions, giving patients a choice of convenient times within a maximum guaranteed waiting time (replacing conventional waiting lists for appointments and admissions). The qualitative judgements of those involved in these changes reinforce the view that they were successful.

In differing forms, several common themes are displayed in these narrative vignettes:

- Change leadership as a stream of activity, an interconnected process in context. Some activities are planned, targeted and intended, while others are responsive.
- Change leadership is illustrated as a range of dispersed roles and tasks.
- Change leaders assist others to understand how things can be done differently. Hybrids have considerable power and play bridging roles.

Emerging themes and conclusions

In reviewing the data presented here, this section seeks to underline some of the themes emerging from our analysis.

Change leadership as a stream of activity, an interconnected process in context

The data illustrate change leadership or change agency as a stream of activity, an interconnected process in context. This suggests the need to adopt an holistic conceptualization of change leadership as a process in context, rather than discrete interventions. While the will to make changes is intentional in many instances, there is considerable evidence of a high degree of responsiveness in agents' behaviour *combined* with deliberative action moving gradually towards goals and desired outcomes. As Plowman *et al.* (2007) illustrate, a mix of intention and responsiveness to local needs and conditions can combine into powerful (and sometimes) unintended changes. They elucidate the processes of amplification whereby the actions of actors can amplify the impact of small step changes. To understand change leaders' activities, one needs to embed them in their specific context and indeed to ascertain the individual agents' interpretation of that context and their process of sensemaking. Many of the individuals featured in this research, exhibit high degrees of sensitivity to their local contexts, as well as frequently maintaining an understanding of the wider influences on their organization. Local contexts then frame actions and responses, creating priorities for attention.

Change leadership: dispersed roles and tasks

The picture that emerges from our data across all of the different organizations is a mixed and messy picture of the leadership roles in change, reminiscent of the evidence of roles performed in the innovation process (Van de Ven *et al.* 1999). There were few indications of organized and recognizable project management roles, though in some organizations such as Diabetes 3, there were more formalized service improvement roles, with the acknowledged tasks of driving organizational change. In most of the organizations, there was a much broader and looser cast of characters. This was not a straightforward 'leadership constellation' model embracing a cadre of senior figures, as seen in some examples of strategic change in health care (Denis, Lamothe and Langley 2001). Here our data provide a profile of hybrids moving across and between organizations and change leaders dispersed laterally and vertically through the organization, similar to models of dispersed or distributed leadership (Gronn 2000; 2002; 2009; Buchanan *et al.* 2007a; Caldwell 2006). While the widespread dispersal of responsibility for driving changes involving various organizations, groups, teams, and roles was striking, one factor that partially explains the dispersal of change leadership is the complex organizational context. Health care is a highly professionalized context, with tribal loyalties apparent. Thus reinforcing prior research (Locock *et al.* 2001), we perceive change agency engaging the members of differing professions by drawing on the complementary skills of change agents from varied professions. In particular, in these examples, we see various change leaders utilizing the evidence base for change in a manner that was sensitized to the recipients professional background (Ferlie *et al.* 2005).

Even in Maternity 3, where change was more directly centred on a single organization, the actors involved had frequently to influence, collaborate with and engage stakeholders in related organizations. Several of the service improvements, such as the improvements in cancer care delivered through the cancer network, involved ongoing inter-organizational collaboration and joint action. Huxham and Vangen (2000) in discussing inter-organizational collaboration critique the notion of leadership as invested solely in a formal role with the remaining organizational members acting as 'followers'. In inter-organizational settings, the hierarchical relationship between leader and followers often does not apply. So any individual who has power and 'know how' can make an impact on the change process.

Reinforcing prior research evidence (Dopson and Fitzgerald 2005; McNulty and Ferlie 2002), the data draw especial attention to the significance of 'hybrid' roles in facilitating change in health care. These individuals are clinical staff holding joint clinical/managerial roles. They play a prominent role in both instigating and implementing change in all our cases. Luscher and Lewis (2008) explore the role of middle managers as boundary spanners and two aspects of this work, in particular, are relevant to the analysis here. They point to the fact that many middle managers charged with implementing improvement experience intense confusion. In our work, it is apparent that 'hybrid' middle managers play dominant leadership roles in service improvement acting as boundary spanners who can facilitate changes by aiding affected staff to interpret and make sense of their changing circumstances. Luscher and

Lewis identify a similarly helpful process evident in their data, where change agents use data and evidence to provoke discussion and challenge 'ingrained modes of thinking' (2008: 235).

Finally, here, we suggest that the vignettes illustrate how the contributions were significant at different times and stages in the change process. For example, the change agenda appears to have been held together, driven and sustained in several of the organizations by a core group of two to four people. There are examples of leadership groups playing a key role, such as in the diad in Maternity 3 and the quartet in Cancer 3. But this activity was not sufficient of itself to produce progress in improvements. What the leadership group did was to supply the direction and set the culture. Bartunek's (2003) work amply illustrates the unfolding nature of the work of a change agent group; the importance of relationships for sustaining the group and the fluidity of roles and contributions. Here we perceive similar features, but with the added bias of change leadership credibility based on clinical, professional practice and evidence-based health care.

The tasks of change agency include a wealth of influencing, of both individuals and groups and in order to persuade, being cognizant of the evidence base to support change. These tasks require a high level of political skill, underpinned by a nuanced understanding of the local context, the positions and power bases of key stakeholders and groups. Other tasks that are frequently apparent are context assessment; scanning and monitoring the external environment and standard project management activities. Ottaway's (1983) categories of change generators, change implementers and change adopters, and indeed, Buchanan and Storey's (1997) broader range of change agency roles, still underestimate the variety displayed here. In particular, we perceive a substantial emphasis on contextual sensitivity.

So, our analysis has emphasized change leadership as a mix of responsive and deliberative action occurring in context. We find a messy picture of change leaders roles distributed throughout the organizations, playing differing roles. The importance of 'bridging' between professions and boundary spanning between organizations emerge as critical elements of the roles. Within health care the influencing processes also have to be underpinned by knowledge of the clinical evidence base for change. But, not everyone is a leader (Grint 2010); we see here credible and legitimated leaders, not distanced, but relatively accessible.

Individual capabilities – skills, knowledge and credibility

In terms of the skills employed by staff in the process of change agency, one might argue that no new insights have emerged and that the skills that are highlighted in these data accord with previous findings (Howell and Higgins 1990; Beatty and Lee 1992). We noted that influencing skills; persuasiveness, especially using data; high levels of strategic competence to interpret the political agenda and develop strategies; and good political skills were all mentioned frequently. They were the skills most likely to be attributed to 'effective' change leaders. In addition, the ability to assess contexts and sensitivity to local contexts, their priorities and politics was also seen as an essential attribute.

This latter attribute is further reinforced when one considers the knowledge requirements in key roles. Our respondents emphasized an interesting combination of areas, stressing the importance of combining a high grade knowledge base in management and organizational development (OD) *and* local knowledge of how the organization worked, its history and relationships, including much tacit knowledge. This finding is more novel because it underlines the issue of combining knowledge and applicability, and this provides an interesting addition to the six characteristics listed in the work of Alimo-Metcalfe and Alban-Metcalfe (2005) in our introduction. Hence, on the basis of these findings, we argue that leadership of change incorporates an addition to the list presented by Alimo-Metcalfe and Alban-Metcalfe:

- contextual sensitivity (including the potential need for personal credibility).

And contingent on this characteristic, we note that credible change agency in organizations involves many activities that require the translation and customization of national policies and concepts and generalized knowledge to local settings. Finally, it is apparent that for some change leaders, credibility in health care settings is partly dependent on continuing clinical practice.

Acknowledgements

The authors acknowledge the support of the NIHR SDO programme in sponsoring this research. However, the opinions expressed are those of the authors and not necessarily those of the NIHR SDO.

References

Addicott, R., McGivern, G. and Ferlie, E. (2007) The distortion of a managerial technique? The case of NHS cancer networks, *British Journal of Management*, 18: 93–105.

Alimo-Metcalfe, B. and Alban-Metcalfe, J. (2005) Leadership: Time for a new direction?, *Leadership*, 1(51): 51–71.

Anderson, L.A. and Anderson, D. (2010) *The Change Leaders' Roadmap* (2nd edn), San Francisco: Pfeiffer.

Avolio, B.J. and Yammarino, F.J. (2002) *Transformational and Charismatic Leadership: The Road Ahead*, New York: JAI Press.

Baeza, J.I., Fitzgerald, L. and McGivern, G. (2008) Change capacity: The route to service improvement in primary care, *Quality in Primary Care*, Special Issue, 16: 401–407.

Balogun, J. and Johnson, G. (2004) Organizational restructuring and middle management sensemaking, *Academy of Management Journal*, 47: 523–549.

Bartunek, J.M. (2003) *Organizational and Educational Change: The Life and Role of a Change Agent Group*, Mahwah, NJ: Lawrence Erlbaum Associates.

Bass, B.M. (1990) From transactional to transformational leadership: Learning to share the vision, *Organizational Dynamics*, 18(3): 19–32.

Bate, P. (1996) *Strategies for Cultural Change*, Oxford: Elsevier.

Beatty, C.A. and Lee, G.L. (1992) Leadership among middle managers: An exploration in the context of technological change, *Human Relations*, 45(1): 957–989.

Buchanan, D., Addicott, R., Fitzgerald, L., Ferlie, E. and Baeza, J. (2007a) Nobody in charge: Dispersed change agency in healthcare, *Human Relations*, 60(7): 1065–1090.

Buchanan, D., Fitzgerald, L. and Ketley, D. (eds) (2007b) *The Spread and Sustainability of Organizational Change: Modernizing Health Care*, London: Routledge.

Buchanan, D.A. and Boddy, D. (1992) *The Expertise of the Change Agent: Public Performance and Backstage Activity*, Hemel Hempstead: Prentice Hall.

Buchanan, D.A. and Storey, J. (1997) Role taking and role switching in organizational change: The four pluralities, in Ian McLoughlin and Martin Harris (eds), *Innovation, Organizational Change and Technology*, London: International Thomson.

Caldwell, R. (2006) *Agency and Change*, London: Routledge.

Callan, S. (2003) Charismatic leadership in contemporary management debates, *Journal of General Management*, 29(1): 1–14.

Cooper, D., Hinings, C.R. and Greenwood, R. (1996) Sedimentation and transformation in organizational change: The case of Canadian Law firms, *Organization Studies*, 17(4): 623–647.

Delbridge, R. and Edwards, T. (2008) Challenging conventions-roles and processes during non-isomorphic institutional change, *Human Relations*, 61(3): 299–325.

Denis, J.-L., Langley, A. and Cazale, L. (1996) Leadership and strategic change under ambiguity, *Organization Studies*, 17(4): 673–699.

Denis, J.-L., Lamothe, L. and Langley, A. (2001) The dynamics of collective leadership and strategic change in pluralistic organizations, *Academy of Management Journal*, 44: 809–837.

Denis, J.-L., Langley, A. and Rouleau, P. (2005) Rethinking leadership in public organizations, in Ferlie, E., Lynn, L.E. and Pollitt, C. (eds) *The Oxford Handbook of Public Management*, Oxford: Oxford University Press: 446–467.

Department of Health (DoH) (1993) *Changing Childbirth, Part 1: Report of the Expert Maternity Group*, London: HMSO.

—— (2000a) *The NHS Plan*, London: Department of Health.

—— (2000b) *NHS Cancer Plan*, London: Department of Health.

—— (2001) *National Service Framework for Diabetes: Standards*, London: Department of Health.

—— (2004) *National Service Framework for Children, Young People and Maternity Services*, London: Department of Health.

DiMaggio, P.J. and Powell, W.W. (1991) Introduction, in W.W. Powell and P.J. DiMaggio (eds) *New Institutionalism in Organizational Analysis*, Chicago: University of Chicago Press.

Dopson, S. and Fitzgerald, L. (2005) *Knowledge to Action? The Diffusion of Innovations in Health Care*, Oxford: Oxford University Press.

Fairhurst, K. and Huby, G. (1998) From trial data to practical knowledge: Qualitative study of how general practitioners have accessed and used evidence about statin drugs in their management of hypercholesterolaemia, *British Medical Journal*, 317: 1130–1134.

Ferlie, E., Fitzgerald, L., Wood, M. and Hawkins, C. (2005) The non spread of innovations: The mediating role of professionals, *Academy of Management Journal*, 48(1): 117–134.

Ferlie, E., Dopson, S., Fitzgerald, L. and Locock, L. (2009) Renewing policy to support evidence based health care, *Public Administration*, 87(4): 837–852.

Fiedler, F.E. (1967) *A Theory of Leadership Effectiveness*, New York: McGraw Hill.

Fitzgerald, L., Ferlie, E., Wood, M. and Hawkins, C. (2002) Interlocking interactions, the diffusion of innovations in health care, *Human Relations*, 55(12): 1429–1449.

Fitzgerald, L., Lilley, C., Ferlie, E., Addicott, R., McGivern, G. and Buchanan, D. (2006) *Managing Change and Role Enactment in the Professionalized Organization, Final Report*, NIHR, SDO Programme, Department of Health. Available at www. sdo.nihr.ac.uk (accessed 30 March 2012).

Greenwood, R. and Hinings, C.R. (1988) Organizational design types and dynamics of strategic change, *Organization Studies*, 9(3): 293–316.

Grint, K. (2005) Problems, problems, problems: The social construction of leadership, *Human Relations*, 58(11): 1467–1494.

—— (2010) The sacred in leadership: Separation, sacrifice, and silence, *Organization Studies*, 31(1): 89–107.

Gronn, P. (2000) Distributed properties: A new architecture for leadership, *Educational Management Administration and Leadership*, 28(3): 317–338.

—— (2002) Distributed leadership as a unit of analysis, *Leadership Quarterly*, 13: 423–451.

—— (2003) *The New Work of Educational Leaders: Changing Leadership Practice in an Era of School Reform*, London: Paul Chapman.

—— (2009) From distributed leadership to hybrid leadership practice, in A. Harris (ed.) *Distributed Leadership. Different Perspectives*, London: Springer.

Hartley, J. and Benington, J. (2010) *Leadership for Healthcare*, Bristol: Policy Press.

Hogg, M.A. (2001) A social identity theory of leadership, *Personality and Social Psychology Review*, 5(3): 184–200.

Howell, J.M. and Higgins, C.A. (1990) Champions of technological innovation, *Administrative Science Quarterly*, 35: 317–341.

Huxham, C. and Vangen, S. (2000) Leadership in the shaping and implementation of collaboration agendas: How things happen in a (not quite) joined up world, *Academy of Management Journal*, 43(6): 1159–1175.

Kanter, R.B. (1984) *The Change Masters, Corporate Entrepreneurs at Work*, London: Allen and Unwin.

—— (1990) *When Giants Learn to Dance*, New York: Simon and Schuster.

Locock, L., Dopson, S., Chambers, D. and Gabbay, J. (2001) Understanding the role of opinion leaders in improving clinical effectiveness, *Social Science and Medicine*, 53(6): 745–757.

Lovelady, L. (1984) Change strategies and the use of OD consultants to facilitate change. Part II. The Role of the internal consultant in OD, *Leadership and OD Journal*, 5(4): 2–12.

Luscher, S.L. and Lewis, M.W. (2008) Organizational change and managerial sensemaking: Working through paradox, *Academy of Management Journal*, 51: 221–240.

McKinlay, W. and Scherer, A. (2000) Some unanticipated consequences of organizational restructuring, *Academy of Management Review*, 25: 735–752.

McNulty, T. and Ferlie, E. (2002) *Reengineering Health Care: The Complexities of Organizational Transformation*, Oxford: Oxford University Press.

NHS Executive (2000) *Manual of Cancer Services Standards*, London: NHSE.

Ottaway, R.N. (1983) The change agent: A taxonomy in relation to the change process, *Human Relations*, 36(4): 361–392.

Pettigrew, A.M. (1985) *The Awakening Giant*, London: Blackwell.

Pettigrew, A.M. and Whipp, R. (1991) *Managing Change for Competitive Success*, Oxford: Blackwell.

Pettigrew, A.M., Ferlie, E. and McKee, L. (1992) *Shaping Strategic Change: Making Change in Large Organisations, the Case of the NHS*, London: Sage.

Plowman, D.A., Baker, L.T., Beck, T.E., Kulkarni, M., Solansky, S.T. and Travis, D.V. (2007) Radical change accidentally: The emergence and amplification of small change, *Academy of Management Journal*, 50(3): 515–543.

Rogers, E. (1995) *The Diffusion of Innovations* (4th edn), New York: Free Press.

Stjernberg, T. and Philips, A. (1993) Organizational innovations in a long-term perspective: Legitimacy and souls-of-fire as critical factors of change and viability, *Human Relations*, 46(10): 1193–1221.

Wallace, M. and Pocklington, K. (2002) *Managing Complex Change. Large Scale Reorganization of Schools*, London/New York: Routledge Falmer.

Van de Ven, A., Polley, D., Garud, R. and Venkataraman, S. (1999) *The Innovation Journey*, Oxford: Oxford University Press.

Yin, R.K. (2009) *Case Study Research: Design and Methods* (4th edn), Thousand Oaks/London/New Delhi: Sage.

Yukl, G. (1999) An evaluation of conceptual weaknesses in transformational and charismatic leadership theories, *Leadership Quarterly*, 10(2): 285–305.

Part II

Leadership style in the public services

Part II

Leadership style in
the public services

5 After privatization

The public management of private employment services

Nicolette van Gestel

Introduction

Privatization can be defined as an increase in private sector involvement, relative to public sector contribution, 'in making programs available to the public' (Sellers 2003: 609). The basic idea behind privatization is that competition will result in improved efficiency and a better quality of public services. It has been widely assumed that private providers deliver flexible responses and develop innovative methods and tailored solutions (Bredgaard and Larsen 2008). One way of privatizing is the contracting out of public services to private business (Miller and Whitford 2006). If public leaders decide in favour of contracting out – that is, private firms competing for public service delivery – they usually promise more efficiency and cost savings, and less government involvement. But this promise is not without pitfalls. As Hefetz and Warner (2004: 174) suggest, public service delivery is more than a business: 'it reflects collective identity, responds to diversity and promotes social equity'. Privatization of public services may thus imply that public leaders have to balance economic and political goals to secure public values. Despite the large amount of public services contracted out in the industrialized countries, there are only a few systematic, empirical studies about the consequences of privatization for public management and leadership (Sellers 2003; Van Slyke 2003).

This study aims at evaluating the situation that occurs after privatization, when public leaders face new contracting relationships with private employment services. The central question of this chapter is: Has public leadership been capable of creating a new market with competition and innovation, where core public values are effectively managed? Studying this question contributes to the theme of this book in two ways. First, the emphasis in the literature on public leadership has usually been on isolated individuals in formal leadership positions in public organizations (Denis *et al.* 2005: 425). This study shows how public leadership evolves in a complex set of relationships, where public managers are dealing with private business for political endeavours. It will illustrate how leadership is negotiated in the new relationships, where public and private managers adhere to various – sometimes competing – values in a dynamic political environment. Second, public leadership is usually thought to focus on strategic change, while public management is for normal times (Hefetz and Warner 2004; Wallace *et al.* 2011). Whereas public leadership has not often been evaluated in its daily practices (Denis *et al.* 2005), this study shows that management is a crucial part of public leadership, since it is in the implementation of strategic change that leadership is accomplished. In studying the implementation process, this study shows that old problems in public services tend to persist in the new governance arrangements with private actors.

With the goal of examining public leadership after privatization, we have conducted a case study on the field of employment services in the Netherlands since 2002. We begin with a review of the literature on the privatization of public services, the creation of new markets, and the safeguarding of public values in contractual relationships with private business. Data from secondary sources and interviews with public managers and private service providers are used to analyze the new relationships between public and private actors empirically. The chapter concludes with the paradoxes that have emerged in public leadership after privatization, where the privatizing of public services is accompanied by growing state involvement and public values are under pressure from the dominant market logic.

New challenges to public leadership after privatization

Even after privatization, the field of formerly public services remains an important area of state intervention: 'Privatization has been dominated by state presence – before, during and after the process' (Wright 1995: 32). In contracting out, the state is still responsible (by law) for providing the public service to the citizens in an adequate manner. There are two specific reasons the state may intervene after privatizing public services. First, eliminating a public monopoly does not automatically produce a level playing field on which the estimated efficiency can be realised (Héritier and Schmidt 2000). The government is thus regulating the new market in terms of equal competition for the private providers. Second, and even more important, core public values that once inspired the grounding of public monopolies, such as social equity and general access, have not disappeared after privatization (Hefetz and Warner 2004; Héritier and Schmidt 2000). Consequently, the government seeks to safeguard these values in different ways than through direct service provision. This calls upon an active rather than a passive mode of public leadership. Hence, the privatization of public service provision usually goes along with additional public regulation and control of market activities (Ajzenstadt and Rosenhek 2000).

In the process of private service production, new roles for public leaders are required (Van Slyke 2003: 296; Hefetz and Warner 2004) to assure, for example, that formerly public activities attract private firms, and that core public values are addressed by the new market. In the growing literature on public leadership (Denis *et al.* 2005; Raffel *et al.* 2009; Wallace *et al.* 2011), it is increasingly recognized that the success or failure of public leaders depends largely on their ability to constitute and maintain strong and durable relationships with other stakeholders such as private businesses and not-for-profit agencies. From this perspective, public leadership is particularly demonstrated in the ability to develop newly profound relationships with other actors, such as private companies, in which these actors feel engaged and are willing to support not only their own private goals but also the aims of public policy (Bovaird 2006; Brookes and Grint 2010). Public leaders thus have to work with actors belonging to different institutional spheres; this requires them to be sensitive to divergent views, interests and values (Ferlie and McNulty 2004; Townley 2002). A key challenge to public leadership is to generate sustainable decisions and strategies in a context of multiple, even conflicting, objectives (Denis *et al.* 2005: 455).

Specific measures such as contracts, incentive schemes and performance indicators may enable public leaders to mediate between different interests and values (Denis *et al.* 2005). For instance, government contracts with private service providers may help to regulate and correct market outcomes (Héritier and Schmidt 2000). The contractual relationship between the government and the private service provider is, however, full of risks and uncertainties for both parties (Verhoest 2005). For the private service provider, it is a new challenge to commit to political goals under the conditions of competition. It means that the private contractor has to fulfil the interests of the government, to satisfy the needs of the customers and to make a profit at the same time (Broadbent *et al.* 1996). Given these objectives, the contractor's primary desire is for stability in the requirements of the government: a clear and specified contract, with limited space for the government to intervene, in order to minimize uncertainty (Héritier and Schmidt 2000). For public leaders, however, the uncertainties and risks shouldered by private companies are not of primary concern. The government, first and foremost, aims to expand its flexibility to react to the performance of the private agents (Miller and Whitford 2006). Yet the government is also faced with uncertainties about reliable information, which is of course necessary to build decent contracts with private service providers and to monitor them effectively. This information is more difficult to obtain after privatization, since the government has lost its direct contact with, and its history of experience with, the public services it formerly provided.

The contracting relationship, then, is typically characterized by a situation of information asymmetry (Rockman 1997). Two types of information asymmetry are best known in the literature as hidden information (or adverse selection) and hidden action (or moral hazard) (Broadbent *et al.* 1996: 266). *Adverse selection* means that the government runs the risk of purchasing a service of low quality, because the private contractor could hide information about the attributes of a service. Another type of opportunism, *moral hazard*, takes place when the private contractor uses its information to act in its self-interest, to the exclusion of the agreed-upon goals in the contract (Van Slyke

2006: 162). An important issue, therefore, is how public leaders can avoid or resolve these uncertainties and risks in their relationships with private contractors in order to align their goals. They may attempt to control the problems of information asymmetry and the attendant risks of adverse selection and moral hazard in three ways (Miller and Whitford 2006; Verhoest 2005). First, they can manage the private agent by specifying criteria for performance and/or processes. A second tool to reduce uncertainty and performance risks is monitoring the process and/or the outcomes, for instance with assessments, benchmarking or conversations. A final instrument is financial incentives, such as 'no cure, no pay'. Below, we will explore how public leadership has managed privatized employment services in a specific situation, and evaluate the use and consequences of these three instruments.

Research setting

Public leadership studies need to develop toward a more dynamic, process-oriented, and contextual vision of leadership in order to add richness and depth to the static conceptions that have dominated in the past (Denis *et al.* 2005: 463). This will require qualitative, longitudinal research methods that follow the development of leadership actions and their consequences over time. The Dutch case is an excellent example for investigating this because it is one of the early cases of privatization in employment services (Bredgaard and Larsen 2008; Sol and Westerveld 2005; Struyven and Steurs 2005), thus providing the opportunity for rich, longitudinal data. In 2001, the Dutch Parliament decided to privatize the core business of the public employment services, its job-finding activities. This decision implied a strategic change, because the implementation of public employment policy in the Netherlands has been in the hands of a government agency for almost a century. Although a few tasks, such as the running of a national vacancy bank and unemployment administration, are still handled by the government, the key objective of the former job centres – the assistance of unemployed people in finding a job – has been contracted out to private companies.

The government's decision to outsource implied the creation of a new market for privatized public services. It also meant that the former Public Employment Service Agency was transformed into a private agency in a system of competition. The national government, through its National Agency for Social Benefits (*Uitvoeringsinstituut Werknemersverzekeringen*, called by its Dutch initials UWV), is the main principal in the new system of outsourced relationships. UWV selects the private service providers with tender (bidding) procedures. When this new market emerged in 2002, around 600 private bureaus for employment services began operating. That number grew to roughly 1800 in 2007 and more than 2,000 in 2010. The large majority of these companies employ fewer than ten people. Only 23 per cent of the private employment bureaus employ between ten and one hundred job coaches, and only a few firms – fewer than three per cent – employ more than one hundred job coaches.

Method

In examining the public leadership of private employment services, we used two main sources: documents and interviews. First, we studied more than twenty documents, mainly evaluation reports, about privatized employment services in the Netherlands since 2002 (see References at the end of this chapter for details of secondary sources). These documents are a very rich and varied source of information, including reports and studies from the Ministry of Social Affairs and Employment, the National Agency for Social Benefits (UWV), the General Audit Chamber, and the Council for Work and Income. In addition, we carried out twenty-three interviews with representatives of the main stakeholders in the outsourcing process: the public managers in their role as principal, and the managers of private service providers as agents. We conducted interviews with nine government officials (from the principal UWV, at both the national and regional/local levels), the chairperson of the main association for private employment agencies, and thirteen managers of private bureaus (six bureaus with more than a hundred employees, seven with fewer than a hundred). The interviews elicited additional information about the newly created public–private relationships, in particular with respect to the tender system, the monitoring of results, and the impact of financial incentives. The interviews were conducted in three rounds, in 2004 and 2005 (six interviews), 2007 (nine interviews) and 2010 (eight interviews), aiming at a dynamic rather than a static understanding of public leadership in the newly created market.

We examined and analyzed the documents and interview transcriptions with respect to the central theme in this study: public leadership in the creation of a market for public services and the safeguarding of public values. We coded the key constructs in the data (i.e., competition, innovation, social justice) and added memos whenever we encountered potentially important insights (Miles and Huberman 1994; Strauss and Corbin 1998). The insights that emerged during the period of data collection were laid down in three interim reports (in 2005, 2008 and 2011). Together, these reports provided detailed information and allowed for a systematic and comprehensive analysis of how the contracting relationship has evolved over time.

Results

Evaluating the public management of private employment services revealed three key problems in terms of effective public leadership. First, creating a new market for public services has resulted in a tender system with centralized standards for the selection and performance of private contractors that impede the potential for innovation. Although the main reason stated for the transfer of public employment services to private agencies was to increase innovation, our findings suggest that the central standards for selecting and monitoring private agents are in fact preventing it. Second, public leaders want private agencies to focus on assisting specific target groups with low chances at the labour market, such as the long-term unemployed. However, an emphasis on improving success rates has achieved the opposite effect: instead of better results for the hard-to-employ, the government's incentives pushed the private bureaus to facilitate the most promising clients. More generally, our findings illustrate that core public values such as social justice are at odds with a dominant focus on short-term efficiency. Third, the management style of public leadership after privatization evolved from 'control at a distance' toward an emphasis on public–private partnership. Despite the rhetoric of partnership, however, public leaders still (even more) employ a hierarchical approach that hampers optimal service delivery. These contradictions in the outsourcing process reveal important limitations of public leaders in this case. Below, the findings are described in more detail.

Creating markets for public services

While competition and innovation are at the heart of the privatization process, this study shows that they are in conflict with the government's desire for central performance requirements and standardized methods. From the government's perspective, standardization of rules for tenders and monitoring are meant to improve efficiency and performance. But according to a majority of private contractors, the central rules hold back competition and hamper their ability to innovate. For instance, in a survey of 169 private bureaus that received contracts from UWV, with a response rate of 32 per cent, a large majority (67.6 per cent) believe that the tender procedures did not contribute to any innovation in their methods or approach to clients (Brenninkmeijer *et al.* 2006: 77). Other studies confirm that the strict conditions for receiving a contract diminish the flexibility and innovative capacity of private agencies. Moreover, the standardized system of tendering and contracting led to competition based on price rather than on the quality of services (Groot *et al.* 2006). The relatively low chances for private service providers to improve their services under these conditions had negative consequences for the overall efficiency and performance of the system (General Audit Committee 2004; PricewaterhouseCoopers 2006; Brenninkmeijer *et al.* 2006; Van Horssen *et al.* 2004; Zwinkels 2007).

The performance measurement systems implemented in contracts have focused on 'placements', an easily quantifiable product that does not take into account the actual quality and contribution of the private employment services to job finding. Moreover, the focus on 'placements' as a rather simplistic measure for performance has emphasized quantity over quality. A public manager perceives this as a disadvantage:

> Placement is the only goal. That is the disadvantage of this tender, you really have to stress a placement. But the unemployed and disabled are increasingly difficult to employ. It would be better if we could not only agree upon placements but also on intermediate results. Those kinds of results are completely lost now.

Performance monitoring was initially restricted to an annual evaluation study. However, since 2004, benchmarks, visits and conversations have been used more frequently in order to gather information about activities in the private sphere and to improve results. Several evaluation studies showed that UWV has increased its attempts to monitor the private agents in detail (Brenninkmeijer *et al.* 2006; Mallee *et al.* 2008). However, the private contractors interviewed in our study have serious doubts about the adequacy of such performance controls. For example, the government does not seem to register the 'drop-outs' in the re-integration projects, giving the impression that performance is not really discussed. As one of the private managers in our study said, 'I do not believe that we keep statistics on clients who drop out and I don't think UWV registers them.'

The manager of another private bureau pointed to the discrepancy between the performance demands in the contract and the actual controls: 'UWV does not use the same criteria for performance control as they describe in the contract. For example, they do not actually check the drop-outs.'

The private managers thus mentioned that there is a lack of quality measurement and transparency about the results, including drop-outs. In particular, the private managers regretted that the system is focused on competition and control (under unclear conditions) instead of investments in meaningful cooperation.

Safeguarding public values

Although the outsourcing of public services is intended to enhance job finding for specific target groups with dismal chances in the labour market, such as older people, ethnic minorities and people with disabilities, both the public managers and the private agents we interviewed stressed that outcomes have not improved in this respect since 2002 (see also Brenninkmeijer *et al.* 2006: 22; Mallee *et al.* 2008; Zwinkels 2007). On the contrary, the job placement figures for people with disabilities actually decreased (Brenninkmeijer *et al.* 2006: 56). Government incentives seem largely inadequate to motivate private agencies to develop job-finding activities for the lower-skilled unemployed (General Audit Committee, 2004). This is even more disappointing since several studies show that the effectiveness of employment services could greatly increase if the less-promising clients received more attention: specific target groups may improve their chances of finding a job to 15 per cent instead of 5 per cent on average (in other words, from 57 per cent to 72 per cent) (De Koning *et al.* 2005; Kok *et al.* 2006).

In order to focus its contractors' activities on the target groups, the government took extra measures in the contracting and monitoring of private service providers. For instance, while the government initially financed job-finding trajectories without taking the results into account, in July 2003 it introduced a 'no cure, no pay' formula – a recipe for difficulty in the target groups (Arents *et al.* 2003).[1] These measures aim at increasing performance, in particular with regard to social outcomes, and have become more stringent over the past decade. However, the stricter financial incentives did not improve performance in terms of more job placements for the target groups, and even led to lower performance in this area (Van Horssen *et al.* 2004; Mallee *et al.* 2008). The private service bureaus point to the financial incentives as the heart of this problem:

> The consequences of 'no cure, no pay' are that we take less notice of individuals and we do job coaching at the group level. This has increased our efficiency a great deal, but there is little room left for clients who need extra assistance.

Another private manager said, 'Automatically you will now make a selection between promising and less promising job seekers to focus on the first group.'

The financial measures thus seem to result in the opposite of the intended effect. Not only the private managers, but also the public managers who are implementing the financial measures, have serious doubts as to whether they will increase the results for difficult target groups. As a public manager said, 'Financial incentives are good, except for the difficult target groups. You may seriously wonder if this is the right method to bring these people back into the labour market.' The dominance of market logic over social values thus seems a direct consequence of the fact that the government put most financial risks in the employment services on the side of private business.

Public leadership in public–private relationships

After the government privatized employment services in 2002 and developed a tender system, no one initially paid much notice to the management of the new public–private relationship. Public leaders took a top-down approach that placed a huge distance between them and private contractors. The private agencies had to apply for contracts but were not seen as partners, even to the point of avoiding personal communication. Interestingly, this management style has changed over time to a preference for frequent, local and personal contacts between public and private managers about clients and services. This move was illustrated by the government's decision in 2005 to appoint 450 public coaches to manage contact with private employment services (Verveen *et al.* 2006), a programme that grew rapidly to 625 full-time equivalents in 2006. The decentralization of control and monitoring on the part of the government initially seemed to imply that a control approach was replaced by deliberation. As one of the public managers of UWV put it:

> Last year, UWV dictated the outcomes. Now it's more like: we both want to bring a group of clients to work. So how can we do that together, what do we expect from each other? In other words, there is more partnership.

However, an important effect of the introduction of the public coaches was that they tended to maximize their own share in client services and to minimize the role of the private bureaus. Even though the public coaches contributed to the increase in frequent and personal communication; instead of acting in partnership with the private bureaus, they effectively started their own business. They motivated their effort to increase in-house provision of employment services with the growing public debate about outsourcing yielding too few results. After the introduction of public reintegration coaches in 2005, a private manager observed that: 'the introduction of the reintegration coach is an invention of UWV to keep the clients themselves now. It is competitive with the private agencies, they grab a piece of the market'.

One public manager admitted that they went beyond the intention of the legislature:

> You see that clients stay long into the hands of the [public] re-integration coach, but this is not what was intended with privatization. The re-integration coach should only have a role as supervisor, and the employment services should be left to the private market.

The apparent move from control to deliberation thus turned out to be a move toward more public provision of (formally privatized) employment services. The UWV reintegration coaches required a central role and they decided more and more whether clients will receive services from private bureaus and for which service modules (Mallee *et al.* 2008). The tendency toward providing more employment services in-house had a large impact on private bureaus, since they began to receive only clients with more complicated problems that could not be solved by the public agency, making it even more difficult to reach their placement targets.

The public managers admitted that the new governance style of partnership and personal communication did not alter their hierarchical relationships with the private bureaus:

> We still have a principal–agent relationship and in reality, the partnership does not alter our targets for performance. These targets are fixed. But the way you treat each other is different, you have a conversation. That is unlike receiving an order.

In summary, beyond the apparent change in the style of public leadership – from a top-down control approach toward negotiation – the hierarchical relationship between the public agency and private bureaus still remains dominant.

Conclusion

Generally, it can be argued that privatization and outsourcing may facilitate the realization of public service goals through greater flexibility (Brodkin 2006;

Sellers 2003; Van Slyke 2006). At the same time, however, privatization gives rise to a dual need for extra regulation: first, in order to make markets work and to prevent market power from being concentrated in the hands of a few actors, and second, to correct the outcomes of market processes in such a way that societal and political goals are met (Héritier and Schmidt 2000). Through an examination of Dutch employment services after privatization, this study has shown major contradictions in how public leaders dealt with the creation of a new market and the balance between different and often competing values.

First, this study indicates a paradox in a public sector that has apparently been subject to both more privatization and publicization. While there has been pronounced movement toward the creation of more devolved forms of service provision, key strategic issues such as resource allocation, financial conditions and performance targets are laid down in detailed, centralized government rules. As our study demonstrated, the reduction in the role of the state in direct service delivery goes along with a strong government intervention to monitor the process and correct the outcomes of private suppliers. We showed that while operations have been outsourced to private businesses, control over policy and resource allocation have increasingly been concentrated within the state. The result seems to be that neither the advantages of privatization in terms of innovation nor the promise of less state involvement are realized.

Second, employment services, like other public services, have to be delivered in an efficient way and achieve social and political goals at the same time. Hence, performance is often defined in terms of both cost effectiveness and social targets. In the previous analysis, we discovered that a strong emphasis on economic performance (a maximum of placements with a minimum of costs) was generally in conflict with the capacity of the private agents to enhance social performance. While the government used selection criteria and financial incentives to focus the private bureaus at the hard-to-employ, the private agents perceived this as an increased risk, which led them to adapt their methods and drop investments in individual clients, in particular the target groups. The strong emphasis in the contracting relationships on short-term efficiency thus leads to the opposite effect for social performance.

Third, the new roles of public leaders that are required in the process of private service delivery (Van Slyke 2003: 296; Hefetz and Warner 2004) are not yet fully developed. This study shows that public leaders were not able to reconcile competing values within contractor relationships. Our study identified two crucial problems. First, public leaders still draw upon a hierarchical, control-based approach and are less focused on accommodating the divergent interests and values of actors from various institutional domains (Bovaird 2006; Brookes and Grint 2010; Townley 2002). Second, the political environment does not seem to support the development of such new roles and skills among public leaders, since there is a strong emphasis on performance standards and top-down accountability. Generating more partnership and strong decisions in the context of multiple actors and conflicting objectives remains a key challenge for public leadership (Denis *et al.* 2005; Ferlie and McNulty 2004).

What are the consequences of these findings for the public leadership debate?

One consequence is that substantial changes in public service provision may require not only better public leadership in managing the new public–private relationship, but also different policies. Without political solutions for balancing social and economic goals and values, current efforts to reform the European welfare states by creating new markets or adopting New Public Management techniques are likely to create new versions of old administrative problems. Our study shows that, although it might be necessary to reform bureaucratic arrangements for public service provision for reasons of innovation and flexibility, this does not mean that new arrangements will automatically resolve the complex problems of performance. This is particularly true in the case of social welfare politics, where implementation is both embedded practically and politically (Brodkin 2006; Moynihan and Pandey 2005). A real improvement in public service delivery will thus require a significant combination of material resources, greater clarity of purpose, and better alignment of different interests and values. Public leaders who aim to improve such services should resolve ambiguities at various levels: the political environment, organizational goals, and the roles of managers (Pandey and Wright 2006). This may also enable the managers and the clients of these services to be heard and taken seriously (Denis *et al.* 2005). Yet, such conditions are not obvious in either the old or new models of public sector reform.

Acknowledgements

I thank the editors of this volume for their helpful comments on a previous draft of this chapter, and Laury Keller, Nannette Broeks and Eveline Dekkers for their support in collecting data and writing interim reports.

Note

1 'No cure, no pay' implies that 40–50% of the costs is paid beforehand, and 50–60% after finding a job of at least six months' duration, of which two months have passed. 'No cure, less pay' means 60–80% financing at the start of a trajectory, and 20–40% related to job finding. The percentages have been adapted to different target groups and over time.

References

Ajzenstadt, M. and Z. Rosenhek (2000) Privatisation and new modes of state intervention. *Journal of Social Policy*, 29(2): 247–262.

Arents, M., M. Peters and R. Dorenbos (2003) *Vormgeving van het opdracht-geverschap: Ervaringen en percepties van reïntegratiebedrijven* (Den Haag: Raad voor werk en inkomen).

Arents, M., R. Dorenbos, V. van Loon and J. van Velden (2004) *Ontwikkelingen op de re-integratiemarkt. Ervaringen van reïntegratiebedrijven en opdrachtgevers* (Den Haag: Raad voor Werk en Inkomen).

Bovaird, T. (2006) Developing new forms of partnership with the 'market' in the procurement of public services. *Public Administration*, 84(1): 81–102.

Bredgaard, T. and F. Larsen (2008) Quasi-markets in employment policy: Do they deliver on promises? *Social Policy and Society*, 7(3): 341–352.

Brenninkmeijer, V., C. Wevers, W. Zwinkels, P. van Eekert, P. Donders, K. van Laarhoven and E. Dorscheidt (2006) *Evaluatie aanbesteding UWV 2001–2005* (Hoofddorp: TNO Kwaliteit van Leven).

Broadbent, J., M. Dietrich and R. Laughlin (1996) The development of principal–agent contracting and accountability relationships in the public sector: Conceptual and cultural problems. *Critical Perspectives on Accounting*, 7: 259–284.

Brodkin, E.Z. (2006) Bureaucracy redux: Management reformism and the welfare state. *Journal of Public Administration Research and Theory*, 17: 1–17.

Brookes, S. and K. Grint (2010) *The New Public Leadership Challenge* (Basingstoke; New York: Palgrave Macmillan).

Buurman, M. (2008) Re-integratiebeleid: Wat zijn de resultaten en wat zijn ze waard? *Tijdschrift voor Openbare Financiën*, 2: 40–47.

De Koning, J. (2004) *The reform of the Dutch public employment service* (Rotterdam: SEOR).

De Koning, J., A. Gelderblom, K. Zandvliet and L. van den Boom (2005) *Effectiviteit van Re-integratie – De stand van zaken; Literatuuronderzoek* (Rotterdam: SEOR).

Denis, J.-L., A. Langley and P. Rouleau (2005) Rethinking leadership in public organizations. In E. Ferlie, L.E. Lynn and C. Pollitt (eds), *The Oxford Handbook of Public Management* (Oxford: Oxford University Press): 446–467.

Ferlie, E. and T. McNulty (2004) Process transformation: Limitations to radical organizational change within public service organizations. *Organization Studies*, 25(8): 1389–1412.

General Audit Committee (Algemene Rekenkamer) (2004) *Bemiddeling en reïntegratie van werklozen* (Den Haag: Tweede Kamer der Staten-Generaal).

Groot, I., D. Hollanders, J.P. Hop and S. Onderstal (2006) *Werkt de reïntegratiemarkt? Onderzoek naar de marktwerking op de reïntegratiemarkt* (Amsterdam: SEO Economisch Onderzoek).

Hefetz, A. and M. Warner (2004) Privatisation and its reverse: Explaining the dynamics of the government contracting process. *Journal of Public Administration Research and Theory*, 14(2): 171–190.

Héritier, A. and S.K. Schmidt (2000) After liberalization: Public interest services and employment in the utilities. In F.W. Scharpf and V.A. Schmidt (eds), *Welfare and Work in the Open Economy* (vol. II) (Oxford: Oxford University Press).

Kok, L., D. Hollanders, J.P. Hop, M. de Graaf-Zijl, I. Groot and T. de Hoop (2006) *Kosten en baten van re-integratie* (Amsterdam: SEO Economisch Onderzoek).

Mallee, L., J.W.M. Mevissen, J.E. Soethout and H.A. Weening (2006) *De re-integratiemarkt geijkt. Evaluatie introductie marktwerking bij re-integratie van niet-werkenden* (Amsterdam: Regioplan).

Mallee, L., J.W.M. Mevissen and W.R. Tap (2008) *Ontwikkelingen op de re-integratiemarkt* (Amsterdam: Regioplan).

Miles, M.B. and A.M. Huberman (1994) *Qualitative Data Analysis: An Expanded Sourcebook* (Thousand Oaks, CA: Sage).

Miller, G.J. and A.B. Whitford (2006) The principal's moral hazard: Constraints on the use of incentives in hierarchy. *Journal of Public Administration Research and Theory*, 17: 213–233.

Moynihan, D. and S.K. Pandey (2005) Testing how management matters in an era of government by performance management. *Journal of Public Administration Research and Theory*, 15(3): 421–439.

Pandey, S.K. and B.E. Wright (2006) Connecting the dots in public management: Political environment, organizational goal ambiguity, and the public manager's role ambiguity. *Journal of Public Administration Research and Theory*, 16: 511–532.

PricewaterhouseCoopers (2006) *SUWI-evaluatie 2006, Een evaluatie van de Wet structuur uitvoeringsorganisatie werk en inkomen (Wet SUWI)* (Den Haag: in opdracht van het Ministerie van Sociale Zaken en Werkgelegenheid).

Raffel, A., P. Leisink and A.E. Middlebrooks (eds) (2009) *Public Sector Leadership: International Challenges and Perspectives* (Cheltenham: Edward Elgar).

Rockman, B.A. (1997) Honey, I shrank the state: On the brave new world of public administration. In A. Farazmand (ed.), *Modern Systems of Government* (Thousand Oaks, CA/London/New Delhi: Sage): 275–294.

Sellers, M.P. (2003) Privatisation morphs into 'publicization': Businesses look a lot like government. *Public Administration*, 81(3): 607–620.

Sol, E. and M. Westerveld (eds) (2005) *Contractualism in Employment Services: A New Form of Welfare State Governance* (The Hague: Kluwer Law International).

Strauss, A. and J. Corbin (1998) *Basics of Qualitative Research: Techniques and Procedures for Developing Grounded Theory* (Thousand Oaks, CA: Sage).

Struyven, L. and G. Steurs (2005) Design and redesign of a quasi-market for the reintegration of jobseekers: Empirical evidence for Australia and the Netherlands. *Journal of European Social Policy*, 15(3): 211–229.

Townley, B. (2002) The role of competing rationalities in institutional change. *Academy of Management Journal*, 45(1): 163–179.

Van Horssen, C., L. Mallee and J.W.M. Mevissen (2004) *De reïntegratiemarkt langs de meetlat van SUWI. Derde inventarisatie van stand van zaken. Eindrapport* (Amsterdam: Regioplan).

Van Slyke, D.M. (2003) The mythology of privatisation in contracting for social services. *Public Administration Review*, 63(3): 277–296.

—— (2006) Agents and stewards: Using theory to understand the government–nonprofit social service contracting relationship. *Journal of Public Administration Research and Theory*, 17: 157–187.

Veerman, T.J., V. Veldhuis, M.C.M. Aerts and J.W. van Egmond (RWI) (2008) *Een markt in beweging. Ontwikkelingen aan de aanbodzijde van de re-integratiemarkt* (Den Haag: Raad voor Werk en Inkomen).

Verhoest, K. (2005) Effects of autonomy, performance contracting, and competition in the performance of a public agency: A case study. *The Policy Studies Journal*, 33(2): 235–258.

Verveen, E., S. Bunt, C. Bos and M. van der Aalst (2006) *Ontwikkelingen op de re-integratiemarkt – Ervaringen van opdrachtgevers en opdrachtnemers* (Den Haag: Raad voor Werk en Inkomen).

Vinke, H. (2004) *Evaluatie aanbesteding van reïntegratiecontracten 2003* (Hoofddorp: TNO rapport 16005/25388).

Wallace, M., D. O'Reilly, J. Morris and R. Deem (2011) Public service leaders as 'change agents' – for whom? *Public Management Review*, 13(1): 65–93.

Wevers, C.W.J, J. van Genabeek, B.M.F. Fermin, E.L. de Vos, S. Dhondt, J.J.M. Besseling and A. Braat (2006) *Evaluatie SUWI 2006, perceel 2: Werk boven uitkering* (Hoofddorp: TNO Kwaliteit van Leven).

Wright, V. (1995) Privatization in Western Europe: Paradoxes and implications for institutions. Paper for the annual conference of the Netherlands Institute of Government: 1–40.

Zwinkels, W. (2007) Effectiviteit van re-integratie: onbenutte potenties van privatisering. *Tijdschrift voor Arbeidsvraagstukken*, 23: 121–131.

6 Medical leadership and management reforms in hospitals

A comparative study

Mike Dent, Ian Kirkpatrick and Indranath Neogy

Introduction

New Public Management (NPM) has been an all encompassing force that has had an impact on the medical profession and threatened its autonomy and influence within hospitals across Europe over recent decades. Yet, hospital doctors continue to dominate the clinical work processes and remain core to the health care division of labour, which underpins their traditional leadership role within hospitals. The challenge has been, how may the doctors' leadership role be incorporated within the new managerialism, rather than be defiant of it?

In this chapter we examine the variation in reform trajectories and its outcomes for hospital physicians and their leadership within four case studies: three national public sector hospital services within Europe (Denmark, the Netherlands and England) plus a 'not-for-profit' health maintenance organization (HMO), Kaiser Permanente, in the USA. The inclusion of Kaiser Permanente, despite it not being a public sector health system within a nation state is justified as it has become almost a reform template for public sector health systems outside the USA; moreover, in membership size and organization it shares much in common with such systems. Kaiser Permanente has a membership of 8 million, larger than the populations of both Denmark (approximately 5.5 million) and the Netherlands (approximately 6.25 million, see Exter, Hermans, Dosljak and Busse 2004: 1), but smaller than the population of England (approximately 49 million). The inclusion criteria for our cases are based on three factors:

1 All actively engaged with health management reforms, designed to directly involve doctors.
2 Each can be categorized within a different welfare regime (social democratic, corporate and neo-liberal) (Esping-Andersen 1999; Dent 2003), which provides analytic leverage for the comparative analysis.
3 All were early adopters of new managerialism.

Drawing on a mix of primary and secondary sources we identify the main variations in medical–management relations, their implications for hospital organization and suggest reasons for the differences, based on sociological as well as organizational analysis. Hospital doctors in the different countries have developed a range of responses to the managerial reforms in an attempt to preserve – if in a modified way – their leadership role within the hospital management structure. The variation in the range of changes in medical–management relations, we will suggest, is largely *path dependent*, shaped by the profession's historical relations with other key actors, including the state (Wilsford 1994; Greener 2002). The medical profession in many countries has had to redefine the basis of its professional status, which has engaged them in new discourses around managerialism and identities (Dent and Whitehead 2002: 3). Hospital doctors have, nevertheless, retained a considerable power base and with it the capacity to facilitate or undermine management reform efforts. This has not meant that the principles of professional bureaucracy (Mintzberg 1983) have remained unchallenged for, with the growing complexities of organization and delivery of health care, there has been a growing interest in the possibilities of a *hybridization* of both the organizational form of health care organizations and the leadership role of the doctors within them (see Fitzgerald, Lilley, Ferlie and Buchanan 2006: 16–17).

For more than 25 years – within all four cases – hospital doctors have had their traditional workplace autonomy and influence increasingly questioned. Yet despite evidence of similar trends in management reforms, there are distinct differences in the responses of the doctors (Degeling *et al.* 2006: 765), for the profession in the different cases has developed along differing historical pathways largely depending on their relations with the state (Wilsford 1994). The key question we address here is: *How, if at all, have hospital doctors adapted their traditional dominance to the new managerial demands for organizational leadership?*

Following a short section setting out our research methods we will move on to the four case studies, focusing particularly on the issues of hybridization and leadership among hospital doctors.

Research strategy and methods

The four cases that we focus on here represent – in broad terms – two variants of health care system organization and funding (Table 6.1): the English and Danish health care systems are both funded directly from taxation and are

Table 6.1 Selected health care systems

State sector/tax funded	Corporate sector/insurance funded
Denmark	Kaiser Permanente (USA)
England	the Netherlands

accountable to the state, whereas funding and accountability of Kaiser Permanente (USA) and the Netherlands health systems are at 'arms length' from the state, being funded via health insurance.

To oversimplify, there are two distinct approaches to the involvement of doctors in management, which reflect two organizing principles ('state' and 'corporate'): one tends to be 'management-led', the other, if not medically led then medically 'shaped'. There are, however, differences within examples of each approach, which will be explored later.

We chose to concentrate on the acute hospital sector on the grounds that, historically, this is where professional power and dominance has been concentrated. In order to disentangle and analyze the differences between the two organizational principles (state and corporate) we have organized the presentation of the four country case studies into two pairs according to whether they are 'state' or 'corporate' sector/funded (see Table 6.1):

•   England and Denmark
•   The Netherlands and Kaiser Permanente (USA)

The research draws on a mix of primary and secondary sources from the health care management, policy and sociology literatures. First, we carried out a thorough but focused review (Charmaz 2006: 166) of the available academic research for the four cases. This search was conducted manually, reading through the (online) contents pages of key journals in following the areas: health management; sociology and health policy; public administration and organizational theory. Second, we drew upon the interviews carried out as part of the earlier 'national inquiry' that focused on the relationship between management and medicine (Kirkpatrick *et al.* 2007). Third, we also carried out a series of semi-structured interviews with hospital managers and senior doctors in Denmark and the Netherlands to further clarify how hospital doctors there were engaging in management. Our approach reflects a 'theoretical sampling' strategy (Green and Thorogood 2004: 102–103; Charmaz 2006). These interviews were useful for triangulating the documentary evidence and clarifying further how the arrangements were implemented and functioned within specific hospitals primarily from the medical managers' perspective.

For the English case we drew upon ten general and medical managers in five acute hospital trusts (Kirkpatrick *et al.* 2007). We visited two hospitals in a major city in Denmark: a university hospital and a large local general hospital, interviewing two medical directors and two chief executive officers (CEOs). In the Netherlands we visited three hospitals: a university centre and two large general hospitals. There we interviewed three senior hospital managers all with medical backgrounds: a medical director; a vice-dean; and a CEO. We also had interviewed a senior health policy person from the Netherlands as well as a senior medical executive with Kaiser Permanente as part of the national inquiry (Kirkpatrick *et al.* 2007). In all the countries our focus was on exploring the extent to which formal 'hybrid' management roles had developed and how doctors have responded to them.

Part I: hospital doctors, path dependency and leadership

Involving hospital doctors in management could be constructed as undermining their professional leadership by incorporating them within management. Before NPM, doctors in all the cases here enjoyed the autonomy that goes with medical dominance. The leadership they provided was rooted in their professional interests rather more than necessarily those of the specific hospital where they worked.

Within health care, particularly in relation to staff development and training, discussions around leadership have tended to be in terms of the 'allocative' and more particularly 'transformative' modes: one reflecting a bureaucratic authority (and hardly a leader at all), the other a charismatic type (Burns 1978; Bryman 1992). This has provided the rhetoric intended to engage clinicians in management with such romantic language as that used by the NHS Leadership Centre when identifying the 'leadership gene' in terms of 'youthful energy, courageous circumspection, winning ways, balance, intuition, and moral fibre' (cited in BMJ Editor's Choice 2002). More recently the English NHS, the Health Service Journal (Neale 2008), was arguing that 'all doctors need to develop skills of transformational leadership'. All of this reflects the significance of transformational leadership in public services more generally (see Newman 2005: 3). It is a discourse that, as Newman observes (2005: 4), has twin associations with the USA (the source of much of the literature) and business. It was concordant with the ambitions of New Labour by seeming to transcend the policy–delivery divide and the general desire to 'make a difference'. The approach has received close attention by Alimo-Metcalfe and colleagues (see Alimo-Metcalfe *et al.* 2007), whose work summarizes the relevant research from an organizational psychology perspective.

In contrast to transformative leadership, there is also what Gronn (2002) has defined as 'distributed leadership'. This take on several forms but essentially it is: 'the aggregated leadership of an organization . . . dispersed among some, many, or maybe all the members' (2002: 429). Alimo-Metcalfe and her colleagues (2007), in part, seek to make transformative leadership compatible with distributive leadership. They do this by distinguishing between 'leaders' and 'leadership'. One concerns individuals, the other is a 'distributed relational process' (2007: 32). In general what one finds within health care is that clinical leadership programmes have focused on training 'leaders' while the research evidence suggests that organizational and strategic change is successful only when there is distributed leadership. It is the latter that this chapter is concerned.

Denis, Lamothe and Langley (2001), drawing on Canadian studies of health care organizations, set out a process theory of strategic change that explains the subtleties very well and provides a useful starting point for our own comparative study. They suggested that there are three levels of 'couplings': (a) leaders; (b) organization; (c) environment. It is virtually impossible to integrate the three levels at the same time and the leadership team or 'constellation' (2001: 811) can only focus on one (or two) of these at a time. To borrow from actor network theory (ANT), in order to *enrol*, rather than *coerce*, the doctors into hospital management it is necessary within the constellation to find ways of dealing with doctors perceived erosion of institutional (professional) independence (see Dent 2003: 123).

The four cases included here reflect different varieties of health care systems, but the environment of each also reflects particular – path dependent – histories, such that, for example, the Netherlands is different from other corporate systems in Europe, and Denmark is not quite the same as other Nordic health care systems.

Health policy and health care organization reflect the strong cultural and political stability of existing institutions (Wilsford 1994; Rochaix and Wilsford 2005: 106–107) – a 'sticky stasis' (Rochaix and Wilsford: 107; see also Pierson 2000: 490). It is a theory that accounts for cross-national variation in health care organization. It is a model that both accounts for the tendency towards 'entropy' (Greener 2002: 164), and, paradoxically, for explaining change too. Wilsford (1994: 257) suggests that change is the outcome of specific 'conjunctures'; those 'fleeting coming together of a number of diverse elements into a new, single combination' (1994: 257), or 'the distinctive short-term mixes of fluid contingencies with sticky structures' (Rochaix and Wilsford 2005: 106), they are the result of exogenous shocks to the system and the consequences are difficult to predict or control. Nevertheless, when a health system is confronted with challenges of exogenous shocks that prevent the continuation of the status quo, then the contingencies may force the pre-existing path onto a new trajectory. This may lead to major changes within health systems and organization.

The institutional arrangements that underpin the work organization of hospital doctors have proven to be particularly 'sticky'. This is in part because many within the ranks of the profession see any change as unattractive; involving a dilution of influence and autonomy. The medical professions within all four countries possess substantial 'countervailing powers' (Light 1995; 2010); however, the outcome of their negotiations with the state and management differs, depending substantially (but not entirely) upon their own organization and priorities.

Part II: managing doctors: four case comparison

While both the English and Danish health systems are tax funded, they differ in some important respects. The Danish system has been more decentralized than the English one; it is the local state (county councils and municipalities) that 'steers' the pattern of health delivery, whereas, in England, local government has had little influence. The Netherlands and Kaiser Permanente

(USA) are both systems funded by health insurance. Medical care in the Netherlands is funded by a system of public and private insurance schemes, but the US citizen has far greater choice than their Dutch counterparts as to which health insurance to buy and, indeed, whether to take out health insurance at all (Moran 2000; Exter, Hermans, Dosljak and Busse 2004). All four cases, however, are predicated on the patient going first to a general practitioner and only then being referred to a specialist if appropriate.

We turn now to the specific issue of the medical involvement in management.

Denmark and England

Danish medical management

The Danish model is known as the 'troika' model. It was introduced in 1984, about the time that general management was introduced into the British NHS (Griffiths 1983). A hospital commission recommended changes to the senior management arrangements within hospitals (Indenrigsministeriet 1984). The commission did not suggest a particular model, but the counties all adopted the 'troika' model, comprising a doctor, a nurse and a general manager as the executive team. The commission also advocated greater decentralization of management to the clinic level, paralleling and predating the introduction of clinical directorates in England (Department of Health 1989). At the strategic level there was considerable pressure from the centre to introduce professional managers onto the executive in order to control costs (Vallgårda, Krasnik and Vrangbæk 2001). However, over a relatively short time the troika model became firmly embedded. In part this was made possible because of the emphasis placed on providing training in multidisciplinary leadership, as Ham and Dickinson (2008: 14) pointed out:

> Denmark stands out . . . as the country where there is an explicit aim of increasing the involvement of doctors in leadership roles . . . [They] are supported . . . through mandatory training . . . [and] consultants . . . are offered a five day leadership course.

All is not complete harmony, however, and some tensions do exist at the clinical directorate level, with nurses pressing for greater management involvement (Interviews: Denmark, November 2006).

Within the troika model, the medical director has largely been able to dominate the executive, despite the formal leadership role of the general manager. This reflects the traditional assumption that doctors are the ascendant occupation within the division of labour. There is now evidence that the troika model is undergoing further managerialization, to shift it from an interdisciplinary to a corporate model. We found evidence of this development at the university hospital we visited. Here there was a greater emphasis on specifically managerial and financial concerns over clinical ones – marking a shift from a professionally/medically led organization to a managerially led one. In principle this meant that the hospital executive no longer had to be composed of a balanced troika of health professionals and managers:

[T]he [new] model is that you can be a doctor or you could be administrative educated on any of these [executive] posts. You could have four doctors, you could have four nurses, you could have four adminis-trators, except that it says, in the leadership of the hospital, you should have the competence to govern the hospital; the medical and the nursing, and the administrative competence you should have in the leadership. And in practice, you will always have some administrative and some medical experience.

(Medical Director 1)

In practice, the expectation is that all the directors will continue to be doctors and nurses. Nevertheless, at the senior management level, the trend is away from 'physician managers' to doctors becoming corporate managers. This is an ongoing process and has at departmental level led to a growing emphasis on management and leadership training for careerist doctors. Masters and MBAs in public management and administration appear to be the favoured qualifications (Interviews 2006; Ham and Dickenson 2008).

The intellectual capital of the chief executive may come from law, economics, business or social sciences, but in order to do well they have to prove their capacity to lead successfully in dealing with the hospitals political, regulatory and financial environment. At the corporate level medical directors may, in principle, be interchangeable; nonetheless, they continue to be leaders for their colleagues. Clinical directors are far more ready to accept hard decisions coming from a medical director than from someone who is not a medical professional. A key aspect of this is the ability:

[to] go into a professional dialogue with [clinical directors] in medical terms as well as general managerial terms. So I see that as a role. I try to integrate the general managerial language and put it into a language that gives meaning for health care professionals in the organization.

(Medical Director 2)

Moreover, this 'translator' role is important to the efficacy of medical involvement in management. As the same medical director pointed out, while clinical directors have been given a lot of autonomy:

They are not so used to it, so they still ask a lot. But as a principle, when we have made a contract from the beginning of the year, here's the money, here's what you should perform, we do not put barriers up for them. They can move around with their salary, money and money for production and so on, as they like. And they can hire another senior doctor if they want.

This is somewhat different from the experience of clinical directors in England, who have limited flexibility, although there are parallels with the 'cluster' arrangements to be found within the Dutch hospitals (see below). It is also the case that Danish hospital doctors have far fewer opportunities than their English counterparts for private practice and are, therefore, far more reliant on their hospital employment to build their career. As a result, management may have more appeal than in the English case. As one chief executive explained:

> I have about 80 consultants at this hospital and 75 of them only work here, they don't have any other work outside, so they are here every day. So those consultants are mine . . . they are not coming from their private practices, going into the hospitals and then going back again every day or so as you're used to in the UK.

The Danish hospital system shares some similarities with the English NHS but operates on a smaller scale. It has had a history of decentralization and democratic engagement and, importantly, higher historical funding than the English NHS. Even so, public management reforms challenged their social democratic ethos with the introduction of the troika model paving the way for realignment between management and medicine. This was achieved, not by challenging the doctors' right to be in control, but by creating space for management to enter onto the stage and make its contribution.

English medical management

There has long been a tension within the English NHS between the principles of national direction and local implementation, which has been characterized as 'one of national accountability with local paternalism' (Greener 2009: 80–1), reflecting a consensus between state and the medical profession (Klein 1990) that started to break down in the 1980s when the then Conservative government began to embrace the new managerialism. This redefined the medical profession more as a pressure group and no longer as a partner in delivering NHS health care. The recent Labour administration was also keen to moderate the profession's 'countervailing powers' (Light 1995) and paternalistic influence on the delivery of services.[1] This was apparent in a raft of policies, including 'patient choice' (Appleby and Dixon 2004; Dent 2006) and the introduction of Independent Sector Treatment Centres (ISTCs) (DoH 2005) that were intended to ensure 'contestability', a hybrid concept normatively defined as follows: 'planning and competition should be used together . . . [to ensure the] possibility that contracts will move [between providers] . . . rather than the actual movement' (Ham 1996: 70).

The increased emphasis on evidence-based medicine has also opened up the profession to external inspection and control (Harrison and Macdonald 2003: 117). This is a process that has been more marked in England than in Denmark perhaps because it is more about *managing* medics rather *engaging* them in management. Nevertheless, managing hospital doctors remains challenging for it means: 'having to negotiate rather than impose new policies and practices, and work in a way that is sensitive to the culture of the [hospital]' (Ham and Dickenson, 2008: 4).

It was the Griffiths report (1983) that first clearly advocated transforming the NHS into a managed organization. The policy saw the introduction of general managers and a rise in the numbers of senior management from around 1,000 in 1986 to 20,842 in 1995 (Pollock 2005: 39). This managerial cadre was intended to be a direct challenge to medical dominance, in part, through the 'tighter measurement and control of clinicians' work' (2005: 107). Yet despite the reform doctors remained 'conspicuously autonomous' (Harrison, Hunter, Marnoch and Pollitt 1992: 146).

Within the hospitals, the managerial innovation that impacted most directly on the hospital doctors was the introduction of clinical directorates (Llewellyn 2001: 597). Introduced after 1990, they have become universal. At about the same time, medical directors were introduced (Kirkpatrick *et al.* 2007). These senior doctors sit on hospital boards as advisors on medical matters, and to act as a 'bridge' between the board and the doctors. The BMA and Royal College of Physicians (RCP) showed a willingness to accept the principle of clinical directorates (Kitchener 2000: 138) and doctors accepted the new clinical director roles, and became hybrid managers (Fitzgerald, Lilley, Ferlie and Buchanan 2006). Llewellyn (2001: 618–19) reported that it was the clinical directors who 'enable[d] cost consciousness, performance review, standardisation and evidence based practice' to become established within English hospitals. Forbes, Hallier and Kelly (2004: 167) even identified a number of doctors who 'actively pursued a management opportunity as an alternative to clinical medicine'. Nevertheless, most doctors do not clamour to become clinical directors (Kitchener 2000: 739; Hoque, Davis and Humphreys 2004; Kirkpatrick *et al.* 2007). In the main this is because it is clinical practice that is the more rewarding (intrinsically and extrinsically) for most hospital doctors. Very few would earn more by engaging more with management than with patients.

The Labour administration was somewhat enamoured with NPM, especially the regulatory frameworks, delegation and networks, rather more than it was about the role of the market (Hood, James and Scott 2000; Dent, van Gestel and Teelken 2007: 2–3). It was, in particular, keen to outmanoeuvre doctors' capacity for 'knavish' behaviour (Le Grand 2003), while the doctors themselves expressed concern about this new form of governance. Crilly and Le Grand (2004) in a survey of over 1,500 managers and consultants reported considerable dissatisfaction with 'the single-minded pursuit of financial targets' within hospitals. Others, including Rundall, Davies and Hodges (2004) and

Degeling *et al.* (2006) reported similar findings. Indeed, management was commonly perceived as: 'anti-patient, anti-clinical freedom and a threat to . . . autonomy and values' (Jacobs 2005: 137).

It is against this background of the generally ambivalent attitudes of doctors that a current initiative to engage them is taking place:

> The Academy of Medical Royal Colleges and NHS Institute for Innovation and Improvement have embarked on an ambitious project, entitled 'Enhancing Engagement in Medical Leadership' which aims, among other objectives, to develop an integrated medical management and leadership competency, education and assessment framework for doctors throughout the UK.
>
> (Clark and Armit 2007: 36)

It is too early yet to know what the impact of this initiative might be. But the intent is there to engage the new generation of hospital doctors unambiguously in management more in line with the Danish-style model. Real convergence, however, is unlikely to occur because of their different histories and path dependencies.

Danish and English medics and management: initial comparison

Any apparent similarity between the English NHS and Danish social democratic models of tax-funded health care systems disguises their different 'pathways dependencies'. These broadly explain why Danish doctors have been far more ready to embrace the new managerialism than their English colleagues. NPM and new governance arrangements have been experienced by the English profession as increased external regulation/control in ways not shared by their Danish counterparts. There are at least two historical reasons for this – first, the marked difference in the profession/state settlement. The Danish and British Medical Associations (DMA and BMA) were established within a year of each other (1855 and 1858), and while the Danish profession saw no conflict of interest with their leaders working within the National Board of Health (Vallgårda, Krasnik and Vrangbæk 2001: 11–12) this was not the case in England. Here, neither the leadership of the profession nor state had any desire to work closely together and the latter were content to let the medical profession dominate the whole process (Macdonald 1995: 77–8).

A second key difference is that there were – and are – far more private hospitals in England than in Denmark, with few obstacles to doctors working in both sectors contemporaneously. This has never been the case in Denmark (Vallgårda, Krasnik and Vrangbæk 2001: 11–12), with the consequence that doctors' career choices in the two countries are differently constructed. Danish doctors have not had the possibility of developing lucrative parallel careers in the private sector in the way that their English colleagues (or many of them) have. In Denmark's case, there has been little evidence of 'conjunctures' (or crises) with the introduction of public management reforms; the trajectory followed a well established historical pathway. This is an oversimplification, but not a distortion, and contrasts with the English case where the introduction of NPM was driven, in part, to undermine the dominance of the profession and redefine doctors as expert clinical workers, rather than a powerful partner with the state.

We turn now to the two 'corporate' cases of Kaiser Permanente and the Netherlands where we will find different configurations of relations between doctors and management and profession and state.

Kaiser Permanente (USA) and the Netherlands

Kaiser Permanente: medical managers and the three-legged race

Kaiser Permanente is the largest non-profit health plan in the USA, with 8.2 million members across nine states, with most (6.1 million) concentrated in California (Towill 2006). Kaiser Permanente is composed of two non-profit organizations: (1) Kaiser Foundation Health Plans and (2) Kaiser Foundation Hospitals, plus (3) the Permanente Medical Groups, which are for-profit professional organizations. The structure of the Kaiser Permanente group comes out of a long history. Originally, in the 1940s, it was set up to provide prepaid, pro-active health care to workers at the Kaiser Shipyards; only later did it become the Permanente Health Plan open to the general public (Smillie 2000).

The attraction of Kaiser Permanente is its cost effective and integrated approach to keeping workers healthier, by 'treat[ing] their problems before they became ill' (Light and Dixon 2004: 763). What is not always recognized is the distinctly different medical organization within the HMO. Indeed, this difference has meant conflict with the organized profession in the USA, which has forced Kaiser Permanente to become self-sufficient in its recruitment and retaining of doctors – adopting a 'whole systems' approach. A medical career within Kaiser Permanente is never the most financially rewarding career option for newly qualified doctors, but it provides an alternative to one within the mainstream liberal competitive and privatized model. One consequence of this has been that Kaiser Permanente doctors have always had a more open and direct engagement with management. This has been fortunate for the survival of Kaiser Permanente for it enabled the organization to better withstand the financial difficulties that confronted the group in the late 1980s and early 1990s and led to even greater doctor involvement in management. There are now 'physician-managers' who are selected by central management and are primarily responsible to them. The formal organizational structure involves a 'physician leader' and 'hospital manager' with equal and over-lapping responsibilities for the functioning of a treatment centre. According to an associate executive director we interviewed (Kirkpatrick *et al.* 2007), the group's structure has ensured that managers and doctors are 'tied together in a three-legged race' through interrelated budget structures ensuring a mutual interdependency: 'managers and the doctors rise and fall together in a very direct financial way . . . [and] has been material to Kaiser being able to . . . get doctors involved and be jointly motivated towards the outcomes'.

The financial incentives are designed to attract clinicians into management roles. In addition, there has been a long-term programme designed to raise the status of the physician-manager:

> we [now] have a very intentional process of choosing younger, clinically inspired, [physicians] to take on these roles, rewarding it, recognising it. We've really – over the last 15 years – made it something that looks attractive to physicians, it creates variety in their work, they're not thrown cold into situations where they don't have the support or the skills.
>
> (Kirkpatrick *et al.* 2007)

This is further underpinned by the prospect of a long career within the organization. Competing organizations offer more money, but few offer the same potential for a structured career path for doctors. This model does not appeal to all medics, for there are few opportunities to engage in research or academic work. The group emphasizes training and development and has established:

> an intentional strategy of building leadership into a sub-speciality of medicine. Training for it, hiring and recruiting for leadership, creating many leadership roles to develop a 'deep bench' from which to select physicians for these senior roles. So in our medical group of 5,500 doctors, we probably have 1,500 physicians who hold some kind of title, administrative title.
>
> (Kirkpatrick *et al.* 2007)

These training programmes and the amount spent on selecting candidates (internally and externally) represent a large investment to ensure the full integration and involvement of the medics in the management of Kaiser Permanente. This contrasts, substantially, with the case of hospital doctors in the Netherlands.

The Netherlands: negotiation not integration

There is a uniqueness to the Dutch hospital medical–management arrangements that stems from a very particular history. The hospital doctors, certainly since the establishment of the Hospital Specialist Association in 1946 (Dent 2003: 55–6), have enjoyed considerable autonomy and medical dominance. This is rooted in the institutionalization of the 'closed hospital' policy introduced in the 1940s (Klazinga 1996: 80–2), which gave doctors exclusive contracts with one hospital without providing the management monopsonist control of the doctors – rather, the reverse was the case. The hospital specialists operated as a wholly independent body within the hospital through the Medical Staff Committee, which represented the individual partnerships (*maatschappen*) and co-existed with the hospital management. This very loosely coupled arrangement reflected the strongly embedded entrepreneurial values held by doctors, which was rationalized on the grounds that they attracted the work and income for the hospital. The specialist partnerships are still central to the medical organization of a hospital and these collectively have been represented by a medical executive committee (MEC), typically the 'sparring partner' of hospital management. This body has been transformed, since the mid 1990s, to become the Staff Executive (Scholten and van der Grinten 2005: 166), a body that has also become an alternative locus of power and influence within the hospital. It has acquired a de facto 'position of juxtaposition in hospital governance' (2005: 165), competing with management in the strategic leadership of the hospital. This was not the intention of the policy (Integration Act 2000) but it is what has emerged in practice (Scholten and van der Grinten 2005: 165). To counter or adapt to this reality, the dominant arrangement to emerge has been the introduction of 'clusters', which are cognate groups of specialties and clinical activities, which have an affinity to clinical directorates[2] but differ markedly in their dynamic. Clusters are headed by a clinician supported by an administrator and possibly a nurse. The relationship between the board and 'clusters' is a 'trading' one between two 'organizations' cohabitating a single hospital: hospital board and medical staff executive.

This apartheid between medics and management is one that the state has attempted to overcome. Different government coalitions have swung the emphasis between politically managed and market-led solutions, but over a period of more than twenty-five years the pressure has not let up. The medical profession, however, has proven itself strongly resistant to alternative ways of working especially when imposed by the state. Scholten and van der Grinten (1998: 36) identified three reform inspired models: 'integrated', 'participative' and 'entrepreneurial', and it is the last of these that appears to be having most success. Hospital specialists, while a mixed group composed of self-employed and salaried doctors,[3] nearly all have a common commitment to their independence from management; they have strongly contested management reforms and have been far more effective in disabling policy initiatives than their colleagues in other countries across Europe and North America. This has been, primarily, because of their unique independent provider status and their *maatschappen* organization. This may be changing, but it is a slow process and the trajectory is unclear.

While the official policy is one of integration, the evidence to date suggests that hospital specialists prefer 'separate development'. The process of reform has reflected a marked tendency for 'muddling through' and an acceptance of 'sedimentation' (Cooper, Hinings, Greenwood and Brown 1996) with old arrangements co-existing with the new (Scholten and van der Grinten 2005: 172). To illustrate, the executive board of an acute hospital typically consists of the chief executive who comes from a business background, a medical director and an administrative director. This does not mean, however, that the medical director will have an effective leadership role over the hospital specialists. As one of Ong and Schepers' respondents commented on his role as a medical director (1998: 384):

> You are vulnerable as a person. People [i.e. fellow doctors] do not make a distinction between function and person, and they do not see the different hats you wear . . . You are given imagined power and people turn against you. That's very unpleasant, especially when you think that you use your influence with integrity . . .

A remark that finds resonance in Klazinga's comment (see also Plochg, Klazinga and Casparie 1998; Plochg 2006) to the Inquiry panel:

> There are . . . many situations where [the new arrangements are] problem-atic and . . . in our hospital system, usually at the end of the day, the doctors win, and the director of a hospital has to go.
>
> (Telephone Interview: 28 September 2006)

There is now, however, a growing realization that somehow there needs to be closer working between medicine and management in order to control costs and it is why 'clusters' have come to be seen to provide a pragmatic way forward. It is important to note that this mode of integration remains an aspiration for much of the hospital sector. Nevertheless, given the particular history of medical–management relations in the Netherlands, one can understand why 'clusters' is the particular and pragmatic strategy that emerged, because it allows the clinicians to retain their autonomy, organizationally, from the hospital executive board, reflecting the institutionalized power of the profession at the organizational level. Yet the arrangement has also provided management with more leverage too, for the contracting process has made the hospital specialists more dependent upon the hospital's executive leadership than they would have ever previously allowed (Exter, Hermans, Dosljak and Busse 2004).

The Dutch health system is the most complex of our international comparisons. Hospital specialists have truly enjoyed medical dominance within the hospitals. The challenge to their supremacy, by the Biesheuval Commission in 1994, was aimed at subordinating them to management, similar to the English case. What has emerged instead over the intervening years has been a reworking of the old dualistic structure of medics and managers based on new contractual terms for the trading relations between them.

Kaiser Permanente and the Netherlands hospital specialists

It may seem perverse to compare these two cases, but they do have some marked organizational similarities. They are both based on versions of the corporate health insurance model and the doctors' careers are tied to specific health care organizations. But, there are key differences too. Kaiser Permanente has been able to produce (i.e. encourage, train and socialize) the hybrid medical manager, to an extent that their 'management' expertise virtually equates to a medical specialism within the organization. This contrasts markedly with the Dutch hospitals, where the specialist groups continue to exist as independent bodies that, through their Staff Executive, exist in antagonistic co-existence with the hospital management board. This unique arrangement is described by Berg and van der Grinten (2003: 117) in the following terms:

> [a] peculiar combination of separation and integration ... [in which] hospital management and the medical specialists are bound up within one hospital organization reflects the *strong reliance in the Netherlands on professional autonomy* and the expected benefits of cooperation. The concrete situation is characterised by a complex negotiation process within each individual hospital ... between medical specialists and hospital management, which are not bound in a hierarchical relation. [*emphasis added*]

This represents the loosely coupled arrangements that underpin the strongly embedded professional values of Dutch doctors; they, as free professionals, are the entrepreneurs that provide the work and income for the hospital and other professionals – rather than being incorporated via means of management education and training,[4] this being achieved, perhaps, through extending the logic of the *maatschapen* in the creation of 'clusters' subcontracted, via quasi market mechanisms, to the hospital within which the doctors work. Unlike their Kaiser Permanente colleagues, the Dutch medical specialists have avoided being directly incorporated into management. On the other hand, they do have management responsibilities in terms of running the 'clusters', but these are smaller scale than the organization-wide responsibilities of the Kaiser Permanente medics.

Discussion: reflections on medicine, management and leadership

In this chapter we have reviewed and compared hospital doctors' involvement in hospital management in four health care systems in relation to the role of leadership and history (path dependency).

Leadership

Discussions around leadership within health care, as we observed earlier in the chapter, have tended to focus on the notion of transformative leadership. Yet reviewing these four case studies, we find little real evidence of transformative leadership, at least, not as an explanation of the systematic engagement of doctors in management. More apposite is the concept of 'distributed' leadership (Gronn 2002). This is particularly apparent in the cases of Denmark and Kaiser Permanente, where the tough (in the US case study) and moderately challenging environments (in the Danish case) have led to a greater incorporation of the doctors into management coupled with greater acceptance of interdisciplinary cooperation (in the leadership 'constellation'), than in the other two cases. Moreover, this redefinition of the 'terms of engagement' between medicine and management has been positively embraced.

Even in the other two examples, England and the Netherlands, where management has been less positively accepted, professional leadership has generally been more 'distributed' rather than 'heroically' transformative. Where they differ is that the hospital specialists (the Netherlands) and consultants (England) have been more resistant – in a distributed sense – to managerial incorporation. In the Netherlands' case this is very clear; the 'cluster' model is one intended to maintain a sense of medical ascendency by creating medically dominated 'constellations' in the form of the relatively autonomous Medical Staff Committees and 'clusters'. The English variant is less clear-cut; there are examples where the hospital management model reflects medical engagement in an interdisciplinary and corporative model of management (Kirkpatrick *et al.* 2007); these, however, are a minority. More often the doctors show ambivalence to management and a wide variation in terms of engagement.

Involvement in management

Involvement in management does not necessarily signify an erosion of autonomy and influence within the health care division of labour and its coordination. Instead it reconfigures their relations and roles within the hospital organization: there has been a move away from physicians' individualized clinical autonomy and towards possibly a more corporate but certainly more collective medical presence and possible leadership within hospital management. It is a process that has generally been resisted and not been accepted without the presence of a significant 'conjuncture'. Yet within all the regimes, elements within the profession have come to recognize the necessity of genuine engagement. The hospital doctors in each of the cases discussed here have adjusted differently to the new managerialism. At one end of a spectrum is Kaiser Permanente, a management-led health care organization within a market-led health economy – where the medics, embracing their hybrid status, have integrated within a single managerial hierarchy. At the other is the Netherlands, where we find a dual structure of managerially coordinated hospitals where the doctors respond to NPM by adapting the traditional '*maatschappen*' model of medical partnerships and the hospital specialists are thereby able to maintain, if in a modified form, their autonomy from management control.

The Danish system 'stands out for its efforts to engage doctors in leadership roles and to provide training and support' (Ham and Dickenson 2008: 4), it also most closely compares with Kaiser Permanente on this topic. In England and the Netherlands, by contrast, most management training and support has 'tended to be ad hoc and episodic' (Clark 2006: 14). What matters to the doctors – in all four cases – is their clinical work; this is far more important than involvement in management *per se*. This is hardly surprising given the traditional focus of the medical education, training and socialization of doctors. Within the English NHS, for example, medics moving into management are often considered, jokingly, by their colleagues as going over to the 'dark side'.[5] A view even more strongly held by Dutch medical specialists, if not with the same cultural reference; on the other hand, this is certainly not the case with the Danish or Kaiser Permanente doctors. However, in these last two cases, involvement in management has been encouraged by strong, positive and material rewards.

The doctors, within all four cases, nevertheless, have moved in some degree to accepting the need to have greater involvement in management. Even where this is reluctant, progress is being made because all parties realize that the old certainties of medical dominance are now dead. As Light (1995: 31) points out, 'the profession and state are in a symbiotic relationship', although as Klein (1990) implied, it is a difficult 'marriage'. Over the years patterns of accommodation have developed in the four cases:

> [which] represents a shift from protected professionalism to contracted professionalism, from autonomy and authority to accountability and performance, with *managers in a pivotal middle position.*
>
> (Light 1995: 31, emphasis added)

Traditionally, doctors within all the cases were able to exercise their autonomy and control within the hospital organization. This is rather less the case, as the state pressures the profession to be more accountable and efficient. In England and the Netherlands the state has directly challenged professionalism, whereas in Denmark and Kaiser Permanente the doctors did not resist their reconfigured incorporation as hybrids within the management arrangements. In all cases the hospital doctors have had to review their traditional dominance within the hospital and have had to adapt to a new reality where they have had to give up some autonomy to retain a dominant but reconfigured form of control of their core work activities and the work of those, particularly the nurses, working alongside them. The reconfiguration, as we have shown, varies between the different health care systems because of their different histories that have shaped the path dependent outcomes. The role of leadership is mediated by this reality, but where medical involvement in management is most firmly embedded it results from a collective, distributed, leadership engaging with the challenge of management.

Acknowledgements

We are indebted to Peter Kragh Jesperson (Aalborg University, Denmark) and Thomas Plochg (AMC, Amsterdam), for their help with our interviews in Denmark and the Netherlands. Sadly, Peter died in 2010. He will be much missed.

Notes

1   This emphasis is not so apparent in the current Conservative–Liberal coalition. To date the focus has been more on doctors working in primary care rather than hospitals (e.g. Department of Health 2010a).
2   Interestingly, the model of 'clinical directorates' was favoured by the Biesheuval Commission (1994) and reaffirmed in the Integration Act (2000). The intended objective was that the executive board would run the hospital in a way that would 'correspond strikingly with those in the United Kingdom' (Scholten and van der Grinten 2005: 166).
3   In 2003 just over 70 per cent of hospital specialists where self-employed – and 30 per cent salaried (Kruijthof 2005).
4   There has been a serious attempt to involve medics in management, including the 'partnership in management' project in the 1990s, but it was unsuccessful in gaining general acceptance by the hospital specialists (Dent 2003: 49).
5   A reference to Darth Vader in the *Star Wars* film series.

References

Alimo-Metcalfe, B., Ryrie, I., Everitt, B., Bryson, T., Walwyn, R. and Lee, J. (2007) 'The impact of leadership factors in implementing change in complex health and social care environments: NHS plan clinical priority for mental health crisis resolution teams', SDO Project-09/1201/022, University of Southampton: National Institute for Health Research. Available at www.sdo.nihr.ac.uk/files/project/SDO_FR_08–1201–022_V01.pdf. Last accessed 6 October 2011.

Appleby, J. and Dixon, J. (2004) 'Patient choice in the NHS: having choice may not improve outcomes', *British Medical Journal (BMJ)*, 329: 61–2.

Berg, M. and van der Grinten, T. (2003) 'The Netherlands', in C. Ham and G. Robert (eds) *Reasonable rationing: international experiences of priority setting*, Maidenhead: Open University/McGraw Hill Education: 115–40.

BMJ Editor's Choice (2002) 'Needed: transformational leaders', *BMJ*, 325 (7 December). Available at www.bmj.com/content/325/7376/0.6. Last accessed 6 October 2011.

Bryman, A. (1992) *Charisma and leadership in organizations*, London: Sage.

Burns, J.M. (1978) *Leadership*, New York: Harper and Row.

Charmaz, K. (2006) *Constructing grounded theory*, London: Sage.

Clark, J. (2006) 'Enhancing medical engagement in leadership', *Innovate/Improve/In View*, 10 (June): 14–15.

Clark, J. and Armit, K. (2008) 'Attainment of competency in management and leadership: no longer an optional extra for doctors', *Clinical Governance*, 13(1): 35–42.

Cooper, D.J., Hinings, B., Greenwood, R. and Brown, J.L. (1996) 'Sedimentation and transformation in organizational change: the case of Canadian law partnerships', *Organization Studies*, 17(4): 623–47.

Crilly, T. and Le Grand, J. (2004) 'The motivation and behaviour of hospital trusts', *Social Science and Medicine*, 58(10): 1809–23.

Degeling, P., Zhang, K., Coyle, B., Xu, L.Z., Meng, Q.Y., Qu, J.B. and Hill, M. (2006) 'Clinicians and the governance of hospitals: a cross-cultural perspective on relations between profession and management', *Social Science and Medicine*, 63(3): 757–75.

Denis, J.-L., Lamothe, L. and Langley, A. (2001) 'The dynamics of collective leadership and strategic change in pluralistic organizations', *Academy of Management Journal*, 44(4): 809–37.

Dent, M. (2003) *Remodelling hospitals and health professions in Europe: medicine, nursing and the state*, Basingstoke: Palgrave Macmillan.

—— (2006) 'Patient choice and medicine in health care: responsibilisation, governance and proto-professionalisation', *Public Management Review*, 8(3): 451–64.

Dent, M. and Whitehead, S. (2002) 'Configuring the new professional', in M. Dent and S. Whitehead (eds) *Managing professional identities: knowledge, performativity and the 'new' professional*, London: Routledge: 1–16.

Dent, M., van Gestel, N. and Teelken, C. (2007) 'Symposium on changing modes of governance in public sector organizations: action and rhetoric', *Public Administration*, 85(1): 1–8.

Department of Health (DoH) (1989) *Working for patients* (Cmnd 555), London: HMSO.

—— (2005) *Treatment centres: delivering faster, quality care and choice for patients*, London: TSO.

—— (2010) *Equity and excellence: liberating the NHS*, London: DoH.

Esping-Andersen, G. (1999) *Social foundations of postindustrial economies*, Oxford: Oxford University Press.

Exter, A., Hermans, H., Dosljak, M. and Busse, R. (2004) *Health care systems in transition: Netherlands*, Copenhagen: WHO Regional Office for Europe on behalf of the European Observatory on Health Systems and Policies.

Fitzgerald, L., Lilley, C., Ferlie, E. and Buchanan, D. (2006) *Managing change and role enactment in the professionalised organisation*, report to the National Co-ordinating Centre for the NHS Service Delivery and Organisation R&D.

Forbes, T., Hallier, J. and Kelly, L. (2004) 'Doctors as managers: investors and reluctants in a dual role', *Health Services Management Research*, 17: 167–76.

Green, J. and Thorogood, N. (2004) *Qualitative methods for health research*, London: Sage.

Greener, I. (2002) 'Understanding NHS reform: the policy transfer, social learning and path dependency perspectives', *Governance*, 15(2): 161–83.

—— (2009) *Healthcare in the UK: understanding continuity and change*, Bristol: The Policy Press.

Griffiths, R. (1983) *National health service management inquiry* (6 October), London: Department of Health and Social Security.

Gronn, P. (2002) 'Distributed leadership as a unit of analysis', *The Leadership Quarterly* 13: 423–51.

Ham, C. (1996) 'Contestability: a middle path for health care', *British Medical Journal*, 312: 70–1.

Ham, C. and Dickenson, H. (2008) *Engaging doctors in leadership: what we can learn from international experience and research evidence*, Coventry House, University of Warwick: Institute of Innovation and Improvement (NHS).

Harrison, S. and Macdonald, R. (2003) 'Science, consumerism and bureaucracy: new legitimations of medical professionalism', *International Journal of Public Sector Management (IJPSM)*, 16(2): 110–21.

Harrison, S., Hunter, D.J., Marnoch, G. and Pollitt, C. (1992) *Just managing: power and culture in the National Health Service*, London: Macmillan.

Hood, C., James, O. and Scott, C. (2000) 'Regulation of government: has it increased, is it increasing, should it be diminished?', *Public Administration Review*, 78(2): 283–304.

Hoque, K., Davis, S. and Humphreys, M. (2004) 'Freedom to do what you are told: senior management team autonomy in an NHS acute trust', *Public Administration*, 82(2): 355–75.

Indenrigsministeriet (1984) *Sygehusenes organisation og økonomi, Betænkning fra Indenrigsministeriets produktivitetsudvalg*, Copenhagen: Direktoratet for Statens Indkøb.

Jacobs, K. (2005) 'Hybridisation or polarisation: doctors and accounting in the UK, Germany and Italy', *Financial Accountability and Management*, 21(2): 135–61.

Kirkpatrick, I., Maltby, B., Dent, M., Neogy, I. and Mascie-Taylor, H. (2007) *National inquiry into management and medicine: final report*, Leeds: Centre for Innovation and Health Management, University of Leeds.

Kitchener, M. (2000) 'The "bureaucratization" of professional roles: the cases of clinical directors in UK hospitals', *Organization*, 7(1): 129–54.

Klazinga, N. (1996) *Quality management of medical specialist care in the Netherlands: an explorative study of its nature and development*, The Hague: Belvédere.

Klein, R. (1990) 'The state and the profession: the politics of the double bed', *British Medical Journal*, 3 October: 700–2.

Kruijthof, K. (2005) 'Doctors orders: specialists' day to day work and their jurisdictional claims in Dutch hospitals', Ph.D. thesis, Erasmus University, Rotterdam. Available at http://repub.eur.nl/res/pub/6763/050610_Kruijthof.pdf. Last accessed 9 February 2012.

Le Grand, J. (2003) *Motivation, agency and public policy: of knight and knaves, pawns and queens*, Oxford: Oxford University Press.

Light, D.W. (1995) 'Countervailing powers: a framework for professions in transition', in T. Johnson, G. Larkin and M. Saks (eds) *Health professions and the state in Europe*, London: Routledge: 25–41.

—— (2010) 'Health professions, markets and countervailing powers', in C. Bird, P. Conrad, A. Fremont and S. Timmermans (eds) *Handbook of medical sociology* (6th edition), Nashville, TN: Vanderbilt University Press: Chapter 11.

Light, D.W. and Dixon, M. (2004) 'Making the NHS more like Kaiser Permanente', *British Medical Journal*, 328(7442): 763–5.

Llewellyn, S. (2001) '"Two-way windows": clinicians as medical managers', *Organization Studies*, 22(4): 593–623.

Macdonald, K.M. (1995) *The sociology of the professions*, London: Sage.

Mintzberg, H. (1983) *Structures in fives: designing effective organizations*, Englewood, NJ: Prentice-Hall International.

Moran, M. (2000) 'Understanding the welfare state: the case of health care', *British Journal of Politics and International Relations*, 2(2): 135–60.

Neale, G. (2008) 'Transformational leadership in a transformed NHS', *Health Service Journal*, 22 September. Available at www.hsj.co.uk/resource-centre/

transformational-leadership-in-a-transformed-nhs/1862571.article. Last accessed 6 October 2011.

Newman, J. (2005) 'Enter the transformational leader: network governance and the micro-politics of modernization', *Sociology*, 39(4): 717–34.

Ong, B.N. and Schepers, R.M.J. (1998) 'Comparative perspective on doctors in management in the UK and The Netherlands', *Journal of Management in Medicine*, 12: 378–90.

Pierson, P. (2000) 'The limits of design: explaining institutional origins and change', *Governance*, 13(4): 475–99.

Plochg, T. (2006) *Building a tower of Babel in health care? Theory and practice of community-based integrated care*, University of Amsterdam: Academisch Proefschrift.

Plochg, T., Klazinga, N.S. and Casparie, A.F. (1998) *Het medisch-specialistich mozaiek: een 'dubbele' integratie tussen de medische beroepsgroep en de ziekenhuisorganisatie*, Rotterdam: Instituut Beleid & Management Gesondheidszorg.

Pollock, A. (2005) *NHS plc: the privatisation of our health care* (2nd edn), London: Verso.

Rochaix, L. and Wilsford, D. (2005) 'State autonomy, policy paralysis: paradoxes of institutions and culture in the French health care system', *Journal of Health Politics, Policy and Law*, 30(1–2): 97–119.

Rundall, T.G., Davies, H.T.O. and Hodges, C.L. (2004) 'Doctor–manager relationships in the United States and the United Kingdom', *Journal of Healthcare Management*, 49(4): 251–68.

Scholten, G.R.M. and van der Grinten, T.E.D. (1998) 'Between physician and manager: new co-operation models in Dutch hospitals', *Journal of Management in Medicine*, 1: 33–43.

—— (2005) 'The intergration of medical specialists in hospitals. Dutch hospitals and the medical specialists on the road to joint regulation', *Health Policy*, 72: 165–73.

Smillie, J.G. (2000) *Can physicians manage the quality and costs of health care? The story of the Permanent Medical Group*, Oakland, CA: The Permanente Federation.

Towill, D.R. (2006) 'Viewing Kaiser Permanente via the logistician lens', *International Journal of Health Care Quality Assurance*, 19(4): 296–315.

Vallgårda, S., Krasnik, A. and Vrangbæk, K. (2001) *Health care systems in transition: Denmark*, WHO Regional Office for Europe: The European Observatory on Health Care Systems.

Wilsford, D. (1994) 'Path dependency, or why history makes it difficult but not impossible to reform health care systems in a big way', *Journal of Public Policy*, 14(3): 251–83.

7 Quality development and professional autonomy in modern hospital fields

Peter Kragh Jespersen

Overview

Based on a review of the literature on professions in modern society this chapter focuses on the possible effects on professional autonomy of the New Public Management (NPM) inspired health quality development policies in Denmark and Norway. Three different kinds of autonomy are conceptualized: traditional autonomy, framed autonomy and competitive autonomy. These concepts are then used in the analysis of health quality development strategies in Denmark and Norway focusing on two different governance systems and the identification and explanation of changes in medical professional autonomy in the two countries. Both professions have experienced changes and differences in institutional contexts and the managerial strategies developed can explain most of the differences, but the strategies of the medical professions and their access to different policy arenas have been important too.

An understanding of the interplay between policymaking, specific governance systems and the reactions of the professionals seems to be crucial in order to understand and develop leadership in the modern professional bureaucracies. But also trans-national processes of standard construction and dissemination and the implication of a two-tier professional system with professional elites and rank and file professionals are important and should be taken into consideration in order to understand the complexities of leadership in the modern hospital.

The sociology of professions and the theme of professional autonomy

The sociology of the professions has evolved from early efforts of mostly Anglo-American sociologists to characterize professions as a distinct type of occupation (Carr Saunders 1928; Millerson 1964; Parsons 1939, 1954). Right from the beginning one of the central 'traits' that separated professions from other occupations was the notion of professional monopoly at the level of society meaning official and often legally approved monopoly of certain types of work and regulation of the boundaries of the professional work. Another was the observation that every individual professional had some kind of technical autonomy in work situations to apply a special kind of knowledge and expertise in professional work (Goode 1957; Etzioni 1969; Freidson 1986). The two kinds of autonomy are interrelated and mutually supportive. Individual autonomy is not possible without a recognized professional monopoly over a body of knowledge that must be actively advanced by the profession in relation to other professions and the employing organizations. On the other hand, according to this tradition, it is not possible for the profession successfully to claim monopoly without securing the ability of individual professionals to act and perform in accordance with the best available expert knowledge when classifying problems, reason about them and take action. Morell (2007) and Murphy (1988: 246) have indicated what is distinctive about professional knowledge and emphasize formal, rational, abstract and utilitarian knowledge and means of control of nature and humans. However the functionalist trait approach did not help understanding the power of the professions compared to other occupations and neither to understand the situation of the professions in contemporary societies or the discourse of professionalism in many occupations (Evetts 2006, 2009).

The so-called 'power' approach (Macdonald 1995) focused instead on how different professions attained their autonomy, especially the ways professional autonomy was extended to prevent interference and management from outside and to obtain dominance over other occupations. A main theme in the American sociologist Freidson's work has been how the medical profession in the USA has developed its position in relation to the state and the patients but also how the autonomy of individual professionals was controlled by the profession through informal control mechanisms (Freidson 1970, 1986, 1994). Sociologists within the 'power' approach raised the question of whether the autonomy and the role of the professions was something fundamentally different from that of other occupations and generally the answer was negative. Larson's (1977) work, especially, introduced a new theme in the sociological analysis of professions where the analytical focus shifted to professionalism, professionalization and especially 'professional projects' (Abbott 1988; Macdonald 1995; Freidson 2001). The professional project was defined by Larson as the coherent and consistent efforts by a profession to secure the profession's special knowledge, high status and social respectability and the support of the individual professional. Central to the professional project is the ability to monopolize jurisdictions of work, the core body of knowledge and the control of access to training, accreditation and labour market and also the ability to construct a 'coherent ideology' to justify their special privileges on the grounds of technical competency and social trusteeship (Brint 1994).Through historical and comparative studies in European countries the dominating Anglo-American conception of market-based professions was challenged and it was highlighted that professions in European contexts (with the exception of the UK) are much more dependent on the interventions of the state (Brante 1988; Bureau *et al.* 2004; Burrage and Torstendahl 1990;

Kuhlmann 2006; Witz 1992). Bringing the state into the analysis of professionalization and professional projects certainly illustrated the nature of the professions as collective agents but also points to the significance of specific national and institutional contexts (Dent 2003; Degeling *et al.* 2006). Governance structures and the interaction between professions and the state in different countries determine the institutional and organizational framework within which the professions and professionals seek to maintain their autonomy (Kragh Jespersen *et al.* 2002; Sehested 2002). The importance of organizational structures, cultures and management strategies was also investigated and it became evident that the strategies of the professions were important also within organizations (Kirkpatrick and Ackroyd 2003). Successful professional projects could in this way imply a form of 'double social closure' whereby professions combined closure in the labour market with control over working routines inside organizations (Ackroyd 1996).

But today professionals are more than ever before employed by large organizations where bureaucratic regulatory mechanisms and authority can conflict with codes of ethics, expert knowledge and collegial influence inherent in professional projects (Hall 1968; Mintzberg 1979; Scott 1982). The central question about professional/organizational relationships has been reframed and new ways of collaborating between managers and professionals are emerging and conceptualized. Montgomery (2001) and Oliver (1997) emphasized the importance of trust and ability to conduct efficient intra- and interorganizational transactions and reduce the need for formal monitoring systems and costly contracts so that professionals can contribute to organizational reforms as well as the efficiency of these reforms. Broadbent *et al.* (1997) suggested three important changes in the relations between organization and professionals as the basis for new forms 1) professional autonomy must be accommodated to organizational needs for strategic control 2) the organizations have to accept professional identities rather than pursue one common organizational identity and 3) organizations have to respect professional practices and at the same time ensure change (Broadbent *et al.* 1997: 10). Freidson (2001) described the assault on professionalism reflecting the economic interests of both private capital and the state, which have changed the position of professions in modern society leading to decreasing credibility (2001: 197). But also that the *institution* of professionalism is still important because neither private firms nor the state wants to do without professional competences. Nevertheless the likely outcome of modern professionalism is jurisdictional changes and more control by the employer maybe through a two-tier professional system with a small elite and a large population of practitioners. This could again minimize professional discretion, emphasize short-term practical needs and cause professionals to loose their ideal-type professional spirit. Freidson introduced, as a possibility, a third (professional) logic besides market and hierarchy: 'The freedom to judge and choose the ends of work is what animates the institutions of the third logic. It expresses the very soul of professionalism' (2001:217). Freidson's idea of a third logic of professionalism alongside the market and the hierarchy emphasizes the potentially positive side of professionalism and represents one alternative to the common interpretation in the NPM literature that professionals are part of the problem with modern service organizations and have to be controlled and managed.

But this is not the only possibility. Professionals might also be hybridized into new kinds of professionalism due to the development of bureaucratic organizations where rational–legal forms of authority and hierarchical structures of responsibility are combined with external forms of regulation and performance measures in order to improve efficiency and effectiveness. This gives rise to new forms of professionalism that are termed 'organizational professionalism' (Noordegraaf 2007; Evetts 2009). This new kind of professionalism often involves both re-stratification within the professions with professional elites drawn into managerial roles as hybrid managers or alternatively bureaucratization of the work of professionals via the use of so-called 'soft bureaucratic' mechanisms (Courpasson 2000). The result is both a new kind of bureaucracy and new kinds of professionalism and such a neo-bureaucracy represents a shift in bureaucratic regulation with a bifurcation of hierarchy and simultaneously centralized and decentralized forms of bureaucratic regulation (Hoggett 1996; Harrison and Ahmad 2000; Harrison and Smith 2007). According to Rhodes (1997) public administration has been hollowed-out with the locus of bureaucracy taken away from middle managers and pushed to the top and the bottom. In health care the new kind of bureaucracy is characterized by professional action becoming much more rule-governed and rule-constrained and the subject of surveillance and sanctions aimed at securing compliance with the rules. It encompasses a range of techniques such as performance reviews, staff appraisal systems, medical and nursing audits, systematic 'customer' feedback schemes, league tables, clinical evidence-based governance and quality standards. It represents a new 'control at a distance' very different from the classic bureaucratic regulation and often involving semi-autonomous institutions and regulatory agencies in the management of results. On the one hand this development of neo-bureaucratic organizational forms of regulation threatens the traditional professional autonomy in occupational professionalism but on the other hand it also gives some opportunities for professionals to influence the regulatory instruments and the standards that are created both at the national level as well as in the individual organizations. But health care professionals are not alone any more when it comes to standard construction and implementation because other professions and the management will interfere and this means competition about the 'content of control mechanisms' where the old professionalism was more about the 'control of content' that is a certain kind of work (Noordegraaf 2007).

Summing up, the question of autonomy has been a central topic in the sociology of the professions. Today, after a period of critique of professions and professional projects, there is more focus on new kinds of professionalism and the positive and negative contributions for clients, organizations, organizational fields and society. Professions are seen as key actors in health care and as mediators between states taking ever more active roles in the reforming and regulation of health care and service for citizens who are more demanding than ever before (Kuhlmann 2006). This is implied in the literature; both a return to professionalism as a normative value, a distinct form of occupational control founded in communities of practice that might restrain both excessive competition and tight hierarchical control and give rise to new forms of organizations and cooperation (Freidson 2001); but also empirical observations about new kinds of professionalism focused on the new regulatory instruments in neo-bureaucratic organizations.

According to these new understandings public and professional interests are not necessarily in opposition and professionalism is now seen both as a possible and maybe also desirable way to develop and provide complex services to the public (Exworthy and Halford 1999; Evetts 2006) but also a professionalism that is controlled and regulated in new ways. If professionals are becoming more accountable both to the state and citizens, this does not mean a simple alliance between the three. New tensions can be expected and new dynamics appear depending on the specific contexts in different countries and the way professionalism is conceived in modern societies. Such a focus on new kinds of professionalism might give new directions and interests for sociologists refocusing on some of the classic questions but especially on the ways professionalism is discussed and used by states, the public, employers and managers, and by the professions themselves (Timmermans 2008). New forms of governance and management do not only challenge and change the health care professions, they also change the state itself and the ways the public organizations interact with professionals and the public (Hewitt and Thomas 2007; Kuhlmann and Saks 2008; Scott 2008). In the following section we shall analyze the challenges from the NPM strategies, which are among the most prominent in relation to health care professions.

Challenges from NPM and quality improvement policies to the autonomy of health care professionals

Reforming management and organization of health care systems and especially hospitals has been common since the early 1980s across most western countries including the Scandinavian (Brock *et al.* 1999; Dent 2003; Byrkjeflot 2005; Byrkjeflot and Neby 2004; Ferlie, Lynn and Pollitt 2005; Walshe and Smith 2006; Magnussen, Vrangbæk and Saltman 2009). Professionals are generally seen as problematic in the NPM literature because their relative autonomy provides problems of control for organizational and managerial reforms. Generally it is believed that the natural response of health professionals will be to resist change and professionals are often seen as part of the problem not as part of the solution (Broadbent *et al.* 1997; Exworthy and Halford 1999) as professionals represent at least two problems in relation to classical leadership and management. They do not automatically accept the role of general managers to control working activities and are generally sceptical in relation to possibilities for standardizing professional work.

But NPM is not implemented in uniform ways across countries. Recently attention has focused on different welfare regime characteristics and political traditions that might lead to distinctive national or regional variants in the relationship between state health care organizations and health care professions (Byrkjeflot and Neby 2004; Dent 2006) and there seems to be a growing recognition that health professionals react in a various ways depending on a number of factors. First the specific NPM strategy and the institutional structure seems to play a role for the reactions of the professionals (Degeling *et al.* 2006; Kragh Jespersen 2006; Kirkpatrick *et al.* 2009). Second the kind of reform plays a role. Reforms such as quality development requiring collaboration across professions are likely to be retarded or decoupled (Ferlie *et al.* 2005; Fitzgerald and Dopson 2005) and top-down initiated reforms requiring changes in professional beliefs and culture and the use of extraprofessional output measures are difficult to implement even if they are sustained for long periods (Kirkpartick *et al.* 2004; Ackroyd *et al.* 2007). Third the governance models and the interplay between professional groups and local management seems to be important for strategic change in complex and pluralistic organizations (Denis *et al.* 2001; Pomey *et al.* 2007).

The understanding of professionals as almost automatically resisting change and defending old positions has been modified and partly replaced by a more nuanced one where participation and dialogue with management and with other professions in defining, interpreting and implementing NPM reforms are emphasized and accordingly more ambiguous reactions of professions in relation to NPM strategies such as systematic quality development should be expected.

Turning to the issue of systematic quality development in health care, this has certainly been part of the NPM template in most countries (Kirkpatrick and Lucio 1995; Exworthy 1998; Christensen and Lægreid 2001; Øvretveit 2005; Blomgren 2007). It has traditionally been medically based, but in the last 30 years it has also been part of the management agenda in hospitals (Colton 2000; Katz *et al.* 2007).

Quality improvement (QI) and Quality Assurance (QA) have multiple origins in systems engineering, biological and medical science and in different areas of organizational theory. Among them are theories of organizational learning and institutional theory (Cole and Scott 2000). The connection between NPM and quality development is also recognized in the literature (Reed 1995; Hasselbladh and Bejerot 2007). However, the specific alignment between the general NPM strategy and the operationalization of governmental quality programmes in organizational practice can be weak and is likely to be characterized by contradictory interests and policies (Sorensen and Iedema 2008).

One central question seems to be the ways that different professions react to QI or QA schemes ranging from overt resistance, various forms of decoupling and transformation to active professional engagement. A recent literature review concludes that different professional groups tend to define quality in different ways and that different professions inhabit separate hierarchies with little interprofessional communication (Davies, Powell and Rushmer 2007: 7). It also showed that professionals may respond positively to national quality initiatives but QI often becomes an arena for 'turf battles' between different professionals especially between managers and doctors. In the sociology of professions it has for a long time been observed that professional jurisdictions among other things are defined by the right to define the content and quality of professional work. And also that the professions themselves regulate both the definition of quality and the extent to which it is realized (Abbott 1988; Evetts 2009; Freidson 2001).

An important question is the impact of local management on quality issues. A review from 2009 concludes that generally speaking there seems to be some evidence that QI can be affected by health care leaders. They can establish structures, systems and processes in their organization for generating improvement and the actions that are most likely to be successful are to create social processes where the professionals agree upon who does what in a collective way (Øvretveit 2005, 2009: xi). In another literature review Nyström (2009) identified 20 organizational characteristics that were important in connection with QI, strategic development, learning and change management. The three most important characteristics were a) that key actors (including leaders) had long-term commitment in QI; b) that employee commitment, participation and involvement are encouraged systematically and c) that change management processes are employed systematically (Nyström, 2009: 290). Leadership style and specifically charismatic leadership and communicative actions seems also to impact the initiative-oriented behaviour of doctors and nurses in a study of six German hospitals (Boerner and Dütschke 2008).

Summing up, the literature seems to indicate that at least three different factors are important in understanding the relationship between QI and health care professionals:

- First QI today is related to the broader template of NPM and its focus on transparency and control of professionals by neo-bureaucratic organizations, consumers and the public at large. Health care organizations are increasingly expected by governments and patients to invent and implement quality control and improvement strategies.
- Second the role of the health professions seems to be important both in defining, interpreting and implementing quality development schemes, but they are not alone. General management and other professions are also important in the construction and implementation.

- Third we can expect to find many different quality strategies and that professionals will react differently because they tend to define quality in profession-specific ways and react differently to various national quality schemes but we need to know more about the 'turf battles' and why there are many examples of lack of engagement from doctors. We also need to know more about the interaction between the central professions' conceptualization of quality issues and the interpretations by local professionals.
- Fourth it seems from the literature reviews that leadership matters. It also appears that social processes and long-term commitment are important as well as collective engagement in teams resulting in continuous quality development.

On the one hand the issue of quality is certainly an important element in NPM strategies as an integrated and necessary part of the efforts to make the health care sector more effective. Reliable data about quality makes it possible for consumers and politicians to evaluate changes in effectiveness over time and to compare institutions. On the other hand the quality issue also affects the core of traditional professional autonomy. At the level of society it is important for the professions to control and protect the knowledge base including definitions of quality and quality measures and faced with NPM strategies the professions conception of quality might be weakened. At the organizational level professionals have to interpret and implement new quality schemes that might affect professional traditions, autonomy and routines, and their own position in relation to other professionals.

In order to understand and analyze such developments we need concepts about the new kinds of professionalism and especially about the changes in the traditional 'double closure' kind of autonomy where the health professions and professionals define quality and quality development. The next section will set up a conceptual framework for analyzing such changes.

A conceptual framework for studying changes in professional autonomy

The concept of professional autonomy has been one of the most important traits in distinguishing between professions and other occupational groups. Some might argue that autonomy is not important any longer because no profession can anymore claim autonomy in the traditional sense faced with the changes in professional work and its regulation (Brint 1994; Noordegraaf 2007). But another way to go is to elaborate the concept of autonomy in order to identify the changes in the traditional occupational autonomy of the professions. This might be fruitful because at least the idea of professional autonomy still plays an important role among health care professionals.

Three different notions of professional autonomy are suggested in order to analyze changes in professional autonomy over time. The *traditional professional autonomy* corresponds to the autonomy position of the health care professions before the era of NPM and implies double closure autonomy both at the level of society and at the organizational level. The *framed professional autonomy* is a way to summarize what happened with the traditional professional autonomy especially in the 1980s and 1990s where efficiency and hierarchy assaulted the traditional autonomy and kept traditional autonomy within economic and regulative frames. Professional autonomy was not affected directly or in principle but its range was smaller. In the post NPM era a new situation seems to be emerging characterized by 'soft' bureaucratic regulation and competition between different kinds of expert knowledge. This is called *competitive autonomy* because no profession has a recognized monopoly on the definitions of work, quality of work or on the ways the health care organizations are managed.

All professions have to engage in dialogue and struggle about such definitions. This development represents a much more direct attack on the traditional autonomy of professionals and professionalism is likely to be changed under such conditions.

The three concepts reflect the ways professional autonomy is conceptualized and discussed in the sociology of the professions, the NPM literature and the more specific literature on quality development in health care. The actual or perceived autonomy of professions and professionals will probably be different from the three ideal-type categories in concrete empirical cases and mixed kinds of autonomy can be expected in empirical analyses.

In the following empirical analysis of changes in the autonomy of the medical profession in Denmark and Norway the three kinds of autonomy are used to make it possible to develop and refine our understanding of the intricate and complex interplay between the health care policies of the state, the medical profession and other professions interacting in hospitals around the issue of health quality. The empirical analysis is based on official documents. White papers from the Governments in Denmark and Norway, the associations of County Councils and the Regions in Norway, official statements from the Medical Associations in Denmark and Norway, and descriptions of the Danish Quality model from the Danish Institute for Quality and Accreditation in Healthcare are the main material. The focus of the empirical analysis is on the dynamics in the hospital field level and the role of medical professions and it is assumed that the official documents and programmes about quality reflect the interests, ideas and concepts of different actors including the health professions. This kind of material implies some limitations especially regarding the organizational level and the autonomy of the professionals inside hospitals but the analysis should be able to identify changes in the autonomy of the professions at the macro level and illustrate what forces are present at the organizational level. It illustrates above all the significance of different governance traditions and versions of the NPM strategies and their consequences for the autonomy of the medical profession.

Health care in Denmark

In Denmark the founding principles for health service such as equal and free access were established already in the eighteenth century. For a long period until 1970 the health care system was governed by the National Board of Health (dominated by doctors) in close dialogue with the medical profession. The political parties certainly played a role, but mostly a reactive one and before 1970 the Danish system seems to represent an almost clear-cut case of traditional professional autonomy with double social closure (Kragh Jespersen 2002). At the national level questions about hospital planning, expenditures and the development of health care were mostly left to the National Board of Health and the scientific medical societies, and the Danish health care sector became institutionalized within a public context characterized by an intimate interplay between the medical profession and the state. During the 1970s the system was reformed and counties became responsible for ownership, financing and running of hospitals and most primary care through directly elected County Council boards. Due to this development the medical profession lost its monopolistic position at the local level in relation to local health care policies and management of hospitals. However the reform did not change the dominating medical logic at the field level and the medical profession maintained its power in relation to important questions such as guidelines for hospital structure and planning (Pedersen *et al.* 2005). In this period the Danish system represented a decentralized model of 'administered medicine' (Freddi and Björkman 1989) with a large degree of clinical freedom for professionals within public administrative and financial frameworks. Since the early 1980s, the hospital field has been subject to NPM inspired reforms such as the introduction of new management models, quality development and control, use of activity-based budgets, internal contracting, outsourcing, free choice of hospital and improved patient rights (Kragh Jespersen 2002). In the years after 2000 a recentralization has taken place (Vrangbæk and Christiansen 2005, Ejersbo and Greve 2005) and a new local government reform has resulted in five regions with no taxation rights and limited political power to the new Regional Boards (Ministry of Health and Prevention 2008).

Quality development in Danish hospitals: from models of inspiration to a national model for quality assurance

Before the 1980s, quality issues were left to the professionals and they developed quality indicators within each profession according to the internal professional hierarchy. In the medical profession the specialized medical societies affiliated with the Danish Medical Associations were crucial but still each individual medical specialist was important and clinical freedom was preserved. The first systematic, organizationally embedded and managed policy about quality development can be distinguished in the late 1980s and early 90s. It was inspired by the WHO European office, which in 1982 recommended all countries to introduce systematic quality development schemes before 1990 (WHO 1981). The WHO concept of quality was adopted by the Danish Health Board in the early 1990s and at the same time a National Danish society for quality development in Health Care dominated by doctors was founded. The society participated in the formation of the first national strategy for quality development published in 1993 by the Danish Health Board. The first strategy did not recommend specific quality schemes but did encourage and inspire the counties and municipalities to use the following principles (Sundhedsstyrelsen 1993, my translation):

1   Implementation of quality as a continuous and systematic activity in the daily routines for all kind of personnel – everybody has responsibility and tasks.
2   Working with quality should be done in relation to well-defined goals.
3   Goals and the actual level of quality should be measured and routines changed if the goals are not achieved.
4   Continuous reappraisal of goals according to new knowledge.

The four principles were inspired by the TQM idea about quality circles and during the 1990s the Health Board published a number of quality recommendations and guides to counties and hospitals. The actual development was, however, diverse and locally determined. Some counties adopted the TQM concept while others focused on clinical indicators.

In 1997 a hospital commission recommended that the issue of quality should be given priority and that the many different initiatives should be coordinated; in 1999 the National Health Board encouraged the local health authorities to give priority to quality issues and to use clinical pathways and a patient-focused approach. Quality development has to: 'Build on a foundation of common values such as professionalism, quality, effectiveness and care' (Sundhedsstyrelsen 1999: 12). The idea was that patients should experience: 'Transition between functions, departments and sectors as one coherent pathway where an overall responsibility has been provided for' (1999: 13, my translation). The committee that wrote the publication was dominated by generalists and health care professionals who had adopted the idea of total quality and patient critical pathways as founding principles. Parallel to this there were other initiatives more focused on clinical indicators and the establishment of clinical databases. The County of Aarhus developed a clinical indicator project with focus on standards and indicators suitable for the measurement of treatment and care results and this project was later developed into a National Indicator Project supported by the Association of County Councils, the health care professional associations and the Ministry of Health and later again incorporated into the Danish Quality Model. The Scientific Medical Societies and the Danish Medical Association, in cooperation with Aarhus county, established the scientific basis for the project and the idea was to develop quality indicators in order to: 'Improve the quality of prevention, diagnostics, treatment and rehabilitation, provide documentation for making priorities and inform about the quality in health care to patients and consumers' (NIP projektet 2008). Alongside the indicator project a number of the Danish medical societies that are affiliated to the Danish Medical Association established their own databases covering the different medical specialities but during the 1990s the operation of the clinical databases was gradually transferred to the counties and the Health Board and later incorporated in the Danish Quality Model. Also most of the counties initiated surveys examining patient satisfaction with treatment and care and in the late 1990s the Copenhagen Hospital Corporation and one more county decided to implement accreditation schemes using the Joint Commission International Accreditation (JCIA) scheme and the British Health Quality Services (HQS) respectively. In both cases the schemes were adjusted to fit the Danish health care system.

In the late 1990s the Danish system for QI in hospitals thus appeared as fragmented and characterized by lack of coordination, different concepts and priorities, and diversity with respect to priorities in the 15 counties and corporations. The Danish medical association preferred the national indicator project and the use of clinical databases and was somewhat sceptical in relation to the use of patient surveys and total quality management inspired concepts. The Association described the role of doctors and others in quality development as follows:

> Quality development in relation to medical service is the responsibility of the profession, because only the profession has the special knowledge needed for the evaluation and safeguarding of quality. This binding professional autonomy is under pressure from outside-patients and health care authorities – who demand insight in the quality of medical services.
> (Legeforeningen [Danish Medical Association] 2005b: 1, my translation)

In 1999 a National Council for Quality development was created in order to coordinate the diverse initiatives and to propose a new national strategy for quality development. The new Council was a corporatist unit with broad representation from the health care field including the medical association and the association of nurses. They proposed a new national strategy for quality development in the health care sector in 2002. They still took as a starting point the WHO quality goals of 1) high professional standards, 2) effective use of resources, 3) minimal risk for patients and 4) coherent patient pathways, and stated that results from all existing initiatives should be used and incorporated in the quality strategy. But they also pointed to the need for systematic benchmarking and other kinds of systematic comparison between hospitals and departments in order to facilitate the patient free choice of hospitals and this was certainly inspired by NPM (Det Nationale Råd 2002). In this way the new national strategy departed from the hitherto decentralized policy-making and it was proposed that a centralized national model for quality development should be designed in order to monitor and evaluate the general development in health care quality (Det Nationale Råd 2002: 23). The new central Danish model for quality was proposed in 2004 (Danish Health Care Quality Assessment Programme 2004). It was founded in an agreement between the Government and the Association of County Councils in 2001 (Finansministeriet 2001). The agreement stated that the new model should imply common quality standards for all hospitals and that the counties were obliged to follow the new standards and to facilitate patient free choice of hospitals which was a government top priority. Now the decentralized model was abandoned and a new and ambitious national model was developed. It was based on the use of external standards for clinical and organizational quality, internal and external evaluation (accreditation), and the publication of results. The official goal of the nationwide Danish Health Care Quality Assessment Programme is to promote effective patient pathways to ensure that the patients' experience improved quality. The fulfilment of this objective is achieved by promoting continuous clinical, professional and organizational QI of patient pathways and by making quality more transparent. It is not clear in the programme itself what is most important. During the years from 2004 to 2007 the programme was developed and a new independent Danish Institute for Quality and Accreditation in Healthcare was established in 2005. The new institute has developed the first operative version of the model in 2008. It encompasses 37 themes and 103 accreditation standards, each with a number of indicators covering clinical pathways, organizational factors and different types of illness. The Danish model is defined by the institute as an accreditation system, which aims at continuous quality development of clinical pathways through learning and benchmarking (IKAS 2008). The Danish Medical Association considered in a hearing in 2007 that the model was appropriate but also that:

> it would be extremely costly in terms of time, education, manpower and money . . . and the use of resources will have to balanced against the time used for treatment of patients.
>
> (Legeforeningen 2007: 1, my translation)

The Danish case demonstrates the importance of governance structures and national traditions in relation to the regulation of the medical profession. The decentralized governance structure with strong counties and a weak Ministry of Health meant that the first national quality policy was either ignored or developed by the professionals who also in the 1990s virtually captured an important part of the policy formation by establishing their own clinical databases and later by exporting them into the Danish national quality model. During almost 15 years the medical profession in this way was able to protect the traditional professional autonomy in all important respects. But this changed with the introduction of the new national quality model from 2008.

It represents a movement away from traditional autonomy to framed autonomy where standard setting has been initiated from the top of the Danish health administration supported by managers in the counties and regions and hospital managers. The choice of accreditation as the main model also represents a move to a model where external Accreditation Standards are imposed on the Danish system. The great number of organizational standards and standards for patient satisfaction is part of this development. But taken together there is no doubt that medical professional clinical standards are the most central element in the Danish model. The construction of clinical standards has to a great extent involved the Danish medical societies and the National Health Board, and in this way the medical elite has been involved in the formation of the quality policy. The implementation of the new national model depends on the Regions and hospitals but has to be kept within the rather narrow frames of the national standards.

Full implementation of the model will be very costly according to a hearing among the regions and the Danish Medical Association and no extra money has been allocated to hospitals in order to facilitate the implementation. It seems likely that local projects will be limited and that accreditation will be at the centre of the Danish model. Because of the heavy medical influence on the construction of standards it does not really encourage the introduction of alternative professional standards for quality and the involvement of patients is limited. The new Danish quality model is clearly inspired by a NPM inspired strategy and represents a framing of professional autonomy with the introduction of activity-based budgets and centralized organizational standards but it remains to be seen how much it will actually change the autonomy of the individual professional. It is also evident that the medical knowledge elite participated in the construction of the national clinical standards and the individual professional will have to comply with these self-imposed standards and this looks more like a neo-bureaucratic regulation of the medical profession. The Danish case thus seems to represent a mixture of framed and competitive professional autonomy with the introduction of the new national quality model.

Health care in Norway

Before 1970 the Norwegian health care system has been characterized as an extension of the medical clinic into the state (Berg 1980, 1987). The medical profession controlled the health system and penetrated the administration and policy system. After this period the Norwegian health system was to a very high degree a public service organization based on principles of free access and financing through the state. But still the system was depoliticized and in fact the state and the medical profession were grown together to such a degree that Erichsen labelled it a 'profession-state' (Erichsen 1995, 1996: 19–23). Until 1970 doctors were in the offensive through their positions in the central state apparatus but also as the most important managers in hospitals and in local health boards. During the 1980s and 90s the Norwegian hospital system was reformed in relation to financing (introduction of activity-based financing), and patients' free choice of hospitals and a unitary management system was proposed. Until June 2001 hospitals were owned and run by the 19 Norwegian counties. After a hospital reform these hospitals are now operated as *regional health enterprises* owned by the government. The hospitals have become separate legal subjects and thus not formally an integrated part of the central government administration. But, in spite of the decentralized provision of health care, standards and quality requirements for the health service provided in the Norwegian health care system are to a large extent determined by legislation.

Quality development in Norway

The issue of QI was introduced in Norway in the beginning of the 1990s and like Denmark it was inspired by the WHO European Office. The first national strategy was published in 1995 and from 1994 internal control systems were required by law (Sosial- og Helsedepartementet 1995). The strategy was based on the following principles:

1   safety for patients
2   efficient use of resources
3   comprehensive and coherent pathways
4   management should be engaged in quality development
5   the culture should encourage quality development and
6   all employees should participate in quality development.

The official goal of the first national strategy was that all organizations within the Norwegian health system should implement effective and comprehensive systems for quality and control before 2000. According to the evaluation of the first national strategy made by the Norwegian Board of Health Supervision in 2002 not every organization had fulfilled the ambitions, but many organizations had increased their competences and qualifications and a lot of projects had been initiated (Helsetilsynet 2002). Among them the so-called 'breaking through' projects based on clinical standards and controlled output measurement. Not every organization had implemented systems for internal control and in 2002 it became compulsory to establish internal control systems for quality in all organizations. As part of the first strategy a range of quality initiatives has been taken: user evaluation surveys and national quality standards concerning, for example, waiting times; a number of 'corridor' patients and discharge summaries has been introduced and patients can now find this information on public websites and through telephone services in order to facilitate the free choice of hospital. It has been the intention to further increase the use of clinical standards in order to produce league tables of hospitals (Byrkjeflot 2005).

The principal viewpoints of the Norwegian Medical Association on the quality issue can be illustrated by a policy paper from 2005. The main point for the association is:

> that professional competency must be the basis for better quality in hospital health care. This implies also that the health care service should be safer for the patient because mistakes and accidents will result in learning . . . Our common goals about the best possible health services for patients will not be reached if we do not find effective and coordinated solutions on the basis of professional judgement.
>
> (Legeforeningen 2005a)

There are great similarities between the policies of the two medical associations in Denmark and Norway. The medical professional knowledge should be the focus and all other conceptions are secondary in relation to that.

The second Norwegian strategy from 2005 is, like the first, a comprehensive quality development scheme and emphasizes the following important goals for quality development:

1   it should be based on solid knowledge about effects
2   mistakes and accidents should be reduced to a minimum
3   users and patients should be involved and given influence
4   services should be coordinated and characterised by continuity
5   resources should be used in order to maximize both the users and society's benefits
6   everybody should have equal access to resources and services.
(Sosial- og helsedirektoratet 2005: 21–25)

In order to obtain these goals the strategy focuses on the following fields:

1   active incorporation of the patient
2   strengthening of the health professional
3   improvement of organization and management
4   improvement of competencies in change and
5   systematic follow up and evaluation of results.

As part of the strategy the Department for Health and Social Services asked six working groups of practitioners to participate in the formulation of recommendations to the health care organizations (Sosial- og Helsedirektoratet 2007). Part of the strategy implies the use of clinical standards but no accreditation scheme is proposed and responsibility for quality development is placed at all management levels. The strategy represents in this way a combination of top-down and bottom-up change strategy and it is very different from the Danish strategy in its focus on interdisciplinary work, patient involvement and local managerial responsibility. In an evaluation of the

Norwegian quality initiatives Hallandvik (2005) claims that the Norwegian policy has moved from classical professional quality schemes to a more organizationally defined policy in the 1980s, then, in the 1990s, to national systems and then back to a more organizational and professionally defined quality scheme.

Summing up the Norwegian case, it seems the medical profession has to cope with a more fundamental challenge from the quality strategies than their Danish colleagues. The medical profession's policies are very much alike and both point to the importance of medical knowledge evidence and clinical standards. But in Norway especially the second strategy in 2005 emphasizes the importance of other professions, other kinds of professionalism and the active involvement of the patient. This means that the medical profession is faced with competition from other kinds of professional knowledge and traditions (mostly from nurses and general managers) and from patient norms and wishes. But it is also clear that the implementation is decentralized and that clinical standards and measurement of results are important parts of the strategy. At the policy level the Norwegian case seems to represent a mixture of different forms of autonomy. Traditional autonomy because the clinical standards are still mostly under the control of the medical profession, framed autonomy because of the weight on organizational standards and comparisons with the intent to facilitate patients free choice of hospitals, and competitive autonomy because the policy explicitly encourages other professional standards and the empowerment of patients.

Discussion and conclusion

In this chapter I have examined the ways in which the medical professions interact with the state authorities at the hospital field level in relation to the development of quality policies and I have investigated the ways that professional autonomy and professionalism are likely to change during such processes.

In both countries systematic quality development became part of the healthcare policy during the 1980s and 90s within the frames of national NPM strategies that changed the governance structures, the financing and the management structures in the hospital field. The medical profession lost some of their former power in this movement from a professionally dominated to a more managed field. But they did not just adapt to the new political and administrative regime, instead they tried to protect and develop their core professional autonomy which should also be expected according to the literature on professions.

In both countries the medical profession has been active in discussions and policy formation about the national quality strategies since the beginning of the 1990s. They have promoted their views both in relation to members by formulating official policies and in relation to public authorities through hearing statements and participation in the construction of standards and indicators. The medical scientific societies who represent the medical knowledge elite and are connected to the international scientific community have been most active. In Denmark scientific medical societies have been invited to participate actively in the construction of clinical standards and indicators and the first version of the Danish National Quality Model from 2008 is heavily marked by the influence from the societies and the international scientific community. In Norway the growing use of clinical standards and documentation has also involved the medical specialists, for example, in the 'breaking through' projects and in the obligatory internal control. Such participation might secure support to quality strategies from medical professions and especially the knowledge elite. But another and more open question is whether it will gain support from the individual doctor who can feel less freedom of action in the treatment of patients if binding standards shall be met in each case. The involvement of the medical elites in the development of quality development schemes in Denmark and Norway illustrates that medical professionalism might be maintained at the field level but maybe at the cost of the individual professional. This can be seen as a response from the medical profession to NPM inspired quality strategies seeking to frame the traditional professional autonomy.

Second, I expected the medical professions to be reluctant and partly dismissive towards other non-medical conceptions of quality because this could lead to loss of the 'content of control' with the quality issue (Noordegraaf 2007). This is only partly the case because they do accept the new focus on patients, but at the same time they seem to transform the new patient focus to fit their own medical concept about evidence-based treatment. Patients are not conceived as an active part in treatment and care and quality strategies should rather focus on the measurement of results for patients. In the Danish case the transformation seems to succeed because the patient oriented standards in the new national model are unspecific and only confirm that processes about patient involvement and registration of patient satisfaction exist, while in the Norwegian strategy it is directly encouraged to promote the participation of patient in decisions about treatment and care and it is explicitly part of management responsibilities. So in the Danish case the medical profession has to some degree succeeded in defining the focus on patients in accordance with a traditional medical autonomy but that is not the case in the Norwegian discussion.

Third, the use of administrative standards to ensure organizational defined quality might also be seen by the medical profession as an example of alternative professional standards imposed by generalists such as economists and general managers. Such standards are included in the Danish strategy as process standards that management have to pay regard to, but no specific levels of performance are required. In the Norwegian case the local management at the hospital and clinic level have to decide upon organizational standards and include them in the local strategy, but the Norwegian strategy also emphasizes the significance of organizational culture and the participation of all personnel and interdisciplinary projects. Additionally, the Norwegian Directorate of

Health announced that it will provide financial support to projects following these guidelines. This implies a focus on the change process and the active incorporation of all health care personnel more than formal accordance with externally defined administrative standards. It is not yet possible to judge what the actual implementation of the two different strategies will be at the clinical level, but in the Danish case the organizational standards can be met without interfering with clinical standards while in Norway it will not be possible within the frames of the strategy. On the other hand there is nothing to guarantee that all local managers will pursue the goals of the Norwegian strategy as intended. If economic/administrative standards are actually imposed in hospital working practices this will be an indication of a change towards competitive autonomy. Again it seems that in the Danish case the competition from organizational defined quality concepts and the inclusion of other professions is weaker than in Norway.

Part of the explanation behind these differences might be found in the different institutional structures in the two countries. Denmark has a tradition for negotiated corporative policies and a relatively weak Ministry of Health (Vrangbæk and Christiansen 2005). The long period of decentralization has encouraged different quality schemes and together with the consensus-oriented policy tradition the result has been the incorporation of existing medically dominated quality schemes in the new national model and the decision to use accreditation as the dominating strategy. In Norway a more centralized governance model has dominated even before the ownership reform in 2002 and the relatively strong position of the Department for Health and Social Services has been important in the Norwegian strategy which also encompasses the social sector with other professions and other traditions for the involvement of clients. Also in Norway there seems to be a tradition for the utilization of organizational and management research about quality development in the formation of new policies, which is not the case in Denmark (Øvretveit 2001). These contextual factors might have influenced the abilities of the medical professions to marginalize the inclusion of patient experiences and the use of organizational quality concepts defined by other professions.

The analysis of patient experiences and organizational standards for quality in the two national strategies and discourses shows that the traditional monopoly of the medical profession to define quality has been challenged in both countries, but also that the struggle takes place at different arenas and that the arenas themselves are changing. In Denmark the struggle takes place at a national and international arena with the construction of accreditation standards in and around the Danish Institute for Quality and Accreditation in Healthcare. This is a new situation following many years of decentralized policy-making and it represents a neo-bureaucratic development with its combination of central control at a distance and local responsibility for the implementation of quality assurance. In Norway the struggle takes place both at the national level in and around the Norwegian Directorate of Health and Social Services but also and probably more important at the local level in hospitals and clinics following the Norwegian hospital reform of 2001 with its weight of the NPM inspired enterprise hospital model. So we might expect a much more diverse picture in Norway dependent upon the local management team than in Denmark.

These results can be understood in terms of changing professional autonomy and the conceptual scheme developed in the first section. The medical profession is faced with shifts from one kind of professional autonomy to another or to mixed forms of professional autonomy following the development of quality policies. In Denmark the overall conclusion is that the autonomy of the medical profession has been maintained as the dominant form, but that the traditional double closure position has been lost and that autonomy has been changed in the direction of framed autonomy within a neo-bureaucratic governance model. In Norway the conclusion is that the medical traditional autonomy is more seriously challenged at both levels. At the national level the quality strategy does not give priority to medically evidence-based clinical standards and at the local level it is directly prescribed that other conceptions shall be incorporated. But it is an open question whether medical standards will become more important in the future and the situation can be characterized as one of competitive autonomy within the frame of a state-controlled and NPM inspired enterprise governance model.

But the conceptual scheme has some limitations. First it seems best suited to the analysis of professionalism at the macro level and does not in an adequate way capture the internal differences between the autonomy of the profession and the autonomy of the individual professional. Second the three kinds of autonomy can become more blurred if we change the level of analysis to the organizational level. Local management both at hospital level but even more at the clinic level is heavily influenced if not dominated by doctors and nurses (Kragh Jespersen 2006, Mo 2008). Quality development at the local level seems, according to the quality literature (Cole and Scott 2000, Nyström 2009), to be influenced by local management long-term commitments and engagements and by multi-professional conceptions of quality perhaps more than changes in the national governance models and quality policies. This means that at the clinical level the autonomy of professionals can be quite different and more diverse than at the field level and that the differences between nations can be more pronounced but also smaller than at the field level.

Third, the analysis of the quality development strategies illustrates another important point about changes in professional autonomy because we might have to break with the understanding of professionalism as a phenomenon connected to the nation state. Even in recent understanding of professionalism (Kuhlmann 2006; Henriksson, Wrede and Burau 2006; Gleeson and Knights 2006) it is common to understand the development of modern professionalism as intimately connected to the development of the nation state and this is reflected in the conceptual scheme. But in the case of medical quality development, it is quite obvious that trans-national forces are at work. The professional associations do certainly, as Scott mentions, function as institutional agents defining, interpreting and applying health quality schemes (Scott 2008) but they are not restricted to the nation-state arena. In their book Brunsson and Jacobsson (2000) emphasize the development of international organizations and international professional associations who labour to develop standards on an international basis. Such standards are often backed by reference to scientific evidence or documented 'best practices' and by international institutions such as accreditation organizations working to institutionalize certain practices in the international community (Djelic and Sahlin-Andersson 2006). Quality development strategies in health care are certainly influenced by such developments as demonstrated clearly in the Danish case. So it seems that trans-national processes are important in the construction and dissemination of standards and best ways of practice in professional service delivery. This must be recognized and conceptualized in future research and our present-day understanding of professions and their autonomy is perhaps to much linked to the nation-state.

The conclusion seems to be that medical professions challenged with national formations of policies about quality development react strategically in order to maintain traditional professional autonomy, but also that they have to adapt their professionalism in the process. Framed autonomy can be observed in the Danish case where the Danish National Quality Model sets the frame within which the medical profession can preserve its autonomy. This takes place within a neo-bureaucratic governance structure where the medical knowledge elite plays an important role in the construction of clinical standards. Competitive autonomy can be observed in the Norwegian case where medical quality has to compete with other professional standards and compulsory participation from patients. In the Norwegian case the governance structure can be characterized as NPM inspired with decentralization of quality development to enterprise model hospitals. In both cases the medical profession has shown a great ability to selectively adopt quality reform elements, neutralize others and in this way partly maintain their professional powers within different national governance structures. In future research two important themes could be important if we want to improve our understanding of the complex interplay between the health care professions and the state in relation to quality issues. First how do international developments and professional networks affect the autonomy and second how does the development of internal hierarchies between elites and the rank and file professionals affect the professions' ability to protect autonomy and develop new kinds of professionalism?

At the organizational level changing professional autonomy at field level represents both challenges and possibilities for local leadership. On the one hand the NPM or neo-bureaucratic strategies to change professional autonomy represents a challenge for local leadership because of professional opposition. But on the other hand the medical professions seem to engage in policy formation and the construction of standards and quality development schemes. This represents a possibility for local management who want to engage professionals in quality development because it legitimizes quality development and according to the literature it would be most effective if local management together with local professionals engaged in long-term efforts about quality development. However, developments at the field level, which seem to bureaucratize and standardize quality development in order to preserve professionalism, might constrain such local initiatives.

References

Abbott, A. (1988) *The System of Professions*. London: University of Chicago Press.

Ackroyd, S. (1996) Organization contra organizations: professions and organizational change in the United Kingdom. *Organization Studies* 17(4): 599–621.

Ackroyd, S., Kirkpatrick, I. and Walker, R. (2007) Public management reform and its consequences for professional organisation: a comparative analysis. *Public Administration* 85(1): 9–26.

Berg, O. (1980) The Modernisation of Medical Care in Sweden and Norway. In A.J. Heidenheimer and N. Elvander (eds) *The Shaping of the Swedish Health System*. London: Croom Helm.

—— (1987) *Medisinens logikk: Studier i medisinens sosiologi og politikk*. Oslo: Universitetsforlaget.

Blomgren, M. (2007) The drive for transparency: organizational field transformations in Swedish healthcare. *Public Administration* 85(1): 67–82.

Boerner, S. and Dütschke, E. (2008) The impact of charismatic leadership on followers' initiative-oriented behaviour: a study in German hospitals. *Health Care Management Review* 33(4): 332–40.

Brante, T. (1988) Sociological approaches to professions. *Acta Sociologica* 31(2): 119–42.

Brint, S. (1994) *In an Age of Experts. The Changing Role of Professionals in Politics and Public Life*. Princeton, NJ: Princeton University Press.

Broadbent, J., Dietrich, M. and Roberts, J. (eds) (1997) *The End of the Professions? The Restructuring of Professional Work*. London: Routledge.

Brock, D., Powell, M. and Hinings, C.R. (eds) (1999) *Restructuring the Professional Organization*. London: Routledge.

Brunsson, N. and Jacobsson, B. (eds) (2000) *A World of Standards*. Oxford: Oxford University Press.

Bureau, V., Henriksson, L. and Wrede, S. (2004) Comparing professional groups in health care: towards a context sensitive analysis. *Knowledge, Work and Society* 2(2): 49–68.

Burrage, M. and Torstendahl, R. (eds) (1990) *The Formation of Professions: Knowledge, State and Strategy*. London: Sage.

Byrkjeflot, H. (2005) *The Rise of a Healthcare State? Recent Healthcare Reforms in Norway*. Working paper 15–2005. Bergen: Rokkansenteret.

Byrkjeflot, H. and Neby, S. (2004) *The Decentralized Path Challenged? Nordic Health Care Reforms in Comparison*. Working paper 2–2004. Bergen: Rokkansenteret.

Carr Saunders, A.M. (1928) *Professions: Their Organization and Place in Society*. Oxford: Clarendon Press.

Christensen, T. and Lægreid, P. (2001) *New Public Management*. Aldershot: Ashgate Publishers.

Colton, D. (2000) Quality improvement in health care: conceptual and historical foundation. *Evaluation and the Health Professions* 23(1): 7–42.

Cole, R.E. and Scott, W.R. (eds) (2000) *The Quality Movement and Organization Theory*. London: Sage.

Courpasson, D. (2000) Managerial strategies of domination: power in soft bureaucracies. *Organization Studies* 21(1): 141–61.

Danish Health Care Quality Assessment Programme (2004) *The Danish Health Care Quality Assessment Programme and the Danish National Health Board: Programme Proposal*. Copenhagen: Sundhedsstyrelsen. Available at www.kvalitetsinstitut.dk/sw1490.asp (accessed July 2010).

Danish Medical Association (2007) *Lægeforeningen debatoplæg til 5 debatmøde om kvalitetsreformen*, 30 marts 2007. Copenhagen: DADL.

Davies, H., Powell, A. and Rushmer, R. (2007) *Healthcare Professionals' Views on Clinician Engagement in Quality Improvement*. London: The Health Foundation. Available at www.health.org.uk/publications/research_reports/clinician_engagement.html (accessed July 2010).

Degeling, P., Zhang, K., Coyle, B., Xu, L.Z., Meng, Q.Y., Qu, J.B. and Hill, M. (2006) Clinicians and the governance of hospitals: a cross-cultural perspective on relations between profession and management. *Social Science and Medicine* 63(3): 757–75.

Denis, J.-L., Lamothe, L. and Langley, A. (2001) The dynamics of collective leadership and strategic change in pluralistic organizations. *Academy of Management Journal* 44(4): 809–37.

Dent, M. (2003) *Remodelling Hospitals and Health Professions in Europe: Medicine, Nursing and the State*. Basingstoke: Palgrave Macmillan.

—— (2006) Post-NPM in public sector hospitals? The UK, Germany and Italy. *Policy and Politics* 33(4): 623–36.

Det Nationale Råd (2002) *Det nationale råd for kvalitetsudvikling i sundhedsvæsenet: National strategi for kvalitetsudvikling i sundhedsvæsenet. Fælles mål og handleplan 2002–2006*. Copenhagen: Sundhedsstyrelsen.

Djelic, M. and Sahlin-Andersson, K. (eds) (2006) *Transnational Governance: Institutional Dynamics of Regulation*. Cambridge: Cambridge University Press.

Ejersbo, N. and Greve, C. (2005) *Public Management Policymaking in Denmark 1983–2005*. Paper for: IIM/LSE Workshop on Theory and Methods for Studying Organizational Processes, 17–18 February. London School of Economics.

Erichsen, V. (1995) State traditions and medical professionalization in Scandinavia. In T. Johnson, G. Larkin and M. Saks (eds) *Health Professions and the State in Europe*. London: Routledge.

—— (1996) *Profesjonsmakt. På sporet av en norsk helsepolitisk tradisjon*. Oslo: Tano Aschehaug.

Etzioni, A. (ed.) (1969) *The Semi-professions and their Organization*. London: Collier-Macmillan.

Evetts, J. (2006) The sociology of professional groups. New directions. *Current Sociology* 54(1): 133–43.

—— (2009) New professionalism and new public management: changes, continuities and consequences. *Comparative Sociology* 8: 247–66.

Exworthy, M. (1998) Clinical audit in the NHS internal market: from peer review to external monitoring. *Public Policy and Administration* 13(2): 40–53.

Exworthy, M. and Halford, S. (1999) Professionals and managers in a changing public sector: conflict, compromise and collaboration? In M. Exworthy and S. Halford (eds) *Professionals and the New Managerialism in the Public Sector.* Buckingham: Open University Press.

Ferlie, E., Fitzgerald, L., Wood, M. and Hawkins, C. (2005) The nonspread of innovations: the mediating role of professionals. *Academy of Management Journal* 48(1): 117–34.

Ferlie, E., Lynn, L.E. and Pollitt, C. (eds) (2005) *The Oxford Handbook of Public Management.* Oxford: Oxford University Press.

Finansministeriet (2001) *Økonomiaftale 2001.* Copenhagen: Finansministeriet.

Fitzgerald, L. and Dopson, S. (2005) Professional boundaries and the diffusion of innovation. In S. Dopson and L. Fitzgerald (eds) *Knowledge to Action? Evidence-based Health Care in Context.* Oxford: Oxford University Press.

Freddi, G. and Björkman, J.W. (1989) *Controlling Medical Professionals: The Comparative Politics of Health Governance.* London: Sage.

Freidson, E. (1970) *The Profession of Medicine.* New York: Dodd, Mead and Co.

—— (1986) *Professional Powers: A Study in the Sociology of Applied Knowledge.* Chicago: University of Chicago Press.

—— (1994) *Professionalism Reborn: Theory, Prophecy and Policy.* Chicago: University of Chicago Press.

—— (2001) *Professionalism: The Third Logic.* Cambridge: Polity Press.

Gleeson, D. and Knights, D. (2006) Challenging dualism: public professionalism in 'troubled' times. *Sociology* 40(2): 277–95.

Goode, W.J. (1957) Community within a community. *American Sociological Review* 22: 194–200.

Hall, R. (1968) Professionalization and bureaucratization. *American Sociological Review* 33: 92–104.

Hallandvik, J.-E. (2005) *Forbedring, endring eller kontinuitet? Den nye kvalitets-politikken i helsetjenesten.* Oslo: Dr.polit.avhandling. Institutt for statsvitenskap, Universitetet i Oslo.

Harrison, S. and Ahmad, W.I.U. (2000) Medical autonomy and the UK State 1975 to 2025. *Sociology* 34(1): 129–46.

Harrison, S. and Smith, C. (2007) Neo-bureaucracy and public management: the case of medicine in the National Health Service. *Competition and Change* 7(4): 243–54.

Hasselbladh, H. and Bejerot, E. (2007) Webs of knowledge and circuits of communication: constructing rationalized agency in Swedish health care. *Organization* 14(2): 175–200.

Helsetilsynet (2002) *Nasjonal strategi for kvalitetsutvikling i helsetjenesten,* Rapport 5/2002. Oslo: Statens Helsetilsyn.

Henriksson, L., Wrede, S. and Burau, V. (2006) Understanding professional projects in welfare service work: revival of old professionalism? *Gender, Work and Organization* 14(2): 174–92.

Hewitt, J. and Thomas, P. (2007) The impact of clinical governance on the professional autonomy and self-regulation of general practitioners: colonization or appropriation? Paper presented at Critical Management Studies conference, Manchester University, July 2007.

Hoggett, P. (1996) New modes of control in the public service. *Public Administration* 74 (Spring): 9–32.

Institut for Kvalitet og Akkreditering i Sundhedsvæsenet (IKAS) (2008). Available at www.kvalitetsinstitut.dk/sw197.asp (accessed July 2010).

Katz, J.N., Kessler, C.L., O'Connell, A. and Levine, S.A. (2007) Professionalism and evolving concepts of quality. *Journal of General Internal Medicine*, 22(1): 137–9.

Kirkpatrick, I. and Ackroyd, S. (2003) Archetype theory and the changing professional organization: a critique and alternative. *Organization* 10(4): 739–58.

Kirkpatrick, I. and Lucio, M. (eds) (1995) *The Politics of Quality in the Public Sector*. London: Routledge.

Kirkpatrick, I., Ackroyd, S. and Walker, R. (2004) *The new managerialism and the public service professions*. London: Palgrave.

Kirkpatrick, I., Kragh Jespersen, P., Dent, M. and Neogy, I. (2009) Medicine and management in a comparative perspective: the case of Denmark and England. *Sociology of Health and Illness*. 31(5): 642–58.

Kragh Jespersen, P. (2002) Health care policy. In H.P. Jørgensen (ed.) *Consensus, Cooperation and Conflict. The Policy Making Process in Denmark*. Cheltenham: Elgar: 144–66.

—— (2006) Institutionalization of new management models in the Danish hospital field: the role of the medical profession. Paper presented at the 22nd EGOS Colloqium, Bergen.

Kragh Jespersen, P., Nielsen, L.L. and Sognstrup, H. (2002) Professions, institutional dynamics, and new public management in the Danish hospital field. *International Journal of Public Administration* 25(12): 1555–75.

Kuhlmann, E. (2006) *Modernising Health Care: Reinventing Professions, the State and the Public*. Bristol: The Policy Press.

Kuhlmann, E. and Saks, M. (eds) (2008) *Rethinking Professional Governance. International Directions in Health Care*. Bristol: Policy Press.

Larson, M.S. (1977) *The Rise of Professionalism: A Sociological Analysis*. London: University of California Press.

Legeforeningen (2005a) *'Rom for faglighet – til pasientens beste!'*. Oslo: Legeforeningen. Available at www.legeforeningen.no/index.gan?id=74600 (accessed May 2008).

—— (2005b) *Kvalitetsudvikling*. Politikpapir. Copenhagen: Lægeforeningen. Available at www.ugeskriftet.dk/portal/page/portal/laegerdk/laeger_dk/politik/politikpapirer/politikpapirer_laegeforeningen/kvalitetsudvikling (accessed May 2008).

—— (2007) *Høringssvar vedrørende Den Danske Kvalitetsmodel – standarder og indikatorer for sygehuse*. Copenhagen: Lægeforeningen.

Macdonald, K. (1995) *The Sociology of the Professions*. London: Sage.

Magnussen, J., Vrangbæk, K. and Saltman, R. (eds) (2009) *Nordic Healthcare Systems: Recent Reforms and Current Policy Changes*. Maidenhead: McGraw-Hill and Open University Press.

Millerson, G. (1964) *The Qualifying Associations: A Study in Professionalization*. London: Routledge and Kegan Paul.

Ministry of Health and Prevention (2008) *Health Care in Denmark*. Copenhagen: Ministry of Health and Prevention.

Mintzberg, H. (1979) *The Structuring of Organizations*. Englewood Cliffs, NJ: Prentice-Hall.

Mo, T.O. (2008) Doctors as managers: moving towards general management? *Journal of Health Organization and Management* 22(4): 400–15.

Montgomery, K. (2001) Physician executives: the evolution and impact of a hybrid profession. *Advances in Health Care Management* 2: 215–41.

Morell, K. (2007) Re-defining professions: knowledge, organization and power as syntax. Paper presented at the Critical Management Studies Conference. Manchester, July 2007.

Murphy, R. (1988) *Social Closure: The Theory of Monopolization and Exclusion.* Oxford: Clarendon Press.

NIP projektet (2008) *Det nationale indikatorprojekt.* Available at www.nip.dk/about+the+danish+national+indicator+project (accessed May 2008).

Noordegraaf, M. (2007) From 'pure' to 'hybrid' professionalism: present-day professionalism in ambiguous public domains. *Administration and Society* 39(6): 761–85.

Nyström, M. (2009) Characteristics of health care organizations associated with learning and development: lessons from a pilot study. *Quality Management in Health Care* 18(4), October–December: 285–94.

Oliver, A.L. (1997) On the nexus of organizations and professions: networking through trusts. *Sociological Inquiry* 67(2): 227–45.

Øvretveit, J. (2001) The Norwegian approach to integrated quality development. *Journal of Management in Medicine* 15(2): 125–41.

—— (2005) Public service quality improvement. In E. Ferlie, L.E. Lynn and C. Pollitt (eds) *The Oxford Handbook of Public Management.* Oxford: Oxford University Press.

—— (2009) *Leading Improvement Effectively. Review of Research.* London: The Health Foundation. Available at www.health.org.uk/publications/research_reports/leading_improvement.html (accessed July 2010).

Parsons, T. (1939) The professions and social structure. *Social Forces* 17: 457–67.

—— (1954) *The Professions and Social Structure: Essays in Sociological Theory.* New York: Free Press.

Pedersen, K.M., Christiansen, T. and Bech, M. (2005) The Danish health care system: evolution – not revolution – in a decentralized system. *Health Economics* 14(S1): 41–57.

Pomey, M., Denis, J.-L., Champagne, F., Gyslaine, T. and Préval, J. (2007) The pluralistic view of governance within healthcare organizations. Paper presented at the EGOS Colloquium, July 5–7, Vienna.

Reed, M. (1995) Managing quality and organizational politics: TQM as a governmental technology. In I. Kirkpatrick and M.M. Lucio (eds) *The Politics of Quality in the Public Sector. The Management of Change.* London: Routledge: 44–64.

Rhodes, R. (1997) *Understanding Governance: Policy Networks, Governance, Reflexivity and Accountability.* Buckingham: Open University Press.

Scott, W.R. (1982) Managing professional work: three models of control for health organizations. *Health Services Research* 17: 213–40.

—— (2008) Lords of the dance: professionals as institutional agents. *Organization Studies* 29(2): 219–38.

Sehested, K. (2002) How new public management reforms challenge the roles of professionals. *International Journal of Public Administration* 25(12): 1513–38.

Sorensen, R. and Iedema, R. (2008) Redefining accountability in health care: managing the plurality of medical interests. *Health* 12(1): 87–106.

Sosial- og Helsedepartementet (1995) *Nasjonal strategi for kvalitetsutvikling i helsetjenesten 1995–2000.* Oslo: Sosial- og Helsedepartementet.

Sosial- og Helsedirektoratet (2005) *Og bedre skal det bli! Nasjonal strategi for kvalitetsforbedring i Social- og helsetjenesten.* Oslo: Sosial- og Helsedirektoratet.

—— (2007) *Hvordan komme vi fra visjoner til handling. Praksisfeltets anbefalinger for at oppnå god kvalitet på tjenestene i sosial- og helsetjenesten.* Oslo: Sosial- og Helsedirektoratet.

Sundhedsstyrelsen (1993) *National Strategi for Kvalitetsudvikling i Sundhedsvæsenet.* Copenhagen: Sundhedsstyrelsen og Sundhedsministeriet.

—— (1999) *Patientforløb og kvalitetsudvikling.* Copenhagen: Sundhedsstyrelsen.

Timmermans, T. (2008) Professions and their work: do market shelters protect professional interests? *Work and Occupations* 35(2): 164–88.

Vrangbæk, K. and Christiansen, T. (2005) Health policy in Denmark: leaving the decentralized welfare path? *Journal of Health Politics, Policy and Law* 30(1–2): 29–52.

Walshe, K. and Smith, J. (eds) (2006) *Healthcare Management.* Maidenhead: Open University Press/McGraw-Hill Education.

Witz, A. (1992) *Professions and Patriarchy.* London: Routledge.

World Health Organization (WHO) (1981) *Global Strategy for Health for All by the Year 2000.* Geneva: WHO. Available at http://whqlibdoc.who.int/publications/9241800038.pdf (accessed January 2012).

Part III

Leadership and public sector professionals

8 Universities under New Labour

Senior leaders' responses to government reforms and policy levers – findings from an ESRC project on public service leadership

Rosemary Deem

Introduction

The focus of this chapter is on the relationship between public service modernization policies in England (1997–2009), leadership development activities undertaken by leaders and their senior teams in six publicly funded universities in England and these respondents' perceptions of themselves as leading autonomous change in their institutions. The empirical base comprises interviews conducted in 2007 with senior leaders and their teams in six universities in England, repeat interviews with some of the same people in 2008 and interviews conducted with current and former higher education policy makers in 2008. These interviews were part of a UK Economic and Social Research Council project (Award number 000–23–1136) exploring change agency in public service organizations, perceptions and discourses of the New Labour government's public service modernization and reform programmes in health and education from 1997 onwards, particularly the extent to which those reforms have focused on the development of leadership capacity in public service organizations and the formation of national leadership bodies (hereafter referred to as the Change Agent or CAP project). The project looked at four public service sectors, schools, hospitals, community health services and universities but this paper is concerned only with the university element of the study.

New Labour came to power in 1997 and for a while their policies were not that different from those of the previous Conservative administration. However, from 2001 onwards, public service reform in general became a major pre-occupation of the New Labour administration, with the formation of an Office for Public Service Reform. As policy researchers have noted, public policies are complex phenomena and rarely get implemented in any straightforward way (Hill and Ham 1997). In the paper we utilize recent comparative work about the governance of European higher education and the notion of England as the prototype 'evaluative state' (Leisyte, de Boer and Enders 2006; Leisyte 2007), notions of distributed leadership (Gronn 2002) and ideologies of new managerialism in universities (Deem and Brehony 2005; Deem, Hillyard and Reed 2007).

Unlike most other public services in England, universities are not necessarily mainly funded from public sources. Some currently still receive the majority of their funding from the public purse (though this is about to change) but others have considerable unregulated income from other sources, including international students. This has two consequences. First, it means that English universities are different from other public services and have become more differentiated since the advent of variable home undergraduate student fees in the mid 2000s. Second, it has also led to a different attitude about the purposes of higher education on behalf of those who lead universities. Increasingly, the leaders of some English universities, particularly the research-intensive universities, do not appear to think of themselves as public service organizations (Deem 2006; Deem, Hillyard and Reed 2007). Thus we might expect to find that university leaders in England are not directly comparable with their other public service peers in health or schools and indeed expect to have considerable autonomy in deciding how their institutions run. On the other hand, this concern with autonomy dates back several decades to the 1970s and before, during which time the UK HE (higher education) system has shifted significantly from being a largely unregulated elite system to being highly regulated (Kogan and Hanney 2000). More recently, this regulation has included quality audit of teaching and research, a National Student Survey leading to league tables and controls on how many Home/EU students can be recruited. These regulatory activities have mostly operated via a series of 'hard' policy mechanisms such as the financial protocols and reporting systems of the Higher Education Funding Council for England, research selectivity exercises and the academic audit systems of the Quality Assurance Agency. However, the CAP project also explored 'softer' policy such as government documents, ministerial emphases on the importance of leadership and the emergence under New Labour of national leadership development bodies in both health and education.

In the paper, the question about how realistic university leaders' perceptions about their independence is carefully considered. Furthermore, there is also the issue about whether leadership development activities provided by the UK Leadership Foundation for Higher Education are entirely innocent of government policy. Both respondents and leadership development providers are deeply immersed, consciously or not, in current ways of doing things. At the same time, it is apparent that the balance between government and universities is shifting as more unregulated income (research/consultancy projects and international students) and variable undergraduate fees, begin to alter the public–private funding relationship. New Labour's term of office ended in April 2010. A new Conservative and Liberal Democrat government was formed in May 2010 but the publication of the Browne Review of university funding in autumn 2010 and the outcome of the Comprehensive Spending Review shortly afterwards have now led to proposals for unprecedented cuts in HE public expenditure on teaching and a plan for even higher Home/EU undergraduate fees but with continued government controls on student recruitment.

The ESRC 'Change Agent Project'

The project on which the paper is based is entitled 'Developing organization leaders as change agents in the public services' (or CAP). It was funded by the UK Economic and Social Research Council (May 2006 to April 2009). Its remit included analyzing the public service reforms in health and education of the New Labour government in England in the period 1997 to 2009 and the extent to which these reforms include a new emphasis on charismatic leadership and leadership development as one means of bringing about change in public service organizations. In addition, the project aimed to examine the views of public service leaders and their senior teams about their understanding of and identity in relation to leadership and change management in their organizations, how they perceived recent government attempts to restructure public services, the kinds of development support that leaders and aspiring leaders had sought, or were planning to seek and the extent to which development support had included using the services of a national leadership development body. A further interest lay in the extent to which national development bodies and other providers of leadership development reflected the ideas and approaches to change of government or encouraged participants to develop their own autonomous approach to change in their organizations. The study focused on four public services in England: secondary schools, hospitals, primary care (community health) trusts and universities. The project examined the development provision offered by three National Leadership Development Bodies (NLDBs), the National College for School Leadership (NCSL), the NHS Institute for Innovation and Improvement (NHSIII) and the Leadership Foundation for Higher Education (LFHE). All were set up since New Labour came to power and appear to be closely connected to their ideas about how public services organizations should be run (O'Reilly *et al.* 2007a; O'Reilly *et al.* 2007b).

In the project fieldwork, we used qualitative methodologies. First we utilized critical discourse analysis (Fairclough 1993; Fairclough 1995; Lukes 1995; Janks 1997) to examine key government, Labour party and national leadership body documents over the period 1997 to 2008. Second, we used semi-structured interviews (Kvale 1996; Gubrium and Holstein 2002) with key informants, including public service leaders and members of their senior teams, NLDB personnel and respondents from key stakeholder organizations (trade unions and professional bodies), in health, secondary schools and higher education as well as current and former policy makers and leadership developers.

In this paper, we focus on data from thirty interviews with leaders and aspiring leaders in six pre- and post-1992 universities in England conducted in summer 2007, repeat interviews with 19 respondents in 2008 and a small number of interviews conducted with current and former policy makers in 2008. The universities we selected ranged from research-intensive to highly teaching-intensive and were: Hopton, Furzedown and Valley (research-intensive universities) and Parklane, Longley and Little Oaks (all teaching-focused ex polytechnics). The names are pseudonyms.

Our respondents were largely chosen from the Senior Management groupings of each institution, and always included the Vice Chancellor (Rector) and at least three others in senior roles, the latter a mix of manager-academics (such as Deputy and Pro-Vice Chancellors and Faculty Deans) and senior administrators (such as finance directors, human resource directors or registrars). Interview questions focused on the respondents' higher education career biography and current leadership role, their work identity in relation to leadership, management and strategy, their views on the notion of leadership as a form of change agency, their experience of and views about the LFHE, the resources they drew upon for their development as leaders and their views on whether the government or institutions or both were responsible for driving the change agenda in UK higher education. In our second interviews we also asked what policy levers respondents thought were most likely to drive universities to do something. Our policy interviews targeted a small number of individuals who had either worked in government or in the HE funding body for England between 1997 and 2008. These interviews concentrated on how the respondents saw the relationship between policy makers and universities and their views on the importance of leadership to higher education and the relevance, if any, of leadership development to the sector.

New Labour, New Leaders? Leadership and change in public services 1997–2007

From when New Labour came to power in 1997, one of its major concerns was public service reform and modernization (rather like its Conservative predecessors), with particular emphasis on health and education as areas of high public expenditure and considerable public concern over standards of provision (especially in England). Subsequently, a series of key documents, including the 2001 and 2005 election manifestos, and various documents and White Papers on health, schools and higher education, set out New Labour's ambitious (and changing) plans for the modernization process of public services (O'Reilly *et al.* 2007a). Some of the content of these documents subsequently made its way into legislation such as the 2004 Higher Education Act, which introduced (among other things) variable fee levels for home undergraduate students.

Though some institutional autonomy has remained alongside government and funding council regulation, comparative studies of reforms to higher education governance have pointed out that the concept of 'steering at a distance' (Kickert 1995) is more applicable to higher education systems like the Netherlands. In that instance, there has been a shift from considerable central regulation of higher education organizations towards more autonomy for universities. By contrast, in the UK the process has moved in the opposite direction, from a laissez faire system in the 1950s to 1970s to a much higher degree of regulation of the higher education system from the 1980s onwards (de Boer, Leisyte and Enders 2006; Leisyte, de Boer and Enders 2006; Leisyte 2007).

New Labour's plans for transforming public services ranged from marketization and public–private partnership to public engagement with services and involvement of voluntary organizations in service provision. Aspects of this such as markets and private sector involvement arguably echoed the policies of the previous Conservative administration (Newman 2001; Driver and Martell 2006). Where New Labour does appear distinctive, however, is in its emphasis on leadership in the running and transformation of public services. As we have noted elsewhere, this emphasis on leadership is apparent through a whole series of different New Labour documents and policy statements from 1997 onwards but particularly since 2001 (O'Reilly *et al.* 2007b). A number of these documents note the importance of inspirational leaders in reshaping public services and the role of leaders as change agents, with freedom to act on the basis of their authority, expertise and skills but also having responsibilities to implement the government's agenda for change. The particular role of leaders in initiating *cultural* (as well as structural) change in organizations is also stressed. Leaders are seen as spearheading the government's efforts to modernize public services (O'Reilly *et al.* 2007a; O'Reilly *et al.* 2007b) and their leadership of front-line staff is emphasized as vital to achieving more responsive, effective and efficient public services.

It is unclear exactly how or why this shift of emphasis from management to leadership came about. However, it seems likely that one source was the concerns about state schools that had failed their Office for Standards in Education (OFSTED) standards inspection and how the difficulties of these schools might be overcome by appointing the 'right kind' of leadership (such as super-heads responsible for several schools or having run successful schools elsewhere).

In higher education, leadership was fostered in a different way than health and schools, which both had government-sponsored bodies. The Leadership Foundation for Higher Education (LFHE) was founded in 2004. Despite ostensibly being independent of government, its establishment was mentioned in the 2003 Government White Paper on the Future of Higher Education (Department for Education and Skills 2003). LFHE funding comes both from course fees and member services and from the four national higher education funding bodies (Leadership Foundation for Higher Education 2006). But it was intended that the public money input would reduce over time (Oakleigh Consulting 2006).

The LFHE itself may be completely free of direct government involvement but given the extensive reforms that both New Labour and the previous

Conservative administration embarked on in relation to UK higher education, leading to a view that England has become the prototype of the evaluative state (Leisyte, de Boer and Enders 2006), it is difficult to see how LFHE could operate entirely without reference to these reforms. In the sections that follow, we examine how our senior management team respondents in six UK universities see their role as leaders, the extent to which they inhabit ideas of inspirational leadership, how these leaders perceive the relative roles of leadership in universities *vis-à-vis* that of the government in reshaping higher education and how policy makers view the same process.

Universities and distributed leadership

As noted in the last section, the New Labour documents about education (and health) that we have been examining mention issues of leadership a good deal. These documents also privilege a form of charismatic leadership in which change revolves round a single individual in each public service organization, rather than distributed leadership which emphasizes a more interactive and collective concept of leadership not simply based on the actions of one person (Gronn 2002; Spillane 2006) and where several people may have a legitimate claim to the leadership and management of a single organization (Bolden, Petrov and Gosling 2008). Distributed and consensual leadership is common in public service organizations as other research demonstrates (Currie, Boyett and Suhomlinova 2005; Denis, Lamothe and Langley 2011). When we asked our university respondents about leadership in 2007, there was little mention of characteristics of charismatic leadership, in contrast to some discussions in a 1990s project on UK university management (Deem, Hillyard and Reed 2007). On the other hand, it was clear that Vice Chancellors did regard themselves as driving what happened in their institutions. Twenty out of thirty respondents explicitly mentioned distributed leadership in their interviews:

> I'm a member of the directorate; my portfolio is everything to do with the academic work of the university, all the student facing side of things, academic administration . . . and in terms of my more general role with the Vice Chancellor . . . I work closely with the Vice Chancellor doing all the things that aren't in that list that are the general things that go on in any university.
>
> (female PVC, Longley, post-1992)

Distributed leadership, with its division of labour, sharing of knowledge and expertise and a pooling of risks, is arguably less glamorous and less focused on one individual. It also does not depend on the qualities and skills of one person, which is the focus of much leadership development. Other researchers have found wide acceptance recently of the notion of distributed leadership in UK higher education, from committees to team-working of various kinds

(Petrov, Bolden and Gosling 2006; Petrov 2007; Bolden, Petrov and Gosling 2008).

As already noted, all six of the universities we researched for the CAP project had some kind of senior management group but the extent to which these groups operated as teams is probably somewhat variable (Kennie and Woodfield 2008). This respondent from a teaching focused university did think her institution operated team-based management:

> Well, my approach to running a department, or an institution, or whatever, is very much to set up a team, to get a team in place, who know what their role is, both individually and collectively, and to all work together to deliver that. Now, I see myself as part of the team, and yet not part of the team, and you have to get the balance right between telling people how you want it done, and not telling people how you want it done, but setting the broad outline and then letting them get on with it, because if you don't give them the responsibility they soon learn to lose the ability to act independently.
>
> (female VC, Little Oaks, post-1992)

On the other hand, we found one example of an approach that suggested a more VC-specific decision-making process, albeit with some element of consultation:

> When I came here I asked how many faculties there were, and nobody could quite answer the question. It was somewhere between eight and nine, it depended who you asked, and there were eighty something departments, maybe more, complete chaos, and it's actually not atypical of where universities were . . . they were in the process of trying to sort out what they should do instead, because they all knew it was nonsense, so I spent a long time with the then eighty heads of department on away days, away-weekends, chewing over the strategy for the institution and a structure. We, first of all, worked out the structure, because I insisted we should have a managerial culture, of some sort, that was better than what we had, and that power should be aligned with accountability.
>
> (male VC, Furzedown, pre-1992)

If nevertheless, our respondents were, in the main, convinced of their distributed approach to leading universities rather than a charismatic approach, which suggests that the 'soft' policy lever used by New Labour has not worked well in the higher education sector, the extent to which our interviewees saw themselves as change agents was more varied. Only eight interviewees identified with 'change agent' as a descriptor. A minority rejected the notion because they saw it as an ideological term associated with government attempts to change things in higher education without paying too much attention to what institutions themselves wanted to do:

Implementing government reform? I think I'm responding to it, and there's a whole set of things that I'm doing at the moment . . . I'd hate to be a sort of 'kept' change agent on behalf of the government, if you see what I mean?

(male DVC, Furzedown, pre-1992)

However, dealing with change *per se* is, according to our respondents, now seen as a key part of most senior roles in UK HE. A small number of respondents with academic backgrounds were particularly keen to be involved in change agency activities, which they felt (or hoped) got easier as they climbed the managerial ladder:

. . . when I was a Head of Department, one of reasons I got very frustrated with the job is that I didn't seem to be able to act as an agent of change, that I was simply reactive and never proactive, and my hope, and my expectation is, in this new role, the balance between reaction and being proactive will alter.

(female Dean, Parklane, post-1992)

Senior administrators interviewed also saw themselves as significantly engaged in change and change management, as in this quote from a finance director:

. . . any change in the organization will have financial ramifications. Either because it's a change that involves restructuring the organization, changing things and therefore you've got to look at what that will mean to income and expenditure streams, and the balances between different activities, because obviously you may look at changing the structure of the institution.

(female Senior Administrator, Longley, post-1992)

The views of our sample, with respect to distributed management then, are somewhat at odds with those ideas expressed in New Labour's writing and pronouncements on the role and type of leadership they wished to see in public service organizations, which tended to eschew distributed leadership in favour of more person-specific notions of inspirational leadership (O'Reilly *et al.* 2007a; O'Reilly *et al.* 2007b). The idea of leaders as change agents was better received if regarded as something not linked to government policy, which leads us on to consider what effect leadership development was perceived to have had on our respondents and their institutions.

The Leadership Foundation for Higher Education: a support for government reforms?

All thirty respondents were aware of the existence and remit of the Leadership Foundation, and twenty-two had some personal experience of using its services, though sometimes this involved only one-off events. Ten people had participated in the LFHE course aimed at potential Vice Chancellors, the Top Management Programme (TMP). The fact that not everyone had experienced more substantial provision is partially attributable to the fact that sixteen of our interviewees were well established in their leadership careers when LFHE was established in 2004. Significant involvement in leadership development was regarded by many of our respondents as something best engaged in at the beginning of a leadership career. At the time of interviewing, most respondents were not currently engaged in any significant leadership development activities unless they were relatively new to leadership work or, if, as in this case, they hoped to become a Vice Chancellor:

> Yeah, I do go to Leadership Foundation things, and so on, but the most recent thing is that I've been accepted on to the Top Management Programme . . . and that starts in September, and I had to have the support of my Vice Chancellor, and the financial support, because it's jolly expensive, I mean it's about, I think, about £14,000, or something now. But, I think, you know, I've . . . that is both to support me in my current role, but I've also got a very strong eye on its use in terms of my further career paths . . . I was interviewed for a Vice Chancellor position recently, and the first question that I was asked was why I hadn't been on the TMP.
>
> (female PVC, Longley, post-1992)

Those who had been on LFHE courses, including the extensive TMP as well as shorter workshops and day events, did not think it was promoting any particular kind of change approach, including government agendas, for HE:

> I mean the thing about the Top Management Programme is really, I mean the best bits of it are about reflection and being exposed to a variety of different ideas, and the other part is just, again, you know, it's the networking thing, sharing common experiences, so, no, they didn't promote any particular . . . I mean they promoted the idea that change was an important thing that you had to deal with, and they said, you know . . . the different ways of meeting it.
>
> (male DVC, Furzedown, pre-1992)

> *Respondent*: It wasn't specifically about [being] a change agent, but it did acknowledge that the one constant in higher education is change.
>
> *Interviewer*: Did it promote a particular approach to managing change?
>
> *Respondent*: No.
>
> (female Dean, Parklane, post-1992)

Though LFHE was criticized by some of our interviewees for the nature of some of its provision, this was not on the basis that LFHE had adopted government change agendas. Indeed, the great majority of respondents did not feel that any of the development activities they had attended (whether provided by LFHE or not) had targeted them as agents for change in support of government agendas. Some respondents mentioned the range of types of LFHE provision as being suited to a variety of different kinds of change activities:

> . . . it wasn't a skills based course . . . it was much, much broader than that. I think it helped you in terms of very much the wider policy agenda, and an idea how different organizations operate.
>
> (female Dean, Little Oaks, post-1992)

So, even if New Labour's public service modernization agendas and associated messages could have potentially been carried by the activities of the leadership bodies for which it was directly responsible as in schools, the independence of the LFHE was firmly asserted by those of our respondents with substantial experience of its work. Nevertheless, there was no evidence that alternatives to the status quo were actively considered in LFHE courses. At the same time, LFHE's provision is nevertheless important in the UK HE sector in a rather unexpected way. Going on the Top Management Programme is entirely voluntary (unlike the National Professional Qualification for Headship, which is run by the National College for School Leadership and is compulsory for anyone wanting to become a English state school head-teacher). But increasingly there is an expectation among panels selecting new UK Vice Chancellors that candidates will have been on the TMP. Most UK Vice Chancellor appointments are now handled by private headhunting agencies (Newman 2007) who often derive lists of candidates from those who are on or have recently completed the TMP. So TMP has become *de facto* the qualification sought, even though attendance on it is completely voluntary.

We now move on to examine how our respondents saw the process of reform and change in higher education. Did they think the current and recent past reshaping was down to the initiatives of the sector itself or attributable to government efforts at becoming an 'evaluative state' (Leisyte, de Boer and Enders 2006)? As we shall see, the responses were somewhere in between.

Reshaping higher education – whose agenda, whose money?

In general, it would be fair to say that the New Labour government's current policy agenda for higher education was regarded with some scepticism by many of our respondents. Indeed, several people felt that government under-valued the contribution that higher education could make to society and, in so doing, also undermined the very notions of leadership that New Labour claimed to espouse:

> Well, I cynically think that they want the leaders to accept government thinking and policy, and to implement them, and to me that isn't really

leadership. I think they undervalue HE and its influence on society, and they see it more as a kind of professional training programme, almost an extension of school, they don't really, I don't think, understand the importance of the research that's done; in all the disciplines, nationally in the universities, and how it's totally important for economic wellbeing in the nation. They think that's all done in industry. My experience is it's all initiated in universities; industry might pick up a good idea here and there, and develop it, but all the quality, innovative initial work . . . is in HE.

(male PVC, Hopton, pre-1992)

Scepticism and cynicism arose not least because of the pace of change over the last three decades but also in relation to the proliferation of contradictory policies (for instance that all universities should embrace widening participation while also continuing to do high quality research) and because the government, at the same time as overtly regulating higher education (e.g. in respect of the fees charged to home undergraduates), also wanted to reduce universities' dependence on public funding:

I resent the fact that the government gives us 30% of the money, they think they can control 100% of what we do. So, I object to that very much, and I'm a very staunch advocate of more autonomy because the more successful universities in the world have the greatest autonomy.

(male VC, Furzedown, pre-1992)

Government, in other words, was seen as wanting compliance with its wishes on higher education despite offering decreasingly less public resource in return and without really understanding how universities function:

I think they want leaders to comply. You know, they come out with some statements from the Department, or from Ministers who are singularly ill-informed, and don't really understand how universities work.

(male DVC, Parklane, post-1992)

There was also some resistance among our respondents to the idea that government played a major role in the reshaping of higher education:

Of course. We have our own initiatives as well, and yes, more that then responding to government initiatives in many ways. Yes, it would be wrong to say that our lives are driven by what the government wants, and neither should it be, and neither should the government want it to be, although that's a much harder point to get over.

(male Vice Chancellor, Longley, post-1992)

We detected some ambivalence about public funding in our interviewees' responses about government policy and government money. On the one hand, respondents in most institutions were somewhat dependent on public funding (particularly for teaching but also for research in the research-intensives) but on the other hand they resented the regulation and constraints that came with it. This view was confirmed by our interviews with policy makers, who declared that university leaders were definitely ambivalent (and contradictory) about public money and its implications, declaring their wish for independence but at the same time asking for public funding for the sustaining of expensive science subjects or initiatives around learning and teaching.

A number of our interviewees certainly did not believe that the government was the main driving force in bringing about positive changes in higher education institutions. Rather, they believed that they worked hard to bring about change that was beneficial for students, staff, employers, parents, industry and the country in general, whether or not this was change that government also embraced. At the same time, Vice Chancellors were also free to internally restructure their institutions as they saw fit. There was some evidence of this, as, for example, in academic unit streamlining at Furzedown, a current trend in a number of pre-1992 universities in the UK (Taylor 2006). Where there was, on occasions, perceived to be a coalescence between what leaders wanted and what the government desired, as with widening participation, this was seen as a happy coincidence:

> ... when I promote widening participation, I don't necessarily think of it as a government policy. I think it's something that I think is really good for people to engage in higher education and be part of it. That's my starting point. It happens that doing that also delivers on a government objective.
>
> (male VC, Hopton, pre-1992)

However, though in this case the value-commitment seems genuine, it is debatable whether the widening participation agenda would be followed as much by English universities if there was no public money involved and if there was no government agency overseeing fair access.

Some interviewees described in detail the tensions of dealing with government. So for instance, it was alleged that government had established a market in which all universities had to operate and that this was problematic. However, it would seem from other indications that most were keen to promote their own institution and that few institutions distanced themselves from international league tables of universities (Deem, Mok and Lucas 2007; Deem, Mok and Lucas 2008). It was also suggested to us that government (or the HE funding body) also promoted various initiatives over which individual institutions had, in theory, more choice about whether to respond or not but in which, in practice, they all felt obliged to participate in case they lost market advantage. One example of this was the 2004 Centres for Excellence in Teaching and Learning initiative, which sought to inject significant funding (including capital for new buildings) into teaching. It was clear that one or two respondents in our study still felt very bitter about not having had their CETL bid funded, a point also emphasized by other research on this topic (Hannan and Gosling 2005). But no one had obliged them to make a bid at all.

One of our policy maker respondents suggested that even when universities were not forced to follow what government or the funding council suggested, they still did so. Indeed the great bulk of university funding has until now come in the form of a block grant but it seems likely that although most universities make some departures from the exact formulae, wide variations are exceptional (for example funding science teaching less generously than arts funding or not giving most Research Assessment research funding to those with the highest quality profiles). One or two respondents suggested that the extent to which government could be ignored depended on the type of institution one worked in:

> We, we are independent; I mean universities are independent institutions. That said, we get the majority of our funding from HEFCE . . . so we have a responsibility to be responsive to the country's needs, but I suspect that a university like this, post-'92, big widening access agenda, sees life in those terms much more than Oxford or Cambridge, or a Russell Group university, who are much more inclined to stand proud of government.
>
> (female VC, Little Oaks, post-1992)

Overall, most respondents described the HE environment in England as one in which there were a series of different external influences, so that universities developed their own 'mission' and then negotiated their own course through the various agencies and influences. In this respect, interviewees saw their leadership responsibilities as principally being to their institution, its development and the nurturing and sustaining of institutional core values. As such, they did not see themselves as implementers of government reforms, but as being much more independent than other public service organizations such as schools or hospitals:

> I always think when I meet anyone senior from the NHS, thank God we don't have to run the NHS, it would drive me mad. I mean just the . . . they're in to change, and of course you're looking at the NHS aren't you, they're in to change but then change to my way of thinking so much more rapid that they're no sooner into one initiative then they're on another, and while higher education is in to initiatives I don't think it's that frenetic.
>
> (male VC, Hopton, pre-1992)

In the second round of interviews with our university respondents, we asked them what policy levers they thought had been particularly effective. Policy initiatives from the Higher Education Funding Council (four responses) and anything linked to money (eight responses) were the most commonly given answers. Though only two leaders mentioned markets directly, the notion of the importance of markets in driving forward change in UK HE was an implicit assumption in several responses:

> Well, this sounds terribly glib, but it's the market, and I mean, you know, it may not be popular and it may not be something mostly I'd like to admit to, but I think it's very difficult to buck the market. We don't of course exist, thankfully, in a complete market ... I think that poses the most significant challenges for leadership, because two aspects, most, a lot of institutions don't know where they are, not a minor point I'm afraid. A lot of institutions don't actually know where they are in the system ... How many institutions claim to be the top post-92, how many institutions claim to be top twenty, how many institutions claim to be research intensive, you know, how many institutions claim to be the best business facing? ... I think we're moving to a market with the connotations of market failure ...
>
> (VC, Valley, pre-1992)

Particular policies that were considered to have led to significant change in recent years were firstly the Research Assessment Exercise or RAE (first established in 1986), which involves periodic peer review, discipline by discipline, of a small selection of academics' outputs plus a narrative about research culture and infrastructure and data about research funding and research student numbers and completions and second, the UK National Student Survey. The latter was initiated in 2005 and is based on a questionnaire to final year undergraduate students about their courses, assessment, personal development, resources and general organization and management. The RAE was seen as having massively changed the quality and quantity of research and the attention paid to research activity:

> ... the RAE has been an overwhelmingly powerful lever. I don't think there are many. I mean there are plenty of people who rail against it, and complain about the amount of time that it takes up and so on, but I think what is pretty undeniable is that there's a very, very close correlation between the introduction of the RAE and the rise of the quality of research, and you know, I don't think that's accidental at all, you know, if people are adept in organizations like these, at looking at the, looking at the rules and seeing how they can use those to their advantage, and I'm chairing one of the RAE panels and it's very interesting to look at the effect that that's had on the returns of individual institutions, and I was on the 2001 RAE and now looking at things five or six years later what is remarkable is the impact.
>
> (Dean, Furzedown)

The NSS, on the other hand, had caused much more attention to be paid to the undergraduate student experience, although often because it was an annual survey there was a particular focus on those 'quick fixes' which could be accomplished in a year. The RAE by contrast, being only every five to six years, allowed more sustained changes to be made:

> ... the biggest lever that I've seen has been the National Student Survey. Now I think that universities are such complicated bodies it's very difficult to characterise them, and so the newspapers' league tables are very influential, but they're not a government, they're not the government thing ... In the National Student Survey we came in a sense top, we actually came below a few, but we came top if you look at universities with undergraduate students on campus ...
>
> (PVC, Hopton)

Finally, one leader gave an interesting response about funding and cultural change, which implicitly underpins much of what has happened to UK HE in the past two decades:

> I suppose it has to be funding ultimately, for this university, but the other powerful levers I think have been, actually I think the cultural change that there's been in universities over the past twenty years has become a powerful lever in its own right. I don't think it's just a response, I think it's actually become a lever itself, in terms of, you know, the generation that I'm in. When I compare myself with leaders twenty years ago there is now just an assumption that we will respond to X, and Y, and Z, there's an assumption that we will, you know, recognise that running university is as much about running 150 million pound organization, as it is about providing academic leadership. I mean all of those things were not givens twenty years ago, but they are givens now.
>
> (PVC, Little Oaks)

All of this suggests, for our interviewees at least, that New Labour's plans and intentions for higher education reform and for the transformation of leadership received a mixed reception, except where they coincided with the values and objectives of university leaders themselves. Indeed new Labour's policies were seen, so we were told by a number of respondents, as a source of considerable ambiguity and uncertainty in the higher education sector. There was a good deal of cynicism and scepticism among our more senior respondents over the extent to which government sought to control higher education in England, while simultaneously urging institutions to seek more money from non-public sources. It would appear from the accounts provided to us that any beneficial reshaping of higher education is believed by leaders to have been as much the result of the efforts of individual institutions and their leaders as the outcome of government initiatives. Add this to our respondents' views that the LFHE does not generally reflect government reform agendas or approaches to change in its activities and services and it is hard to see how the government reform agenda for HE could be fully accomplished in the face of such clearly expressed resistance from the university senior leaders to whom we talked. However, had we conducted the research in 2010–11 when very radical changes to funding began to be suggested (such as the abolition of all public funding for social science and humanities) then maybe we would have reached a different conclusion, as Vice Chancellors put up barely any opposition to the plans of the coalition government. We could conclude that soft policy levers (discourses of charismatic leadership, leadership development) definitely did not work in New Labour's favour while hard levers, such as taking away funding, do work. From the outside, it appears that many universities in England do seem to have complied with what government wants on a wide variety of issues, even if this is not entirely consistent with the accounts leaders give.

Conclusion: following government agendas or subverting them?

In the paper we have briefly explored some of the dimensions of the UK New Labour administration's attempts to modernize public services by promoting particular concepts of leadership and facilitating the establishment of national leadership development bodies. We then examined recent interview data from senior management groups in six universities, one strand in the CAP project on public service modernization, change agency and leadership development in England. We have noted the extent to which New Labour's efforts to become an 'evaluative state' (Leisyte, de Boer and Enders 2006) in relation to higher education and their endeavours to present leadership as an individual inspirational activity designed to transform public services have not been embraced by our interviewees.

There was little support evident in the accounts we were offered for a notion of university leadership that relied on inspiration and charisma. Rather, most spoke of the significance of distributed leadership in their senior management teams. This is consistent with other research on public service leadership that talks of process driven consensual distributed leadership (Currie, Boyett and Suhomlinova 2005; Denis, Lamothe and Langley 2011), though as noted earlier, English universities are far from fully publicly funded and are also arguably more globally oriented (at least in respect of student recruitment and research) than other public services in England, such as health or state schools. So it is interesting to note that they still display some features of the leadership of other more heavily state funded services in western societies.

Respondents did not believe that the role of the recently established Leadership Foundation for Higher Education was one that particularly supported government policies and plans for the higher education sector. Insofar as interviewees had experienced significant LFHE development provision (and only nine had), its training was seen to focus on broad notions of institutional change, conceptions of leadership and change strategies, not on strategies of which government might approve.

When asked about the extent to which change occurred in universities as a result of government reform policies in higher education, there was an emerging consensus that these policies were complicated, lacked consistency, were often at odds with each other and were frequently not properly resourced. What organizational leaders claimed that they tried to do was to mediate these policies in the context of their own institution and in relation to shared institutional values, as well as pursuing reform agendas of their own, such as streamlining organizational units. There was also a strong reaction among many of our respondents to the manner in which the current UK government wanted to control what universities did, without fully recognizing either the extent to which private as well as public money was now flowing into the sector or really understanding how universities actually worked. Thus, the accounts emerging from our university interviews supported a view that it is university leaders, working in a distributed fashion, who by mediating government policies are reshaping universities. Such a perception adds weight to the view, which has been stated by both Universities UK and by the Leadership Foundation for Higher Education (Deem 2006), that UK universities are no longer a public service. It also suggests that New Labour's attempts to reform and change UK universities in particular ways and its efforts to promote inspirational leadership in public service organizations may have met with considerable resistance in higher education in England. Hence the soft policy levers of charismatic leadership discourse and leadership development do not appear not to have worked well, though direct policy and market levers are acknowledged to have worked much better, as is becoming evident in the more far reaching changes made to funding by the coalition Conservative and Liberal Democrat government formed in 2010. Resistance and mediation by university leaders may prove no longer sufficient to retain university autonomy despite huge reductions in public funding.

Acknowledgements

We would like to thank the six universities that allowed us access to their Senior Management Teams and the former and current policy makers who were willing to be interviewed. Thanks are also due to the other members of the ESRC CAP project team at Cardiff, especially Dermot O'Reilly and Mike Wallace for their work on the framework of the study, which we have drawn on here, and Paula Mullins, our skilful project administrator. Participants at an invited symposium on leadership held at Windsor in April 2008 also provided very useful feedback on an earlier draft of the paper.

References

Bolden, R., G. Petrov and J. Gosling (2008) *Developing Collective Leadership in Higher Education*. London: Leadership Foundation for Higher Education. Retrieved January 2010 from www.lfhe.ac.uk/protected_login_form.html?item=bolden.pdf.

Currie, G., I. Boyett and O. Suhomlinova (2005) Transformational leadership within secondary schools in England. Panacea for organisational ills? *Public Administration* 83(2): 265–296.

de Boer, H.F., L. Leisyte and J. Enders (2006) The Netherlands: 'steering from a distance'. *Reforming University Governance: Changing Conditions for Research in Four European Countries*. Eds B. Kehm and U. Lanzendorf. Bonn: Lemmens: 59–96.

Deem, R. (2006) Changing research perspectives on the management of higher education: can research permeate the activities of manager-academics? *Higher Education Quarterly* 60(3): 203–228.

Deem, R. and K.J. Brehony (2005) Management as ideology: the case of 'new managerialism' in higher education. *Oxford Review of Education* 31(2): 213–231.

Deem, R., S. Hillyard and M. Reed (2007) *Knowledge, Higher Education and the New Managerialism: The Changing Management of UK Universities*. Oxford: Oxford University Press.

Deem, R., K.H. Mok and L. Lucas (2007) Transforming higher education in whose image? Exploring the concept of the 'world class' university in Europe and Asia. Retrieved September 2007 from http://recordings.wun.ac.uk/id/2007/.

—— (2008) Transforming higher education in whose image? Exploring the concept of the 'world class' university in Europe and Asia. *Higher Education Policy* 21(1): 83–97.

Denis, J.-L., L. Lamothe and A. Langley (2011) The dynamics of collective leadership and strategic change in pluralistic organizations. *Organizing Health Services*. Eds G. Currie and M. Kitchener. London: Sage.

Department for Education and Skills (2003) *The Future of Higher Education*. London: DfES. Retrieved June 2006 from www.dfes.gov.uk/highereducation/hestrategy/.

Driver, S. and L. Martell (2006) *New Labour: Politics after Thatcherism*. Cambridge: Polity Press.

Fairclough, N. (1993) Critical discourse analysis and the marketisation of public discourse. *Discourse and Society* 4(2): 133–168.

—— (1995) *Critical Discourse Analysis*. London: Longman.

Gronn, P.C. (2002) Distributed leadership as a unit of analysis. *Leadership Quarterly* 13(4): 423–451.

Gubrium, J.F. and J.A. Holstein (eds) (2002) *Handbook of Interview Research Context and Method*. Thousand Oaks, CA and London: Sage.

Hannan, A. and D. Gosling (2005) Responses to a policy initiative: the cases of Centres for Excellence in Teaching and Learning. Unpublished paper presented to the Society for Research into Higher Education Annual Conference, 13–15 December, University of Edinburgh.

Hill, M. and C. Ham (1997) *The Policy Process in the Modern State*. London: Prentice Hall.

Janks, H. (1997) Critical discourse analysis as a research tool. *Discourse* 18(3): 329–342.

Kennie, T. and S. Woodfield (2008) 'Teamwork' or working as a team? The theory and practice of top team working in UK higher education. *Higher Education Quarterly* 62(4): 397–415.

Kickert, R. (1995) Steering at a distance: a new paradigm of public governance in Dutch higher education. *Governance: An International Journal of Policy and Administration* 8(1): 135–157.

Kogan, M. and S. Hanney (2000) *Reforming Higher Education*. London: Jessica Kingsley.

Kvale, S. (1996) *Interviews: An Introduction to Qualitative Research Interviewing*. London: Sage.

Leadership Foundation for Higher Education (2006) About us. Retrieved June 2006 from www.lfhe.ac.uk/about/.

Leisyte, L. (2007) University Governance and Academic Research. Centre for Higher Education Policy Studies, University of Twente, Enschede, the Netherlands. Ph.D. dissertation.

Leisyte, L., H.F. de Boer and J. Enders (2006) England: the prototype of the 'Evaluative State'. *Reforming University Governance: Changing Conditions for Research in Four European Countries*. Eds B. Kehm and U. Lanzendorf. Bonn: Lemmens: 21–58.

Lukes, A. (1995) Text and discourse in education: an introduction to critical discourse analysis. *Review of Research in Education 21*. Ed. M.W. Apple. New York: American Education Research Association.

Newman, J. (2001) *Modernising Governance: New Labour, Policy and Society*. London: Sage.

Newman, M. (2007) Headhunters' picks dominate V-C hiring. Retrieved May 2008 from www.timeshighereducation.co.uk/story.asp?storyCode=311295&sectioncode=26.

O'Reilly, D., M. Wallace, R. Deem, J. Morris and M. Reed (2007a) The discursive representations of leadership development in the reform of UK health and education public services. Unpublished paper given to the Political Studies Association Conference, 11–13 April , University of Bath.

—— (2007b) The managerial innovation of national leadership development bodies: acculturating change agents for public service reform in England. Unpublished paper given to the International Research Society of Public Management Conference, 4–7 April, Potsdam, Germany.

Oakleigh Consulting (2006) *Final Report: Interim Evaluation of the Leadership Foundation for Higher Education*. Retrieved September 2006 from www.lfhe.ac.uk/about/history/evaluation.html.

Petrov, G. (2007) 'No more heroes?' Rhetoric and reality of distributed leadership in higher education. Retrieved August 2007 from www.bristol.ac.uk/education/research/networks/henetsw.

Petrov, G., R. Bolden and J. Gosling (2006) Developing collective leadership in higher education: interim report summary. Retrieved August 2007 from www.lfhe.ac.uk/research/projects/goslingsummary1.pdf/.

Spillane, J.P. (2006) *Distributed Leadership*. San Francisco: Jossey Bass.

Taylor, J. (2006) 'Big is beautiful'. Organisational change in universities in the United Kingdom: new models of institutional management and the changing role of academic staff. *Higher Education in Europe* 31(3): 251–273.

9 Academic leadership and its effects on professional autonomy

Christine Teelken

Introduction

As a result of socio-economic and political developments, such as budget constraints, accountability for quality, 'massification', and decentralization of higher education (e.g. Bryson, 2004), universities all over Europe have adopted organizational strategies, structures, technologies, management instruments and values that are commonly found in the private business sector (Aucoin, 1990; Deem, 1998). This trend of copying techniques of the private sector by public organizations is 'one of the earliest features of New Public Management, and remains one of the most enduring' (Boyne, 2002: 97) and may even go further back then the actual term NPM or 'managerialism' (Hood, 1991, 1995; Pollitt, 1993).

Some researchers suggest that ' "some dose" of "managerialism" in the right proportion and in the right context' may be useful in universities and that it positively affects the quality of job performance (Chan, 2001: 109). This research is challenged by others who argue that managerialism works against its own intentions of efficient and effective quality improvement (see also Bryson, 2004; Davies and Thomas, 2002; Thornhill *et al.*, 1996; Trow, 1994).

It is within this changing context of a more managerial university that we want to investigate and further discuss the role of the academic leader. For this purpose, we analyzed data, which has been collected in a study that involved the impact of NPM and managerialism on the university systems in three countries, the Netherlands, Sweden and the UK (Teelken, forthcoming), and consisted of document analysis and extensive interviews with forty-eight academics carried out in 2007. Particular emphasis will be laid on the perceptions of the respondents (the academics) and their academic leaders.

In line with Chapter 4 by Fitzgerald *et al.*, the focus of this chapter aims at the micro-processes of change and the roles of actors. Several authors have drawn attention to the need for further research on the roles of individuals, implying a need for a distinct micro institutional perspective (DiMaggio and Powell, 1991). This contrasts with the former focus of institutional theory, which largely concentrated on the organizational and inter-organizational level of analysis recording the conditions for stability and tracks of change (Greenwood and Hinings, 1988; Cooper *et al.*, 1996). As Fitzgerald *et al.* explain, other authors such as McKinlay and Scherer (2000) and Balogun and Johnson (2004) plead for further examination of leadership roles in change, focusing on the increasingly problematic role for middle managers attempting to lead change in complex settings.

While Fitzgerald *et al.*'s chapter focuses on the (clinical) leaders themselves, this chapter attempts to analyze and describe how the academic leaders are perceived by the academic workforce.

The concept of academic leadership

The introductory chapters of this book have laid out the main schools of thought on leaders and leadership, e.g. Bess and Goldman (2001) distinguished the situational, charismatic, transformational, path-goal, leader-member exchange models as influential approaches to core leadership theories.

In line with Verbree *et al.* (2012a), we define academic leadership here as 'the ability to organize, manage and lead researchers and the research group, consequently leading to a variety of tasks, with both a more managerial as well as an academic character.' Verbree *et al.* (2012b) distinguish three practices of academic leadership: 1) Organizational design, which refers particularly to acquiring and combining resources, 2) Internal leadership and management, which involves the management of the research process and the direction of researchers, 3) External leadership and management, implying directing the activities of the group within their academic and societal environment.

On the basis of these concepts, definitions and practices, we intend to answer the following research questions:

1 What does academic leadership mean and how do academics perceive academic leadership within a context of managerialism in the higher education sector in the Netherlands, Sweden and the UK?
2 What are the implications of the growth of a more managerial approach for leadership in current public services organizations?
3 What kind of responses to the leadership discourse and practices can we find, when academic professionals are moving into more managerial roles? What kind of impact do the academics experience in their daily work?

While public leadership in general should be considered as under increased scrutiny, for example through the effects of the recent financial crises (Westen, 2011), as well as through older, persistent developments such as New Public Management (NPM), this scrutiny is particularly crucial and draconian in the academic sector. Through NPM or its more nuanced conceptualization 'managerialism' (e.g. Deem, Hillyard and Reed, 2007) academics find themselves under increased pressure for accountability towards their organizations. This accountability is visible in the form of publication pressures and an emphasis on fundraising, but also towards students, colleagues, competing research groups, the university management and, at different levels, department, faculty, university and even at (inter)national policy level including international research bodies.

Managerialism has a dual impact on the nature and activities of academic leadership. On the one hand, it provides the academic leaders with more and more extensive tools at hand, consequently enlarging their possibilities in setting targets for their department or research group, evaluating the performances of academics and giving rewards or issuing sanctions. On the other hand, it makes the position of the academic leader much more complex and diffuse; it is time consuming, frustrating and encourages contradictory behaviour. This is because the measurability of the actual quality of research and teaching is limited and therefore the tools available to the department or research group leaders (e.g. measuring the number of publications) do not always do justice to the academics and their work (Teelken, 2008).

In order to deal with this dual impact, academic leaders have to draw up a balance between various forms of leadership. An important distinction can be made between the content and the process of academic leadership. While focusing on the content of their work, which refers to the primary process of academic work such as teaching and research, academic are, for example, involved in forming a coherent research group, trying to 'assemble all faces in the same direction' (quote from one Dutch interview). Concerning the leadership process, this involves having to deal with increased control and bureaucratic measures, such as the impact from external forces such as visitation and accreditation procedures, which may result in more stress, a limited autonomy for the academics and reduced availability of funding.

The question remains whether academic leaders are equipped to deal with such challenges. Should we consider these leaders as representing public tasks or as managers with a preliminary internal focus? Or should we see them as charismatic leaders who precede their group of academic followers through the current flow of reorganizations? Can they combine this type of leadership with their administrative responsibilities – for example, focusing on financial issues, preparing for accreditation procedures and the registration of publication? How do they combine their different logics in such a 'Janus faced' position and how do they manage such potentially conflicting demands and expectations? Are they able to impose bureaucratic measures and sanctions upon academics who consider their professional autonomy as an established right?

After this brief introduction into the dual character of academic leadership and the formulation of the research questions, we will provide an overview of the current research available, followed by the findings of my own research. Subsequently, the research questions will be answered in the conclusions, leading to a brief discussion.

Current status of research on academic leadership

Before we attempt to answer the research questions, a broader overview of current empirical research in the area of academic leadership will be provided. With academic leaders, we refer here to vice-chancellors, deans, head of departments and professors, for example. For this purpose, we have reviewed three different streams of empirical research on academic leadership, in order to shed light on the diversity and broadness of this current topic. Consequently, the available research will help us to choose the mayor themes in this field, which will structure the presentation of my own empirical research and assist in answering the research questions in a more contextual manner.

First, we will discuss the extensive empirical research as has been carried out by Rosemary Deem and others (2010) since 1990, based on interviews among a large number of vice-presidents as well as other sources. She also draws significantly from her own experiences as vice-principal, dean and research director at the Universities of Lancaster, Bristol and Royal Holloway, providing further depth to her research.

Second, we provide various studies carried out by Van der Weijden *et al.* (2009) and Verbree *et al.* (2012a, 2012b), focusing on research leaders of bio-medical groups in the Netherlands, based on longitudinal data, which is mainly quantitative.

Third, we will go into the issue of grass root leadership in the academic sector as discussed by Hartley (2009) and Kezal (2009). These three streams of empirical research will allow us to examine the complexity of academic leadership. Consequently the issues and findings are further explored on the basis of my own, empirical study (Teelken, forthcoming), involving 48 interviews carried out in three countries.

The inaugural lecture by Rosemary Deem (2010) provides us with five reasons for considering the widening scope of the purposes of universities, and then the important issue of leadership within them. These reasons explain to us why they are making their tasks more strenuous and more ambiguous:

1   The move of the higher education system from an elite to a mass system, making concerns of the institutional missions and differentiation within the system (for example, creating a so-called hierarchy within the university sector) a much broader discussion, which we do not have the space to discuss further here.
2   The traditional focus on teaching and research has expanded towards more entrepreneurial activities, including the increased emphasis on obtaining external funding.
3   More emphasis on leadership and management, for example, new managerialism and corporate management, which resulted in new forms and techniques, such as especially performance measurement.
4   The expansion and use of new technologies, enabling a weaker link between location and communication, and stimulating the massive rise of social networking sites and other forms of ICT-communication.
5   Engaging a wider public than students and alumni.

A couple of interesting observations are derived from the research carried out by Deem and others (Deem, Fulton *et al.*, 2001; Deem, Hillyard and Reed, 2007). They used the term 'manager-academic', hence emphasizing the ambiguous nature of such a profession. From her earlier research can be derived that 'how successful academics ended up travelling down a management and leadership path . . . did not necessarily lead anywhere in career terms' (Deem, 2010: 9), particularly in the 1990s and in the established UK universities. Another interesting remark involves the deliberate tendency to choose leaders who are amateurs and do not have the skills or the expertise, and sometimes not even the intention to take up a leadership role. This may explain why there is little tendency towards excellence in leadership among academics (Deem, 2009). In addition, Deem (2010) explains that the tendency for externally appointed leaders (if not carefully controlled) can result in headhunters actually upsetting the fundamental values of universities, while often little attention is paid to diversity, consequently continuing the male, white dominance of universities, while transparency of appointment procedures remains still far off (e.g. Van den Brink, 2009).

The study carried out by Van der Weijden *et al.* (2009) concerns an investigation of bio-medical research groups in the Netherlands, with particular emphasis on the management and leadership within these groups, and their impact on the group performance. The data have been collected in two stages (2002 and 2007) among respectively 137 and 188 research leaders, consequently enabling a longitudinal comparison. A third round of data collection has been carried out in 2010. The research groups showed an ideal span of control of about 10 persons or FTEs.

Despite acknowledging that the research groups are under closer external scrutiny and being forced to obtain their own funding (e.g. through the Dutch research council and charity funds), internal management features still play a crucial role. Verbree *et al.* (2012a) distinguish three developments in the current science system itself, which have direct consequences for the role of academic leadership, particularly stimulating the entrepreneurial roles of the leaders:

1   Increased pressures towards academic excellence, e.g. through specific funding programmes and the concentration of researchers in 'centres of excellence'.
2   Emphasis on societal relevance of research, including knowledge transfer and research activities that stretch beyond the traditional academic world.
3   More competition between researchers and within as well as among research organizations, e.g. in terms of funding. This has consequences for the willingness to collaborate, to share knowledge and the networking strategies of research leaders.

This study shows clearly that leadership plays an important role in the research groups, and that despite the amount of time spent on management tasks, the leaders feel strongly committed to the actual content of the research carried out in their group. For example, they are well informed about the latest developments of their research and actually contribute to the operational research. They are considered a source of information for their group members and highly competent researchers.

About half of their time is spend on research or supervision of research. The actual research management involves several tasks, which has remained more or less stable in these five years (in terms of nature of the tasks, as well as their distribution in time). Their actual research management concerns such tasks as intense internal communication about their research, and the organization of meetings involving the long-term research policy of the group. Internal quality assurance is important, particularly concerning the composition of research proposals, in order to obtain external funding and create a productive research climate.

This helps to achieve the major purposes of these research groups: a high scientific output. The number of publications grew substantially between 2002 and 2007; this growth coincides with a slight increase in the percentage of external funding as well as less freedom and flexibility for the employees (e.g. in terms of working at home).

A comparison with the most prominent research groups (the best 12 per cent in terms of output and impact, 22 out of the total 184 research groups) revealed that the research leaders in these groups are more directly involved in the primary process of the operational research, as active researchers. They are more likely to appear as first author for major journals, and, on average, spend slightly more time on (supervision of) research. They expose a broader, more varied style of leadership compared to the other research leaders. They carry out a greater variety of tasks (e.g. lab experiments, research activities, external and internal management, teaching, patient care, supervision) but spend on average less time per task, while their time division between tasks is more equally distributed. This larger variation of tasks is also visible in the greater diversity of financial resources obtained, their time is spent on a greater diversity of activities and they make more strategic considerations when choosing new topics for research.

The third stream of research on academic leadership involves a relatively unknown issue as it refers to so-called 'grassroots leadership'. This is particularly relevant for academic organizations, as it can increase their readiness for change (Kezal, 2009). What is so interesting about this type of leadership is that it does not only include distributed leadership – for example, bottom-up leadership in top-down efforts – but goes a step beyond that. It attempts to investigate bottom-up change initiatives independent of top-down sanctioning, perhaps even contradicting the interests of those in formal authority, involving day-to-day changes that 'often go unnoticed and undocumented' (Kezal, 2009: 305).

Until now, we know virtually nothing about grassroots leadership in higher education, and it has only recently been recognized that leadership in higher education takes place at multiple levels, including staff and students (e.g. Rhoads, 2009).

Hartley's study (2009) on grassroot change and leadership is based on interviews with a subset of 38 prominent leaders of the civic engagement movement, and discovered that certain individuals had a disproportionate influence on the trajectory of the movement, showing rather modest type of leadership, which involved 'an eagerness to engage in dialogue, a penchant for quiet persuasion, and dogged persistence' and which was strongly based on 'the power of their ideas' (Hartley, 2009: 332–333). Hartley provides us with an interesting overview of the various types of leadership, as has been distinguished in the 'social movement' literature, and explains that these types are best understood as archetypes, that influence broad-based change efforts, and not qualities of individuals. He concludes that what matters most in any change effort are inspiring ideas that result into committed actions with a compelling purpose.

Both Verbree and Van der Weijden as well as Deem emphasize the increasingly widespread focus on academic leadership, consequently making it a more complex and demanding function as it requires a broader range of skills. These requirements can be contributed to the more competitive and high standard situation of the science system. It seems that academic leadership can be considered as a more diverse and increasingly broad occupation, involving a greater variety of skills, such as multitasking, flexibility and being able to do everything at the same time.

This increased broadness and variety of tasks seems to be required by the external environment, making the role of the academic leader less univocal and less a job or a function to be carried out. While conversely, the organization seems to rely more on the individual features of such leaders and the 'authenticity of their character'. While emphasis on quality of research and teaching is increasingly important by the higher education organizations (and their controlling bodies), the requirements of academic leadership seem to go beyond such measurable standards of quality, although this may sound controversial within the context of NPM. For academic leaders informal, networking skills are increasingly important, such as the ability to signal trends, possess a certain uniqueness as well as the ability to deal with unexpected situations. Paradoxically within NPM, skills such as 'playing with the rules' are perhaps even more important than meeting the quality standards.

After this overview of current literature on academic leadership, we will continue with our own research. We will start with a brief methodological section, followed by the findings of our comparative study.

Method of data collection

The data presented in this chapter are part of a larger, European study on managerialism and organizational commitment in higher education institutions. In an earlier phase, in order to investigate the impact of managerialism at universities, a questionnaire was conducted in eighteen universities within six European countries with 2325 respondents, among academic as well as support staff (Smeenk *et al.*, 2006). This comparability does not extend to the levels of managerialism as these clearly differ between faculties and universities (e.g. Shattock, 1999). The findings of this survey showed that there are many differences between the countries and universities, which made the generalized results rather inconclusive. Because 'levels of managerialism' differ among countries (Pollitt and Bouckaert, 2004), universities (Ball, 1990; Shattock, 1999), faculties (Chan, 2001; Trowler, 1998) and even in the perception of individual academics (Davies, 2007; Ylijoki, 2003), the first study did not reveal a direct positive or a negative effect of managerialism on organizational commitment. Since social interactions clearly have a positive effect on university employees' organizational commitment, it appears that collegiality and social contacts are core aspects of an academic institution, regardless of the level of managerialism. The nature of our survey did not do enough justice to the diversity between countries and universities. Several questions, particularly concerning the exact nature, the direction and the context of the relationship between managerialism and commitment, remained unanswered (Smeenk *et al.*, 2006).

We therefore decided to organize a second round of data collection, in order to investigate which effects of managerialism the respondents experienced in their daily work in higher education and how they coped with these managerial changes. In the summer of 2007 in the Netherlands, Sweden and the UK, interviews were performed with academic staff within the same universities as in the previous phase. The faculties and departments are all featured by a 'gamma' background, in other words, they are related to the social, economic or management sciences. The respondents were asked to focus on the last three to five years, meaning that the findings cover a period from approximately 2002 or 2004 to 2007. The interviews in Sweden and the UK were carried out in English by three masters students, the interviews in the Netherlands were in Dutch, and conducted by the author.

We interviewed seventeen women and thirty-one men (forty-eight interviews in total) who held positions as administrative officers, Ph.D. students, lecturers, senior lecturers, (assistant and associate) professors, (associate) deans and vice-chancellors. Most respondents (80 per cent) worked fulltime and had a permanent contract. The age of the respondents varied between 28 and 67 years. Table 9.1 provides an overview of the interviews conducted. In order to distinguish the various respondents and provide some background on their situation, we used codes (e.g. S1a). Some of the respondents actually function as an academic leader, while others experience the influence of such leaders in their daily work.

To ensure comparability, interviews were carried out by means of a topic list, and were audio taped and transcribed fully. The texts were analyzed with the help of Kwalitan, a software application particularly designed for investigating interview data.

Table 9.1 Overview of respondents

Country: University	Faculty	Number of interviews and codes used
The Netherlands:		
Amsterdam	Social and Behavioural Sciences	5 (Nl1a–e)
VU University Amsterdam	Economics Sciences, Social Sciences	4 (Nl2a–d)
Groningen	Management Sciences, Social Sciences	4 (Nl3a–d)
Sweden:		
Gothenburg	Sociology, Pedagogy	6 (S1a–g)
Uppsala	Educational and Economic Sciences	6 (S2a–e)
Växjö	Social Science Department	6 (S3a–f)
UK:		
Cardiff	Cardiff Business School	6 (UK1a–d, UK2a, b)
East Anglia	Norwich Business School	6 (UK3a–f)
Edinburgh	Department of Education	5 (UK4a–e)

The general findings of this second phase will be reported in *Studies in Higher Education* (Teelken, forthcoming). For the purpose of this chapter, with its focus on academic leadership within a changing context of increased managerialism, the available data have been re-analyzed.

Academic leadership in a comparative perspective: main themes

As reported in Teelken (forthcoming) the respondents in the three countries generally agree that they experienced substantial changes, particularly, an increased emphasis on performance measurement and more assessment of quality of research and teaching. It is within the context of these perceived changes that the respondents see themselves or their manager in an altered role as academic leader.

The main changes as perceived in this academic leadership that could be derived from the data involve the following. The character of these changes may appear somewhat arbitrary, but their impact on the daily work of the respondents is clear.

1   A changing balance between managerialism and leadership/leaderism.
2   A clear ambivalence about whether leaders and managers actually have an impact on the academics and their organization.
3   More focus on accountability and administrative issues, in research as well as teaching.
4   A restructuring of departments, usually encouraged by financial constraints or 'external' considerations (e.g. mergers, increased scale, taking out middle management level).

1 A changing balance between managerialism and leadership/ leaderism

Through the interviews, we perceive a general 'managerialization' of academic work. The respondents in all three countries generally experience a more managerial approach towards academic leadership. This changed emphasis has not been received with much appreciation (Teelken, forthcoming). We perceive 'leaderism' here as has been described by O'Reilly and Reed (2012), as leadership in a more 'ideological form. Because it can be used both as a framing metaphor and as an emergent discourse, 'leaderism' is a key element of this process of cultural re-orientation and political resettlement in UK public services.

It seems that the main tasks of academics, teaching and research are more controlled and determined by the central level, referring to the faculty or university level. This increased emphasis on administration coincides with less time for informal contacts, e.g. informal cooperation, reading and commenting on each others' work. Many respondents complain that efficiency prevails over academic freedom and quality, by emphasizing these administrative measures.

By taking out the middle management layer or diminishing its decision-making capacity, there is more influence and power for the head of department or institution. The respondents expressed in several ways why and how they disagree with this more managerial, hierarchical approach, as one Swedish respondent explained 'I have quite a hard time with this, the way the efficiency is running at the universities' (S1c). Another, a senior lecturer, explained that: 'it is my feeling that the top leadership of the university is trying to have a tighter control, from top-down. Much because of that knowledge, well I think that is the main reason' (S3a).

A British respondent confirmed this hierarchicalization by saying that:

> . . . the university is reasonably hierarchical in the sense that you have got your lecturers, you have got our head of school who reports then to the faculty, who then reports into the pro-vice chancellors and the vice chancellors. So in that sense there is a hierarchy. But in a lot of ways you do not feel like you have a boss. I mean, in a sense, you have somebody you can go to, and you have somebody who comes and asks you to do things now and again. But on the whole, compared to being in industry, I do not feel here like I have a boss.
>
> (UK3d)

While a further Swedish respondent (S1d – female, head of research, age 45) stated that:

> So I think that there is a kind of tendency towards professionalization of the managerial kind of position, of course there is. I think that would

probably only increase. The managers are more and more professionals. ... Professionals are people being more trained for organizational leadership, about organizational structures, workplace organization.

Several Dutch respondents spoke of a more managerial approach towards the organization of teaching, as this is no longer the responsibility of their direct line manager or the leader of their group but the director of education. This implies a more distanced and more 'managerial' approach towards teaching, to illustrate the point:

> At some cases, it is this educational director who is breathing in your neck. Or to put it positively, provide you with relevant feedback. As a professional lecturer, who is paid by the state, you should take your responsibility.
>
> (Nl3a)

A respondent from the UK considered the matter in a more fundamental manner:

> *Interviewee*: But managerialism contradicts the very foundations of education, particularly as I see it, it should be available to a group of people who are motivated to be educated, freely as well. So managerialism adopted from the private sector has a different focus.
>
> *Interviewer*: So it's not suitable for the academic life?
>
> *Interviewee*: Exactly. First of all the whole managerialist idea that we can dissect an employment process for higher education, which has multiple stakeholders and multiple voices into its essential components. But what they don't realise is that this dissecting of activities does not lead to a better overall process.
>
> (UK3c)

Maybe that is the reason why a Swedish respondent appreciated his superior so much: 'I only see my manager in positive matters, so I'm lucky . . . once a year there is a development conversation . . . That works well, because . . . we do not have any professional managers. Everyone is academic' (S2c).

However, the increased emphasis on managerialism results into less committed and more cynical employees, while the university is no longer considered a fruitful employer. As one Dutch respondent commented: 'From my year, I'm one of the losers' (Nl2c). This current situation contrasts with the previous one, where the line manager (often the 'professor') in Netherlands universities protected his or her 'own' employees from outside influences:

> My previous professor was what I call an old-fashionable boss, he considered me as one of his group, or clan. And it was his research group

that he tried to protect from external influences, from others who wanted us to do certain things . . . while now, you are simple 'under the mercy' of the educational or research director.

(Nl3a)

Although on the one hand respondents complain about lack of 'leadership' at their university, on the other hand, the more professional and managerial approach towards leadership encourages that (potential) leaders are provided with specific training and coaching, sometimes even in a very structured manner, for example, through certain leadership programmes. One of the Dutch respondents (assistant professor) explains that he feels that his own, personal development as academic professional is increasingly part of a larger framework, involving a longer development with several levels, where the managerial intentions are actually part of the institutional and departmental policy. There is more coherence with organizational policy and intentions are written down, and consequently more serious and constructive feedback. This indicates that academic leadership of itself is compatible with academic professionalism and *not necessarily* a managerial imposition. One respondent, from the UK, went even further stating that leadership was much more important than management:

I think we need more leadership, which will embrace the spirit of academia and can give enthusiasm to people, but not managerialism. So encouragement, leadership and a more 'follow the leader' kind of attitude is much better in academia. A leader who cares about your wellbeing.

(UK3c)

This is similar to that stated by one Swedish head of administration (S1d – female, head of research, age 45):

I also like being the head. I really like being in a position where I can initiate things and try it and talk to people. I really like that. I think it is really important that we as academics need to develop us . . . In all our networking, we need these skills.

This contradiction between the manager and the professional is even more visible in the interview with a Swedish Vice-Chancellor who explained that:

As I said, I changed my mind about that, I'm thinking a lot of management positions at universities and how to harmonise the old university tradition with of course more management . . . I like that very much . . . But then, when you change your hat, and you sit down as a researcher, then I can be very irritated or angry because of many of those decisions.

(S1e)

A British respondent puts it even stronger when he explained:

> You know the reason that I am doing academic work is that I did not want to become a manager. Definitely, I feel really repulsed when people suggest me to manage a thing, manage people, manage processes. I just go OK, if I have to do it, but it is not something that I personally want, but there is now more. I think there are more people who are coming in through the new university sector with ideas to manage and control processes. That is so vulgar in higher education. Just go and work in industry. It is disgusting!
>
> (UK3c)

2 The ambivalence of the impact of leadership

In reaction to the actual influence of leadership on academic life and the academic organization, the respondents demonstrate a certain amount of ambivalence. Some experience a greater impact of their academic leader, through more steering and hierarchical involvement, while others refer to the limited impact of such positions in academic organization. Particularly concerning the potential of academic leaders to interfere in the staff population, the respondents quite contradict each other. While some state that it is practically impossible to dismiss somebody with a tenure track contract from his or her employment, others (e.g. policy maker) explain that this was always possible, but that a dossier had to be composed in order to enable a lay-off.

For example, when referring to performance measurement and its possible consequences, a British respondent explained that: 'I think the university still has not got the teeth to enforce anything, it is just probably identifying, more formally, which members of staff are not performing as well as they should do' (UK2a). So it is formalized, but not more effective.

Respondents speak of these so-called limited possibilities of leadership; there is little the management can do, for example, there is only a limited focus on the improvement of employee abilities. A Dutch respondent stated that: 'The actual possibilities of interference are very limited, in the case of malfunctioning and a tenure contract, there is not much the organisation can do' (Nl3c).

A British respondent made a similar point on the evaluation of teaching quality explaining that 'I'm not influenced, because I have a very secure job.' He recognized the process did have some effect by adding 'If you are a part-time lecturer or if you are a new lecturer there may be some pressure on you' (UK3c).

Concerning the focus on the improvement of employee abilities, a Dutch lecturer observed:

> What surprises me is that nobody in the organization says, you should work on this, try to improve on that. For example, I'm not so good at giving

large lectures, then my manager should discuss that with me, and suggest a trajectory for development. In the private sector, there is much more coaching and training. And we don't do that at all. As soon as you have tenure contract, I can do what I want. In some cases, it is unthinkable that [for example] a professor should be required to be trained in teaching skills.

(Nl2b)

3 More focus on accountability and administrative issues

From the 1980s onwards, as NPM took hold, research policy increasingly focused on making academic research more efficient, relevant and accountable, coinciding with the growing pressures for greater transparency in government expenditure and effectiveness (Westerheijden, 1997). Academics experienced increased time pressures and demands for greater accountability within their organizations. It seemed that academic work itself (teaching and research) was being converted into 'numbers'. This emphasis coincided with the 'extensive attempts to make everything measurable', as one Dutch respondent commented, and went on to state that the increased administrative burden meant the faculty has to carry out:

Increased efforts to make things more measurable in the area of research, making production more measurable, and stimulate employees to produce more ... There are certain expectations concerning the amount of publications. They are not formulated very clearly, but [they are] increasingly explicit.

(Nl3c)

The respondents agree that there is generally more steering, and direction in terms of research. One of the respondents expressed her frustrations concerning the issue of economizing on journals, and their allocation of a list of A or B journals: 'It has been decided by the faculty, by the research director, that every research group can only have 15 or 20 journals. There was no discussion possible, it was simply implemented in a top down manner' (Nl2d).

It seems that this administrative burden is placed upon the researchers themselves and tends to 'eat up' their precious research time. As one Swedish respondent states:

I dislike the fact that there is more and more administrative work, more forms to fill out, a lot of time is spend to trying to make, when you conclude projects you have to conclude the books when it comes to financing, you have to show you have done certain things you promised to do, whether it is publication or that you have seminars or whatever.

When teaching there are a lot of things which the researchers or teachers have to do themselves with regards to administration: 'In my case it probably is not 10 but 5% of the time of the course. I have no problems with introducing new IT systems or whatever it might be as long as they have a clear purpose' (S1a).

The administrative burden does not only refer to increased accountability but it also (re)emphasizes the hierarchical structure of the organization, a point made by one British academic:

> So all of the deans are appraised by the vice chancellor. The deans themselves by appointment appraise my performance. They also appraise the performance of the head of research, and for the departmental heads. I appraise the performance of the heads of teaching, because we have got the schemes now . . . It is a form filling system, you look at your . . . what you have done in the past year, what your performances are and if you have checked them, and you revisit a year later.
>
> (UK1c)

Another respondent from the UK added that the increased focus on accountability does not improve the actual quality of research or of the organization:

> I think it is generally a very boring trend in higher education to try to fit systems which are not linear into linear logics. This kind of making things accountable, without really thinking that these systems are actually more sophisticated than we envision in our minds.
>
> (UK3c)

A third UK respondent feared that employees will be increasingly promoted for the wrong reasons, as they are pursuing the research goals, but do not care for the organization, do not attend meetings or come into work, but simply stay at home and write for the high quality journals:

> I think there is an element that when you get more senior in the organization you get exposed to more of the kind of ludicrous bureaucracy and stuff. So you perhaps get a bit more cynical . . . I am having a feeling that you kind of have to play the game to a degree. And those that play the game better, get on better.
>
> (UK3d)

One Dutch respondent very cynically commented:

> . . . it involves all false pretentions; the really excellent researchers do not fulfil a high position, nor aim for it. The ones involved with their career, those who 'strike the back of the dean', those are not the true top

researchers. The management is just looking at impact scores, not at actual quality.

(Nl1b)

It seems that trying to achieve a management position is considered an alternative way of moving up the career ladder, and the main way of doing so in post-1992 universities in the UK is described by a UK respondent: 'Especially in new universities you get these people who become professors by administration and then they become managers, and managerial posts are prized posts and that is disgusting' (UK3c).

Concerning research management, there appears to be a distinction between content of research and keeping track of publications; the research director is responsible for keeping record of everybody in the school, which would appear to be a largely administrative task. At the same time, there seems to be no enforced cooperation within the research groups, for instance, as one UK academic commented: 'my colleagues are international, I publish with people from abroad mostly. So it would be impossible because our research is generally extremely specialized' (UK3c).

The administrative pressure is not only felt in research, but in teaching as well. One Dutch respondent added that concerning the accreditation process:

> Yes, it is an incredible administration. But it is very important for the accreditation, etc., in order to determine, what are aspects for improvement, what should we do about it, etc. On one hand it is very good. On the other hand, the workload imposed upon the department is very extensive. You are increasingly careful to do certain things, you tend to think more strategically, e.g. you decide not to change course as it might seem as if we are continually changing.

(Nl2d)

One Swedish respondent explained when referring to the new administrative systems, such as filing travel expenses through a web page: 'But I think that the system is currently missing [the] connection. Introducing a lot of new things, which should make it simple but just make it more complicated. It is a contradiction. You lose a lot of time' (S1a).

It is within this issue of increased administrative pressure that the academic leaders seem to find themselves in a rather 'Janus-faced'-position, within which they are forced to combine different logics, quite similar to what Witman *et al.* (2011: 491) describes in the medical profession, where heads of departments have to look at two different worlds with two different logics. They have to combine managerial behaviour with professional and collegial behaviour as a health worker. Likewise, the academic leaders feel forced to bridge both positions as explained under the first development 'A changing balance between managerialism and leadership/leaderism'.

4 Restructuring of departments

When restructuring or reorganization is required, external considerations seemed to prevail over the internal quality. A Dutch lecturer:

> Since the merging of two faculties has our department been taken over by a new management team, which consists of relative outsiders, people who know little of our teaching and research. This coincided with substantial financial reductions ... This new kind of management resulted into a negative story towards externals and abolishment of certain core courses (e.g. in the area organizational design). The new teaching programme looks excellent from the outside, but it is not our own programme any more. It seems that the management team only perceived the organization from a distance.
>
> (Nl3b)

One Swedish respondent explained that the faculty structure had been changed recently, and that the middle management level had been taken out resulting into moving up responsibilities to the head of department, consequently involving a centralization:

> The whole idea of efficiency ... but that means that everything I do has to go on to my director of undergraduate studies who ... already got burned up because he is so stressed and does not have enough time for that what he needs to do. There are just so many loops you have to jump through.
>
> (S1d)

However, despite the external pressure imposed upon them, through reorganizations and emphasis on accountability, the academics try to 'play the game', as this UK academic commented:

> Yes, I think we have only felt a faint echo of what perhaps in other departments have felt. We have managed successful in a way and by this we have safeguarded our way of running the institute here. In that sense the intrusions have been relatively limited. You know, there has been some formal adjustment, that bureaucratic adjustment had to be made and you might question some of it, but you go along with it, because there is no way out of it. We are part of the university, and if the university sets up some rules, *you have to play by those rules!*
>
> (UK4a – respondent's emphasis)

Although the picture drawn by the various quotes concerning these four developments is rather draconic, it still seems that restructuring and reorganizations play only a minor role in the daily work of the academics.

The respondents are worried about the lack of leadership demonstrated by their management, the increased emphasis on management and managerialism and, particularly, the enlarged administrative pressure on accountability and control. We will continue now with the conclusions and discussion, after attempting to answer the research questions.

Discussion and conclusions

When trying to solve the *first* research question, 'what does academic leadership mean and how do academics perceive academic leadership within a context of managerialism in the higher education sector in the Netherlands, Sweden and the UK?', we can generally speak of a shifting balance between leadership and managerialism, resulting in an increased managerialization and hierarchicalization of academic work, with a specific, administrative focus on efficiency and output measurements. However, this managerial focus coincides with an increased broadness and variety of tasks, as seems to be required by the external environment. This is making the role of the academic leader less univocal and less a role or a function to be carried out. The respondents consider leadership ideal typically as a sort of visionary role, which refers to the charismatic leader who leads his/her troops through difficult times. The academic leaders are expected to carry out their leadership tasks by creating enthusiasm among the followers and stimulating a sense of commitment and 'group feeling'.

However, in the day-to-day reality of the positions of leaders, it appears that typical managerial measures, such as financial cutbacks, redundancies of staff and complex visitation and accreditation processes, for example the Research Assessment Exercise, play a very important role for the survival of their research groups. Concerning these managerial measures we have found some similar developments between the three countries, without clear differences between universities or countries.

While the respondents generally agree on the increased emphasis on management and managerialism, they are unable to appreciate such a tendency, particularly because it (re-)emphasizes the hierarchy within the university. It seems that a research manager is much more an administrator, who keeps track of the publication records, than an actual leader. However, some state that more 'leadership' would be very welcome but not in its current status. Some respondents find even that managers should stay as far away from the primary process as possible and interfere is little as possible with the content of research. The Janus faced position, as described in the above, seems to evolve into a more dynamic but no less ambivalent position.

Concerning the *second* research question: 'What are the implications of the growth of a more managerial approach for leadership in current public services organizations?', we see an increase of the administrative burden. This burden is placed upon the organization, in research as well as teaching, and remains a central issue. This has been emphasized by the focus on the quality of research and teaching by the higher education organizations (and their controlling bodies). This involves substantial developments, such as output measurements, keeping track of publications and research assessments, and takes up a lot of time and energy and has consequences for the functioning of academics and their support staff. Despite this increasingly administrative focus, the requirements of academic leadership go beyond such measurable standards of quality. It seems that informal, networking skills are still just as important, and perhaps even more than before, than the ability to meet the quality standards. Attempts to 'strike the deans' back' and create an international network in order to work together in international teams are still as important, particularly because the actual possibilities of interfering in the faculty are often quite limited, specifically if it concerns tenure track staff.

The *third* research question concerns: What kind of responses to the leadership discourse and practices can we find when the professionals are moving into more managerial roles? What kind of impact do the academics experience in their daily work?

The respondents generally acknowledge the importance of a more managerial leader in the current higher education situation, someone who takes care of the 'administrative burden' and keeps everything going. Some regret the loss of the involved and committed group leader, who would try to protect the research group from external influences. Currently, the respondents feel more part of a larger system, a larger framework, where the actual 'leader', in fact the research or educational director, is positioned much more at a distance. As an academic, different types of reactions are '*fruitful*', you have to play the game, be cynical, . . . work very long hours, etc. There are different types of reactions, which all intend to 'keep things going'.

Being an academic leader in the current higher education system is very challenging, and few academics will be able to unite both the administrative as well as the collegial and professional practices on an equal basis, particularly in the current dynamics of financial cutbacks and staff redundancies. Unfortunately, these current developments only emphasize the disparity between the current reality of the academic leaders involved with administrative tasks and running research and teaching in a rather distanced manner with the utopian principle of the academic leaders as a pursuer of intellect and truth, allowing the researchers and lecturers to develop themselves to the best of their ability.

References

Aucoin, P. (1990) Administrative reform in public management: Paradigms, principles, paradoxes and pendulums. *Governance: An International Journal of Policy and Administration*, 2: 115–137.

Ball, C. (1990) *More means different: Widening access to higher education*. London: Royal Society of Arts.

Balogun, J. and Johnson, G. (2004) Organizational restructuring and middle management sensemaking. *Academy of Management Journal*, 47: 523–549.

Bess, J.L. and Goldman, P. (2001) Leadership ambiguity in universities and K-12 schools and the limits of contemporary leadership theory. *Leadership Quarterly*, 12: 419–450.

Boyne, G.A. (2002) Public and private management: What's the difference? *Journal of Management Studies*, 39(1): 97–122.

Bryson, C. (2004) The consequences for women in the academic profession of the widespread use of fixed term contracts. *Gender, Work and Organization*, 11: 187–206.

Chan, K. (2001) The difficulties and conflict of constructing a model for teacher evaluation in higher education. *Higher Education Management*, 13(1): 93–111.

Cooper, D., Hinings, C.R. and Greenwood, R. (1996) Sedimentation and transformation in organizational change: The case of Canadian law firms. *Organization Studies*, 17(4): 623–647.

Davies, A. and Thomas, R. (2002) Managerialism and accountability in higher education: The gendered nature of restructuring and the costs to academic service. *Critical Perspectives on Accounting*, 13: 179–193.

Davies, C. (2007) Grounding governance in dialogue? Discourse, practice and the potential for a new public sector organizational form in Britain. *Public Administration*, 85(1): 47–66.

Deem, R. (1998) 'New managerialism' and higher education: The management of performances and cultures in universities in the United Kingdom. *International Studies in Sociology of Education*, 8, 47–70.

—— (2009) Leading and managing contemporary UK universities: Do excellence and meritocracy still prevail over diversity? *Higher Education Policy*, 29(1): 3–17.

—— (2010) The 21st century university: dilemmas of leadership and organisational futures. Inaugural lecture, Royal Holloway, University of London.

Deem, R., Fulton, O., Johnson, R., Hillyard, S., Reed, M. and Watson, S. (2001) *New managerialism and the management of UK universities. End of award report.* Working paper. Swindon.

Deem, R., Hillyard, S. and Reed, M. (2007) *Knowledge, higher education and the new managerialism: The changing management of UK universities.* Oxford: Oxford University Press.

DiMaggio, P. and Powell, W. (1991) *The new institutionalism in organisational analysis.* Chicago: University of Chicago Press.

Greenwood, R. and Hinings, C.R. (1988) Organizational design types and dynamics of strategic change. *Organization Studies*, 9(3): 293–316.

Hartley, M. (2009) Leading grassroots change in the academy: Strategic and ideological adaptation in the civic engagement movement. *Journal of Change Management*, 9(3): 323–338.

Hood, C. (1991) A public management for all seasons? *Public Administration*, 69: 3–19.

—— (1995) The 'new public management' in the 1980s: Variations on a theme. *Accounting, Organizations and Society*, 20(2/3): 93–109.

Kezal, A. (2009) Guest editorial. *Journal of Change Management*, 9(3): 305–308.

McKinlay, W. and Scherer, A. (2000) Some unanticipated consequences of organizational restructuring. *Academy of Management Review*, 25: 735–752.

Pollitt, C. (1993) *Managerialism and the public services* (2nd edn). Oxford: Blackwell.

Pollitt, C. and Bouckaert, G. (2004) *Public management reform: A comparative analysis* (2nd edn). Oxford: Oxford University Press.

O'Reilly, D. and Reed, M. (2012) 'Leaderism' and the discourse of leadership in the reformation of UK public services. In C. Teelken, E. Ferlie and M. Dent (eds) *Leadership in the public services: Promises and pitfalls.* London: Routledge.

Shattock, M. (1999) Governance and management in universities: The way we live now. *Journal of Education Policy*, 14: 271–282.

Smeenk, S., Teelken, C., Doorewaard, H. and Eisinga, R. (2006) Predictors of academics' organisational commitment, a study of influences of HRM and antecedents in higher education, pilot study. *International Journal for HRM*, 17(10): 1–20.

Rhoads, R.A. (2009) Learning from students as agents of social change: Toward an emancipatory vision of the university. *Journal of Change Management*, 9(3): 309–322.

Teelken, C. (2008) The intricate implementation of performance measurement systems in public, professional-service organizations. *International Review of Administrative Sciences*, 74(4): 615–635.

—— (forthcoming) Compliance or pragmatism: How do academics deal with managerialism in higher education? A comparative study in three countries, *Studies in Higher Education*.

Thornhill, A., Lewis, P. and Saunders, M.N.K. (1996) The role of employee communication in achieving commitment and quality in higher education. *Quality Assurance in Education*, 4: 12–20.

Trow, M. (1994) Managerialism and the academic profession: The case of England. *Higher Education Policy*, 7: 11–18.

Trowler, P.R. (1998) *Academics responding to change: New higher education frameworks and academic cultures.* Buckingham: Society for Research into Higher Education and Open University Press.

Van den Brink, M.C.L. (2009) Behind the scenes of science: Gender practices in the recruitment and selection of professors in the Netherlands. Ph.D. thesis, Nijmegen.

Van der Weijden, I., Verbree, M. and Van den Besselaar, P. (2009) *Management en Prestaties van onderzoeksgroepen.* The Hague: Rathenau Instituut.

Verbree, M., Van der Weijden, I. and Van den Besselaar, P. (2012a) Generation and life cycle effects on academic leadership. In S. Hemlin, C.M. Allwood, B. Martin and M. Mumford (eds) *Creativity and leadership in science, technology, and innovation.* London: Routledge.

—— (2012b) Academic leadership of high-performing groups. In S. Hemlin, C.M. Allwood, B. Martin and M. Mumford (eds) *Creativity and leadership in science, technology, and innovation.* London: Routledge.

Westen, D. (2011) What happened to Obama? *New York Times*, 6 August.

Westerheijden, D.F. (1997) A solid basis for decisions. *Higher Education*, 33, 397–413.

Witman, Y., Smid, G.A.C., Meurs, P.L. and Willems, D.L. (2011) Doctor in the lead: Balancing between two worlds. *Organization*, 18(4): 477–495.

Ylijoki, O.-H. (2003) Entangled in academic capitalism? A case-study on changing ideals and practices of university research. *Higher Education*, 45: 307–335.

10 The university and the public and private good

Jürgen Enders

Introduction

In modern societies, universities have flourished as central public institutions. Higher education and research became overwhelmingly a public responsibility and universities were perceived as contributing to the public good. Universities were heavily subsidized by governments, publicly provided by employees of the state, and closely regulated in respect to curriculum, teaching and research staff, infrastructural facilities, and achievement standards. In historical terms this is a recent phenomenon in which the development of a public mandate in higher education and research took the form of establishing publicly controlled, state-funded, state-owned institutions. Certainly, the well-established tradition of direct, extensive public responsibility for elementary and secondary education had created an important precedent for public involvement in higher levels of education. The public role of universities was reinforced by the prominent role that higher education played in building nation-states and their public sectors. Further, the emergence of the research university linked the research function to the educational one bringing science and technology into the public realm.

The 'publicness' of universities, including the important role of government responsibility, oversight, and funding, the legal status of the organizational providers and their staff, is not only a recent phenomenon, viewed historically, but is currently being challenged in many ways. We currently observe that traditional boundaries and understandings of the public and private spheres in higher education have become blurred, in a similar way to other sectors of society that were previously under tight public control. This can be seen, among other things, in the delegation of public policy to semi-public organizations, non-governmental, arm's-length agencies, independent regulatory bodies, or public–private policy networks. It also relates to a process by which elements of the fabric of higher education and research are withdrawn from the public sphere, with universities setting up private companies, outsourcing research, teaching or support services, and the emergence of public–private partnerships or new private organizations. The opposite is also observed: the introduction of elements of the private sphere into the public realm of the university. Examples involve the state-induced enforcement of competition, the increasing role of private funding, and the rise of New Public Management (NPM) in universities. Here the term 'private' relates to market-type coordination mechanisms: price, competition, and managerial decision-making.

The importance of innovative knowledge in modern societies places public universities as knowledge institutions in a central position, which, however, is not uncontested (Weber and Bergan 2005). The attributes traditionally associated with the 'public' and the 'private' in higher education and research have become unclear and contested, while the 'private' aspect is growing in incidence and importance. These developments challenge the traditional public provision of higher education and research, and the high confidence placed in public institutions that they will provide education and research efficiently and effectively (Enders 2005). What is at stake as a result is the way higher education and research are governed and managed, financed and provided. Overall, the blurring boundaries and changing contexts thus impact on traditional beliefs and practices of leadership and administration within universities. Notions of a university leader serving as a *primus inter pares* symbolically representing the academic community seem to become as out-dated as traditional bureaucratic practices for organizational administration. Like in other public services, 'managerialism' and 'leaderism' have become dominant themes in the narrative of change.

In elaborating this changing context of the public–private dynamics in higher education and research, this chapter maps the overall theme and its various manifestations. I address the different meanings of the 'private, the public, and the good' that tend to be confused in the often heavily politicized discussion around the transformation of the modern university. First, I will have a closer look at the issue of 'the public good' in higher education and research. Second, issues of governance and leadership (who decides?), financing (who pays?), and ownership (who provides?) will be discussed, followed by a reflection on the contributions of higher education and research (who benefits?). The conclusion summarizes major arguments and elaborates on some promising avenues for future research.

The public, the private and the good

An important issue for contemporary higher education and research is that of the 'public good', or, better, the conflict around the 'public good'. The various tasks that a university performs and its various outputs are currently scrutinized with respect to their value for the 'public' as well as the 'private'. In such a situation, a clear definition may be helpful, such as that provided by classical economic thinking. According to economic theory, a good (or service) is 'public' if it is 'non-rival' and 'non-excludable' (Samuelson 1954). Non-rivality in consumption implies that my consumption of a good does not prevent others consuming it too. My reading of a scientific article, for example, does not necessarily prevent others from reading the same article. Knowledge, the central product of universities, may thus serve as a classical example of a non-rival good. Non-excludability implies that it is difficult, if not impossible, to limit access to a certain good. The production of knowledge may serve as a prime example of a good that is non-excludable because it is difficult to make such knowledge exclusive or to control it privately. The consequence is that such a product cannot be left to the market because the market is primarily interested in selling for exclusive use to consumers who pay for the privilege. In theory, we may thus conclude that the central product of higher education and research has characteristics of a pure public good.

Things may, however, look different in practice. Research outcomes may not be codified in publications or physical products and may only be available to those who have access to tacit knowledge. Scientific knowledge may be encoded in publications in a language that is only accessible to a limited community of scholars in the field, who have previously invested in the capacities needed to understand this language. Secrecy and patenting provide means to exclude others from research outcomes, at least for a certain period of time. Access to taught knowledge is certainly restricted too, given the fact that study places are limited. In such a case, my consumption does prevent that of others. Legal barriers (such as a *numerus clausus* in certain disciplines) or financial barriers (such as high tuition fees for access to elite universities) may enhance further rivalry and exclusion. Finally, higher education and research in real life are produced by private providers who sell their products on the market, as well as by public providers who may charge a fee for access to their knowledge. There is thus no reason to argue that such products can only be provided as public goods and free of charge. Some economists applying this perspective have concluded that universities provide services that are not public goods (e.g. Barr 2004); others have concluded that universities' services are 'impure public goods' (e.g. Schoenenberger 2005) or 'quasi public goods' (e.g. Jongbloed 2004).

In sum, higher education and research are certainly not pure public goods, and they allow for a private as well as a collective return on investment. Examples of outputs that are closer to public goods include an informed citizenry, better public health, better parenting, lower crime, wider political and community participation, and greater social cohesion (OECD 1998). Outputs that are closer to the private good include, for example, credentials leading to high-paying jobs or marketable technologies. All of these goods are likely to lie somewhere between public and private goods, or have elements of both. Universities are not only multifunctional, multi-product institutions; their reality does not always correspond to ideal types of public and private goods.

A related discussion concerns the external economies and information asymmetries that may play a role when it comes to the provision of higher education and research. For one thing, education and research are both potentially characterized by external economies. A characteristic of education in general, and higher education more specifically, is that those who have not directly benefited from it may benefit indirectly because the general level of education in a given society may benefit all. Likewise, research may produce new insights and innovations that are not only beneficial to those who invent or exploit new knowledge but to society at large. Obviously, this does not necessarily imply that such goods are governed by the state exclusively, that they are fully publicly funded or can only be produced in public institutions. The important question of which institutional setting of governance, financing, and ownership conditions is likely to generate such externalities is not a normative one but an unresolved empirical one (Stephan 1996). The potential externalities of higher education and research imply, however, that markets are unlikely to generate the public good purely on their own. This implies that there is a role for government – representatives of the commons, say – in assuring the production of goods that benefit society at large. Again, whether the commons are best represented by the government of a nation-state is an empirical question and is not a normative given.

A certain public responsibility for universities is also legitimated by the relative paucity of information on the private and public returns of higher education and research. Citizens may not be aware of the individual and collective returns of higher education. The consequence may be that their individual demand as well as collective support for higher education is inferior to what would be in the individuals' or societies' long-term interest. Likewise, information on research-based knowledge, on its potential usefulness for the public, as well as on its accessibility for the commons may be restricted. Again, the consequence may be that individual access as well as public support fall short, having consideration to the potential benefits. Markets for higher education and research are imperfect because they do not spontaneously produce solutions to these problems. From an economic point of view, these (and other) market failures justify public intervention in higher education and research.

Public debate on that matter has a perennial tendency to be less concerned with such useful definitions and questions that are open to empirical investigation. Traditionally, many advocates of the modern welfare state were, for example, convinced that the notion of the public good in higher education and research can be defined by a normative theory of public administration. The related belief that higher education and research are to be publicly provided, financed and controlled, though, is a political value statement and nothing else. In fact, policy-makers and leaders of universities both tend to focus increasingly on the contribution of teaching and research to private goods, and the extent to which the public goods produced (may) have a marketable value and contribute to economic wealth. Belief systems are thus susceptible to change; they are nested in culture, policy sensitive, and sensitive to actors' interpretations. This is not to say that such belief systems are irrelevant, though. Institutional theory constantly reminds us of the importance of shared beliefs for the on-going construction of social reality. Therefore, the study of such changing belief systems is important in understanding part of the social forces at work in the re-definition of the public, the private, and the good in higher education and research. The boundaries of any democratic polity are always contested. As those boundaries are contested, so is the nature of the public good and the public governance of universities.

Governance

Throughout the world, governments are experimenting with new models and instruments for the coordination of public service provision, including higher education and research. Traditional state instruments of close top-down control are losing ground and governments are seeking new ways to coordinate their higher education and research sectors. Overall, awareness is growing that the wisdom of the visible hand of government in running increasingly complex social systems, such as higher education and research, is limited. Potential deficiencies of the public hand include, for example, the short time horizon of elected politicians, the separation of the costs of decisions from their benefits, inefficient production under conditions of near-state-monopoly provision of goods and services, unintended costs and unanticipated effects of government intervention due to incomplete information, and the lack of strategic actorhood and leadership in universities. There is also 'no doubt that a great deal of government output is not well defined and its measurement is complex and difficult. The relationship between input and output is vague, uncertain or even unknown' (Schoenenberger 2005: 83). Many universities will probably retain important ties to the state through systems of oversight, contractualization, and funding. However, the overall trend towards a changing role of the state in public provisions supports a change in the publicness of universities and other public providers of higher education and research. This trend is by no means new and may take quite different forms that provide an interesting field for cross-national comparative studies (Toonen 2007).

The introduction of market-type coordination mechanisms in higher education and research provides a most obvious alternative to government and also raises the most controversy. In many countries, important ingredients of markets are still not in place in higher education and research, while quasi-market elements are becoming increasingly popular in higher education policy-making. As Teixeira *et al.* (2004: 4–5) have shown, experimentation with market mechanisms takes three main forms.

The first is the promotion of competition between higher education providers. The second is the privatization of higher education – either by the emergence of a private higher education sector or by means of privatization of certain aspects of public institutions. And the third is the promotion of the economic autonomy of higher education institutions, enhancing their responsiveness and articulation to the supply and demand of factors and products.

'Marketization' in higher education and research thus is a complex and multi-faceted process, while it enforces developments towards universities becoming more tightly coupled organizations increasingly cooperating and competing on quasi-markets. Leadership and management are expected to facilitate such organizational change and to set the strategic agenda for organizational survival and prosperity.

Organizational hierarchical self-regulation is thus increasingly stimulated by governmental actors. Government attempts to enhance the autonomy and leadership capacities of universities as corporate actors (de Boer *et al.* 2007) provide an interesting example of 'enforced self-regulation' (Jongbloed 2004). One of the important elements of shifting governance arrangements in higher education is the growing expectation as regards the leadership and management capabilities of higher education organizations. The university – traditionally described as a 'loosely coupled organization' and as an 'organized anarchy' – was in many countries for a long time almost invisible as an independent actor in the higher education policy arena. Organizational leadership and management in general appeared rather weak and not very professional. In countries where higher education was mostly public the two most powerful groups of actors were the public authorities and the academic oligarchy. As a result, universities operated as bureaucratic interest organizations of their academic staff rather than as managed work organizations with hierarchical leadership. This picture is changing, partly as a consequence of the reshuffling of authority and responsibilities across the different levels in the system. Academic leaders have been encouraged to become managers and to develop strategic management for their organizations. The introduction of new management tools and devices, as well as the recruitment and training of more qualified leaders and management, are supposed to further develop their capacity for internal governance. In consequence, universities and other higher education providers have already become or are on their way to become more important actors in the system's coordination. At the same time, the new freedom that higher education organizations experience is by no means unconditional. In many cases, the new freedom was accompanied by new measures of accountability, the 'contractualization' of the relationship with governments, and other new regulations to control organizational behaviour and performance. One of the consequences of such an external system of surveillance and control is that it gets, at least partly, internalized and translated into an intra-organizational system of risk management. Under such circumstances, leadership might not mean much more than the management of a never ending stream of new bureaucracies due to audits, evaluations, performance targets, multi-annual planning, and daily time-writing (see Chapter 9 by Teelken).

The increasing use of networks that include public and private actors, such as business and consumer groups, in setting research priorities or in encouraging public–private partnerships provides another example for public–private governance. Science and technology policy nowadays routinely postulates the efficiency and effectiveness of steering in and by heterogeneous networks. Innovation networks, regional clusters, science poles, excellence networks, and competence networks are spreading as a means to encourage cooperation between heterogeneous partners as well as a means of neo-corporatist policy-making in these areas.

Faith in the market is based on the fundamental tenet that competition creates efficiencies, cost savings, and productivity gains. In summing up the findings of their book on markets in higher education, Dill *et al.* (2004: 345) point to 'the strong indications that the pressure on universities for more market-like behaviour has had a positive impact in terms of cost per graduate and scientific productivity.' Obviously, higher education is nowadays hosting more students, while research is delivering more outputs with overall funding that has not followed this growth. Dill *et al.* (2004) also point to the contribution of market mechanisms to the transparency in the system and the operation of universities, their growing flexibility, resilience, and responsiveness. At the same time, serious concerns are raised about the costs of an increasingly fierce, globalizing 'academic arms race' (Dill 2005). In such a race, institutions and scholars prefer to invest in their standing in the positional market for reputation than respond to genuine market needs. Facing competition in markets and quasi-markets for customers and funding, the competition in informal and formal ranking systems for academic reputation can become an end in itself (Calhoun 2006). Public money may increasingly be used to reproduce or enhance the reputation of institutions and scholars, rather than as a means of serving the private and the public good.

Faith in networks is based on the tenet that cooperation and trust will create efficiencies, productivity gains, and legitimacy. Enhancing further linkages between actors from different social systems, such as politics, university, industry, and representatives of civil society, is part and parcel of the increasingly visible move from top-down steering and hierarchical forms of governance to interactive processes and policy networks. The basic assumption apparently is that the social relationships between these systems are limited and thus have to be enhanced by government incentives. The policy network literature argues that policies are no longer the result of the efforts of government only, but rather subject to negotiations between a wide range of actors that differ in nature. The inclusion of different stakeholders, Mayntz (1997) argues, helps to overcome functional differentiation, thereby making the policy process more effective. Furthermore, the inclusion of different actors might enhance the legitimacy of policies (Sørensen and Torfing 2007). The extent to which policy networks might be a more effective and efficient mode of governance than hierarchies and markets is, however, empirically contested. Networks do not always deliver, and various studies have shown that governments' attempts to stimulate networking for research and innovation in a top-down way may not be as productive as bottom-up approaches. In the case of the USA, for example,

it was the combination of high industrial demand for research and the relative high quality of the US science system's output that helped to generate the new networks bridging science and innovation. It was demand that created the new networks, rather than the networks that created the demand. In the case of Europe, policy has often created networks that are in search of demand.

(Geuna *et al.* 2003: 399)

Obviously, governance arrangements and instruments are becoming more complex and mixed. It is thus not surprising to note that organizational leaders in universities find themselves nowadays in a quite complex and mixed situation.

Acknowledging that managerial autonomy as such would be too simplistic to portray the complex relationship between universities and the state, Neave (1988: 46) already assumed that universities are only autonomous on condition that their policies and missions are in line with national or governmental norms and expectations that are constantly subject to renegotiation in light of public policy. This concepts comes close to the notion of 'regulated autonomy' (Hogett 1996) or 'freedom within boundaries' in the wider public administration literature. Under such circumstances, university leaders might experience a double-bind between governmental expectations for strong strategic leadership on the one hand and expectations for exercising (shifting) public priorities and policies on the other hand. Deem (in Chapter 8 of this volume) provides illustrative examples for such leadership dilemmas. University leadership might even try to anticipate the political and administrative position of governments and up-coming policies, which is a well-known mechanism from the study of decision-making within the ministerial bureaucracy (Mayntz and Scharpf 1975). As a consequence, universities work 'in the shadow of hierarchy' and the strategic autonomy of the university might be limited because the government's position is anticipated by university leadership.

Further, NPM inspired reforms of university leadership and management are likely to face serious implementation problems. One reason for this is that universities have traditionally been different from other public organizations. They had a rather limited internal administration; there was loose coupling between the ways universities were organized as part of the public bureaucracy and the specialized academic core activities; and the academic staff had much more professional autonomy than most other civil servants. The formal organization as well the culture of universities have been different and quite alien to a reform agenda that has been inspired by other types of organizations in the private sector.

Moreover, Musselin (2007) and Whitley (2008) have provided arguments to assume that universities' capacities to develop firm-like strategic actorhood will be limited even under conditions of decreased state control, increased organizational autonomy, and growth of internal managerial control and surveillance. Such limitations are ascribed to inherent characteristics of universities as part of the public science system, i.e. the inherent technological uncertainty of their core activities; their deeply embedded fragmentation; and competing sources of coordination that universities share with governments, funding agencies, academic professionals, and their epistemic elites. Limitations in the coordination and direction of research by universities stem from the perennial uncertainty of scientific research production about processes and outcomes. As organizations, universities thus possess limited discretion over expected outcomes and also have to rely, at least to some extent, on second-hand assessments of performance within scientific communities and evaluation exercises. Further, systematic planning, coordination, and integration are limited by the division of academic labour along the lines of fields of research and teaching with their specialist knowledge and skills. Central coordination and integration for collective goal achievement will have to rely on the contributions of loosely coupled parts of the organization to the whole. Under such conditions 'strategic choices are more similar to those of holding companies and investment portfolio managers than entrepreneurial decision-making in more authoritatively integrated and directed work organisations' (Whitley 2008: 25).

Finally, horizontal integration associated with network governance approaches generates quite different – and partly contradictory – leadership challenges than the vertical integration of universities into a governmental regime that uses autonomy to control public sector organizations, and the related attempts at strengthening vertical integration within universities via hierarchical leadership. Network governance calls for more trust-based relationships, bottom-up approaches in strategy-making and network building, and an emphasis on team-based leadership and the management of external stakeholder relations. Such a narrative of change does not easily go together with notions of surveillance and control, hierarchical leadership, and line management. Instead, university leadership has to build on the many but deeply fragmented ties that academic members can explore to their communities and other external stakeholders.

Financing

The belief that universities contribute to the public good, both in teaching and research, has traditionally legitimized the public financing of higher education and public research. After World War II, the coincidence of various phenomena had contributed to a political climate that allowed a substantial increase of the expenses for higher education and research: namely, the belief that blue-skies research best serves society's needs for scientific and technological innovation; the boom of the economics of education – that is, the belief that substantial educational investment is needed in order to ensure economic growth; and the readiness to reduce inequality of opportunities in education. 'Massification' of higher education, though possibly interrupted by relatively short periods of stagnation, became a major global trend (Trow 1974) and produced significant effects, one of which was retaining the research function under the conditions of the mass university (Schimank and Winnes 2000).

Research has also been affected by growth and expansion, as well as the search for societal and economic relevance. 'In a self-amplifying cycle of effects, research and scholarship steadily fashion more cognitive domains – disciplines, specialisms, interdisciplinary subjects – whose respective devotees then push on with new specialized categories of research' (Clark 1991: 103). Restless research has moved out in many directions to new frontiers and has thus undergone its own 'massification'. In addition, the rise of 'big science' (Solla Price 1963) with its large-scale facilities and huge budgets called for serious investments in research infrastructure and research-related personnel.

Throughout the world, costs of higher education and research have been increasing while pressures on public expenditure for universities have grown. At the same time, state appropriations were declining, at least in relative terms, due to competing commitments. Increasing costs and fiscal stringencies thus generated discussion and action as regards new forms of external, non-government funding for higher education and research. Revenues from non-state resources play a growing role or are expected to do so in the future. Fees paid by students and their families, commercial cross-border education and courses for adults, commercial e-learning, external research funding from the private sector and the non-profit sector, and direct ties with business (licensing and patenting, partnerships to develop new research and products) all play their role in this development.

The tendency of many governments to place greater emphasis on the contribution of higher education as a private good also needs to be viewed against this background. The advantages that graduates derive from higher education diplomas in particular legitimize a call for greater individual contribution to the funding of higher education. One can see a world-wide trend towards increasing cost-sharing – that is, the shift of some of the costs-per-student from government and taxpayers towards students and their parents. This trend can be detected in the increasing tuition fees in countries that are already used to such cost-sharing as well as in the introduction of tuition fees in countries where they were previously unknown. Since the 1980s, research in higher education has increasingly come to rely on private sources of funding as well (Vincent-Lancrin 2006). This trend is usually supported from the side of policy-makers because of their hope that science and scholarship may be used more quickly and more efficiently for practical purposes – and the related belief that the market is the most efficient mechanism to achieve such practical purposes. It remains clear, however, that enormous public benefits may be derived from the role universities are playing in the overall innovation system. What is less clear is how to organize public investments in such a way as to secure public benefit for public money.

Geiger (2007) points, for example, to the role of public funding for private institutions in the USA. For the past quarter-century the dominant trend in higher education in the USA and throughout much of the world has been privatization. Less conspicuous has been the tendency of private institutions to claim growing amounts of public resources. The public–private dynamics in the USA included both an extraordinary increase in the prosperity of selective private colleges and universities and an explosive growth of for-profit institutions of higher education. In both cases the trend towards privatization has been fuelled in important ways by government policies and public funds. Using public funds to enlarge the purchasing power of students has produced great rewards for selective private colleges and universities, making it possible for them to differentiate on the basis of quality and thereby raise prices. Corporate universities have also been able to exploit this system by effectively competing for highly subsidized (hence, price insensitive) lower-income students and minimizing opportunity costs. The loser in this kind of system has been public higher education, which has seen its subsidies siphoned off by increasing public support for the private sector. And this has compromised its ability to maintain a mixed strategy of reasonably low costs and reasonably high quality for the majority of traditional students.

Further, public spending is increasingly allocated according to formulae and mechanisms borrowed from private, for-profit sectors or NPM approaches. As a consequence, revenues from state sources tend to be provided on more competitive and conditional terms (Salerno *et al.* 2006). Such funding may have many faces. It may be indicator based or review based, or both; it may come as the outcome of a negotiation, or as the direct outcome of a performance contract. It may apply to the basic subsidies given to an institution or group, to additional money given for special purposes, or both. We also notice that some of the funding schemes cover teaching and research activities while others cover either teaching or research activities. In any case, it is remarkable how public resource flows into higher education and research have changed in recent years.

Both resource diversification (due to increasing private contributions) and changing public funding (due to competitive public funding and output control) have substantial implications for the leadership and management of universities and the organization of academic work. One consequence concerns the management of multiple-resource dependencies and related reputation and expectation management. Contrary to common expectations, growth in private contribution and reduction in public funding does not necessarily lead to more organizational autonomy from the government. Instead, governments have been very creative in substantially strengthening strings of accountability and control while substantially reducing direct public funding for their universities. Australia and England provide illustrative examples for such developments. Less public money thus does not necessarily imply greater independence from the government. In addition, university leadership will have to balance state control against the need to pro-actively manage their reputation among other resource providers and to manage the expectations of parents and students who control part of their income. Revenue diversification spreads the risk but also increases the need for risk management.

Another consequence of the changes in financing universities concerns the rise of financial considerations in almost all decisions made for universities and their academic units. Running universities and academic groups as full-cost units implies that decisions are, more than in the past, finance-driven. Full-cost thinking has severe implications, nested with procedures that strengthen the search for efficiency, performance monitoring, and target setting. Overall, funding is becoming more competitive, more conditional, bound to more detailed target setting and deliverables. 'Markets', external and internal, ask for a continuous stream of proposals, deliverables, and accountability reports that not only increase paper work, but also lead to a decrease in financial stability and a distraction from actual teaching and research. Full-cost thinking also implies that apart from learning to 'earn their own money' academics have to cross-subsidize those who are managing them in old and new ways.

For most academics it is probably the policies of cutting down direct and unconditional funding while setting priority areas for research and teaching that most interests and troubles them. Such attempts to control academics' work are a considerable source of tension between their personal priorities and criteria for success and the leadership and management of universities. The maintenance of less fashionable lines of work that are difficult to find funding for becomes a serious problem for research groups and departments. This generates policies at the institutional level to elaborate strategies for resource mobilization and staff management in order to adapt to changing funding environments.

Ownership

In much of the world, universities have been public organizations that fall under the realm of overall public service, its rules and regulations, its funding and supervision. Moreover, the legal status of the bulk of universities around the world is usually a public one. This aspect of the 'publicness' of universities is challenged by two developments: the rise of private universities and the blurring of the concept of the 'public university'.

First, the idea of the state relying on private institutions to provide public services has never been foreign to modern societies, while today it has certainly gained in popularity. Some countries have known a long tradition of universities as private corporations, typically organized on a non-profit basis. Usually, they tend to be treated as quasi-public organizations in recognition of their public mission in teaching and research. Private, for-profit universities have been the exception to the rule of publicly owned or publicly acknowledged universities. The rise of private higher education is thus one of the most remarkable developments in higher education in recent decades (Duczmal 2006). As a result, the amount of research and analysis on this topic has increased dramatically (for a recent international bibliography, see Maldonado *et al.* 2004).

Taxonomic and analytic descriptions of the functions of private higher education have identified three roles of private higher education (Geiger

1986). The first function of private higher education is to provide *better* services. Such private elite institutions have existed for a long time in countries such as France, Japan, and the USA. More recently, this type of private provider has also emerged in other countries in response to the decline of quality in the public higher education sector or in cases of severe competition for access to high quality public providers. A second function of private providers is supposed to provide *different* services. The obvious examples are religious-based providers that serve the preferences of religious communities. The third and most prominent driver of recent growth in private provision consists of institutions that provide *more* higher education and absorb demand that is not met by public providers. This non-elite option is a characteristic of developing countries as well as developed countries that have to accommodate a massive increase in demand. Usually, governments lack the resources or the responsiveness to fund a massive expansion of the public higher education sector.

Second, the concept of the public university is becoming increasingly blurred. In the first instance universities are trying to escape the straightjacket of public control by changing their ownership status overall (e.g. becoming foundations) or by creating sub-units with a private or semi-public status. In the second instance revenues from private sources such as tuition fees and private research funding gain in relative importance next to governmental funding. If state provision is becoming a less important component of the overall revenues, the public character of the institution is becoming more ambiguous. In the third instance more and more public universities are actively engaged in profit-making activities through entrepreneurial initiatives such as the sale of research outputs, the provision of paid services and the like. Institutions seek a profit from these activities in order to reinvest the surplus in basic functions that are supposed to serve the public interest. Dill (2005) has recently argued that the concept of the public university is changing into the reality of the publicly supported university and that this publicly supported university is in fact better described as a 'not-for-profit' institution. Overall, such processes imply that the distinction between public and private institutions is blurring. Universities are becoming hybrids. And as Deem (Chapter 8 in this volume) is showing this might eventually make university leaders believe that they are no longer working in a public but in a private organization.

But does ownership matter? Basic and applied research, teaching and academic degrees, and consultancy and services to the community are provided by public institutions and also by private non-profit and private for-profit institutions. Obviously, there is no reason in principle to argue that academic services can only be provided by public institutions. Moreover, private institutions provide public goods while public institutions provide private goods. Research has also put forward the hypothesis that the more substantial the external conditions (for example regulatory oversight and competition), the smaller the differences in the strategic behaviour between non-profit and for-profit organizations (Powell and Clemens 1998). Duczmal and Jongbloed

(2007) have studied such public–private dynamics in Poland after 1989 where higher education went through a rapid period of reform and a large private higher education sector emerged. They analyze the effects of the injection of market forces into the higher education system by looking at the strategies of private and public higher education institutions. Most private higher education institutions in Poland, as in other countries facing an undersupply of higher education, have been vocationally and commercially oriented colleges. They primarily strove to survive in the marketplace rather than to boost the broader public good. Their study offer was oriented towards low-cost study programmes in high-demand disciplines; research played a very limited role. However, over recent years some changes can be observed, such as private institutions offering an increased variety in programmes and investing in research, and public institutions reaching out to fee paying students in high demand fields. Private institutions increasingly go public while public institutions increasingly act like private ones due to changes in the market demand and the governance and funding arrangements.

It is thus difficult to argue that institutions have to be public or private. The main task is to study the impact of external conditions on the behaviour of institutions and their leadership and to study under which conditions universities assure quality and efficiency as well as accessibility.

Benefits

An unintended consequence of the growing importance of issues related to governance, funding, and ownership is that questions of efficiency, cost-effectiveness, and practicality dominate much of the discussion around higher education and research. These issues are crucial ones but are obviously related to performance. Performance is related to the idea of the public good and to such questions as: which public? And for whose good?

One of the main arguments for the 'publicness' of higher education has been the role of universities for social mobility and the assurance of equality of opportunity by governmental oversight. Experience shows, however, that the 'publicness' of higher education by no means always assures fair access and equity based on merit and talent. In the days of elite higher education large government subsidies and overall government responsibilities were usually uncontested, even though higher education served a happy few with a privileged parental background. Interestingly enough, the important contribution of public higher education to the self-reproduction of a societal elite was not a matter of principal concern. The massification of higher education – that is the increasing demand for and supply of higher learning in many societies – was partly supported by a widespread belief that more higher education would open access to formerly excluded groups in society. Many public systems and universities are, nevertheless, still quite far removed from open, fair access. It is thus not surprising that in many parts of the world newly emerging or expanding private providers serve those groups in society that are excluded from public provision of higher education. These developments are not without a certain irony. In most parts of the world, public universities that served the training of an elite benefited from largely uncontested, quite substantial support from the public purse. In times of mass higher education and more open access to higher education, public support for higher education becomes more contested. Often it is private providers that serve previously marginalized student groups, who have to pay, while privileged groups are served by the publicly funded sector free of charge. Profit-making institutions have a greater incentive to compete on educational value added, since they cannot make money by contesting on the reputational market of academic research. 'Therefore, for-profit universities were more likely than their public and private not-for-profit peers to invest resources in activities designed to meet the needs of enrolled students rather than in efforts designed to boost institutional prestige' (Dill 2005: 7).

A related argument concerns the increasing call for societal relevance of science and scholarship. Put very simply, two alternative though not mutually exclusive arguments challenge the view that public science and scholarship are serving the public good. According to the first argument, science and scholarship are just not doing enough to serve the public good. In this context it is widely agreed that the most important challenges facing us today can be met only with the massive support of research-based knowledge. Scientists and scholars, however, are continuously preoccupied with communicating within their own system, *viz.*, their scholarly communities, instead of being responsive to the societal needs of today and tomorrow. New forms of governance, financing, and organization are thus needed to encourage 'new modes of knowledge production' (Gibbons *et al.* 1994) and interaction between science and its publics.

According to the second argument, science and scholarship are not only serving the public good but also the 'public bad'. In this context, it is widely agreed that science and scholarship are not only the solution to the problem but also the very reason for major problems, such as global warming. Beck (1992) has built these notions of the public losing faith in science into his theory of the risk society that calls for a new public understanding of science as well as a new scientific understanding of the public.

Last but not least, globalization as 'the widening, deepening and speeding up of worldwide interconnectedness' (Held *et al.* 1999: 2) raises questions, old and new, about the provision and access to higher education and research on a global scale. Globalization is more frequently and easily affiliated with the 'private', global production and consumption of private goods, marketization, and competition in higher education. Global communication, global learning, and global understanding are less frequently set on the agenda of the debate on higher education, and, if they are, they tend to be regarded as utilitarian means towards a better functioning of global economic markets. But growing global flows of knowledge, people, and money, and the restrictions that limit access to these resources, are playing a dramatically increasing role in higher education and research. In effect, international relations in higher education and research have become more visible, as have their positive and negative effects. This applies most obviously to the dramatic and continuing global inequalities in access to higher education and research between the global South and the global North. It also applies to the increasing competition between nation-states and global regions for innovative knowledge that provides first-mover advantages in the production and sale of global private goods and services. We simply cannot confine ourselves any longer to the question 'who benefits?' on a national scale; we probably never could (Marginson 2007). In consequence, the issue of the public, the private, and the good goes global, while questions related to governance and leadership, as well as ownership and financing in higher education and research, are no longer limited to national coordination and regulation.

Conclusion

All over the world new ideas and practices emerge not only on how to organize a higher education system and its institutions, but also on how to organize its relationship with society and economy. Universities are driven by this transformation while they are also drivers of the knowledge-based society. The old regime of a more or less strict separation between the public and the private is diminishing. The blurring of boundaries brings about entirely new institutional settings in relation to the cooperation and interfaces of universities with governments, other stakeholders, allies, and competitors. Governance and leadership, and ownership and financing are not given institutional characteristics but form dynamic relationships that undergo change and reform as well. The on-going and multi-faceted public–private dynamics in the field thus form part and parcel of a broader transformation towards a new social contract for universities (Neave 2006) in the knowledge-based economy. We are currently observing the rise of a new political economy of higher education and research. This chapter has made an attempt at putting some of its constituent elements into place.

The field of higher education and research is entangled with changing beliefs and related normative statements about 'the public, the private, and the good'. To many, the direction into which the revised social contract is leading higher education and research is a world in which economic values dominate over cultural values and the advancement of scholarship. However, even in a renewed social contract that stresses economic contributions, public goals and benefits can still stand up next to the more instrumental and economic values increasingly attached to the university. It is a major task to challenge these normative statements, to turn them into open research questions, and to test their underlying rationales as well as their empirical reality. Therefore, the study of changing belief systems is important in understanding part of the social forces at work in the re-definition of the modern university. Understanding the various and sometimes conflicting claims that stakeholders place on higher education is key to understanding the system's institutional dynamics.

Higher education and research find themselves in an increasingly complex governance mix of governmental steering, competition on quasi-markets, and policy networks. It is remarkable how public resource flows into higher education and research have changed in recent years, while not much is known about how the changing funding shapes possibilities and practices in the system. Obviously, the search for the smart governance and funding mix continues and makes cross-national comparative studies on the search for functional equivalences of 'good governance' in higher education and research a relevant and fascinating topic. Hierarchies are not likely to vanish, even if market-based or network-based coordination continues to gain ground; while traditional state-dominated governance is increasingly accompanied by other forms of public–private coordination, funding, and organization. This holds all the more in a situation where policies aim to unlock academic systems to strengthen their function as a key engine of innovation and economic development. Shifts in governance invite for multi-criteria analysis of their legitimacy, effectiveness, and transparency as well as their transaction costs.

Equally important, the impact of managerial change on organizational identities and leadership practices on the one hand and performance on the other hand deserves further attention. Here, the link between organizational capacities for self-steering and the primary processes in teaching and research is at stake. How do institutional policies impact upon efficiency, outputs, and quality of teaching and research? An increasingly relevant object of study is whether more business-like leadership and management approaches are suitable to reach organizational goals and how they affect the nature of faculty members' work. Does leadership and management matter for the performance of universities and other higher education providers? If so, what are the correlates of leadership capacities and professional performance?

Studies as suggested above are expected to lead to a stronger analysis of the public–private dynamics in higher education and research. Equally, from a normative point of view such studies are essential to support a policy search for universities that will be both solid and dynamic in their contribution to the public and private good. This is no sinecure given the current tensions between the demands for high performance under increasingly competitive conditions and contradictory demands.

References

Barr, N. (2004) *The Economics of the Welfare State*. Oxford: Oxford University Press.

Beck, U. (1992) *Risk Society: Towards a New Modernity*. New Delhi: Sage.

Calhoun, C. (2006) 'The University and the Public Good', *Thesis Eleven*, 84(7): 7–43.

Clark, B.R. (1991) 'The Fragmentation of Research, Teaching and Study: An Explorative Essay', in M.A. Trow and T. Nybom (eds) *University and Society:*

Essays on the Social Role of Research and Higher Education. London: Jessica Kingsley Publishers: 101–111.

de Boer, H.F., Enders, J., and Leisyte, L. (2007) 'Public Sector Reform in Dutch Higher Education: The Organizational Transformation of the University', *Public Administration*, 85(1): 27–46.

Dill, D.D. (2005) 'The Public Good, the Public Interest, and Public Higher Education'. Paper prepared for the conference 'Recapturing the "Public" in Public and Private Higher Education'. 22 April, City University of New York.

Dill, D.D., Teixeira, P., Jongbloed, B., and Amaral, A. (2004) 'Conclusion', in P. Texeira, B. Jongbloed, D.D. Dill, and A. Amaral (eds) *Markets in Higher Education: Rhetoric or Reality?* Dordrecht: Kluwer: 327–352.

Duczmal, W. (2006) *The Rise of Private Higher Education in Poland. Policies, Markets and Strategies*. Doctoral dissertation. Enschede: Center for Higher Education Policy Studies (CHEPS), University of Twente.

Duczmal, W. and Jongbloed, J. (2007) 'Private Higher Education in Poland', in J. Enders and B. Jongbloed (eds) *Public–Private Dynamics in Higher Education and Research: Expectations, Developments and Outcomes*. Bielefeld: transcript Verlag: 415–442.

Enders, J. (2005) 'Higher Education in Times of Discontent? About Trust, Authority, Price and Some Other Unholy Trinities', in I. Bleiklie and M. Henkel (eds) *Governing Knowledge. A Study of Continuity and Change in Higher Education*. Dordrecht: Springer: 31–48.

Geiger, R.L. (1986) *Private Sectors in Higher Education: Structure, Function, and Change in Eight Countries*. Ann Arbor, MI: University of Michigan Press.

—— (2007) 'The Publicness of Private Higher Education', in J. Enders and B. Jongbloed (eds) *Public–Private Dynamics in Higher Education and Research: Expectations, Developments and Outcomes*. Bielefeld: transcript Verlag: 139–156.

Geuna, A., Salter, A.J., and Steinmueller, W.E. (eds) (2003) *Science and Innovation, Rethinking the Rationales for Funding and Governance*. Cheltenham: Edward Elgar.

Gibbons, M., Limoges, C., Nowotny, H., Schwartzman, S., Scott, P. and Trow, M. (1994) *The New Production of Knowledge*. London: Sage.

Held, D., McGrew, A., Goldblatt, D., and Perraton, J. (1999) *Global Transformations: Politics, Economics and Culture*. Stanford: Stanford University Press.

Hogett, P. (1996) 'New Modes of Control in the Public Service', *Public Administration*, 74(1): 9–32.

Jongbloed, B. (2004) 'Regulation and Competition in Higher Education', in P. Texeira, B. Jongbloed, D.D. Dill and A. Amaral (eds) *Markets in Higher Education: Rhetoric or Reality?* Dordrecht: Kluwer: 87–112.

Maldonado, A., Yingxia, C., Altbach, P.G., Levy, D., and Hong, Z. (2004) *Private Higher Education: An International Bibliography*. Chestnut Hill, MA: Center for International Higher Education, Boston College.

Marginson, S. (2007) 'Five Somersaults in Enschede: Rethinking Public/Private in Higher Education for the Global Era', in J. Enders and B. Jongbloed (eds) *Public–Private Dynamics in Higher Education and Research: Expectations, Developments and Outcomes*. Bielefeld: transcript Verlag: 187–220.

Mayntz, R. (1997) 'Policy Netzwerke und die Logik von Verhandlungssystemen', in R. Mayntz (ed.) *Soziale Dynamik und Politische Steuerung: Theoretische und methodologische Überlegungen*. Frankfurt am Main: Campus Verlag: 239–262.

Mayntz, R. and Scharpf, F.W. (1975) *Policy-making in the German Federal Bureaucracy*. Amsterdam: Elsevier.

Musselin, C. (2007) 'Are Universities Specific Organisations?', in G. Krücken, A. Kosmutzky and M. Torka (eds) *Towards a Multiversity? Universities Between Global Trends and National Traditions*. Bielefeld: transcript Verlag: 63–84.

Neave, G. (1988) 'On Being Economical with University Autonomy: Being an Account of the Retrospective Joys of a Written Constitution', in M. Tight (ed.) *Academic Freedom and Responsibility*. Buckingham: Open University Press.

—— (2006) 'Redefining the Social Contract', *Higher Education Policy*, 19: 269–286.

Organisation for Economic Cooperation and Development (OECD) (1998) *Returns to Investment in Human Capital*. Paris: Centre for Educational Research and Innovation, OECD.

Powell, W.W. and Clemens, E.S. (eds) (1998) *Private Action and the Public Good*. New Haven and London: Yale University Press.

Salerno, C., Jongbloed, B., Slipersaeter, S., and Lepori, B. (2006) *Changes in University Incomes and Their Impact on University-based Research and Innovation*. Final report for the 'Changes in University Incomes: Their Impact on University-Based Research and Innovation' (CHINC) project. Seville: Institute for Prospective Technology Studies.

Samuelson, P.A. (1954) 'The Pure Theory of Public Expenditure', *Review of Economics and Statistics*, 36(4): 387–389.

Schimank, U. and Winnes, M. (2000) 'Beyond Humboldt? The Relationship Between Teaching and Research in European University Systems', *Science and Public Policy*, 27(6): 397–408.

Schoenenberger, A.M. (2005) 'Are Higher Education and Academic Research a Public Good or a Public Responsibility? A Review of the Economic Literature', in L. Weber and S. Bergan (eds) *The Public Responsibility for Higher Education and Research*. Strasbourg: Council of Europe Publishing: 45–94.

Solla Price, D.J. da (1963) *Little Science, Big Science*. New York: Columbia University Press.

Sørensen, E. and Torfing, J. (eds) (2007) *Theories of Democratic Network Governance*. New York: Palgrave Macmillan.

Stephan, P.A. (1996) 'The Economics of Science', *Journal of Economic Literature*, 34(3): 1199–1235.

Texeira, P., Jongbloed, B., Dill, D.D., and Amaral, A. (eds) (2004) *Markets in Higher Education: Rhetoric or Reality?* Dordrecht: Kluwer.

Toonen, T. (2007) 'Public Sector Reform in the Knowledge Based Economy', in J. Enders and B. Jongbloed (eds) *Public–Private Dynamics in Higher Education and Research: Expectations, Developments and Outcomes*. Bielefeld: transcript Verlag: 39–62.

Trow, M. (1974) 'Problems in the Transition from Elite to Mass Higher Education', in OECD (ed.) *Policies for Higher Education*. Paris: OECD: 51–101.

Vincent-Lancrin, S. (2006) *What is Changing in Academic Research? Trends and Future Scenarios*. Paris: Centre for Educational Research and Innovation, OECD.

Weber, L. and Bergan, S. (eds) (2005) *The Public Responsibility for Higher Education and Research*. Strasbourg: Council of Europe Publishing.

Whitley, R. (2008) 'Constructing Universities as Strategic Actors: Limitations and Variations'. Paper presented at the conference 'The University in the Market', Wenner-Gren Center, Stockholm.

11 The making of professional public leaders

Leadership as practical myth

Mirko Noordegraaf

Introduction

Most public and non-profit managers portray and organize themselves as 'professional public leaders'. Policy managers, police commissioners, school superintendants and health care executives established professional associations that define, standardize, inform and regulate managerial work. Since the 1990s, most of these associations focus on transforming their members into 'leaders' who are able to enact strategic choices, inspire people and add social value. Even groups of managers who are traditionally not seen as managers, let alone leaders – such as policy administrators – want to become professional leaders as well. Leadership models and programmes are set-up and competent leaders are trained.

This chapter analyzes how this is done, by using a critical, constructionist perspective. Professionalization is seen as setting-up and institutionalizing professionalization 'projects'. Empirically, this chapter focuses on how two types of policy administrators are turned into leaders, in order to illustrate how different projects actually evolve. In this way, it shows how the abstract, if not mythical notion of leadership is turned into a practical phenomenon. Two Dutch professionalization projects are highlighted; we study how Dutch national secretaries-general and municipal secretaries are turned into professional public leaders. We conclude that *distinctive contingencies* count. The making of managers/leaders depends on institutional conditions and is heavily influenced by outside events, how these events are translated and which terms and texts are enacted to frame managerial work. The making of leaders is not about formalizing work content; it is about managing the ambiguities of managerial work in changing circumstances.

This casts a distinctive light on the promises and pitfalls of leadership: there are no definitive promises and pitfalls. The promises of leadership do not come from the competencies and skills of public leaders, but from the fact that leadership models and programmes construct an appealing, almost mythical promise. Leadership models promise the rise of competent leaders, who are able to produce results in complex circumstances. The pitfalls of leadership relate to the fact that these promises are taken too literally. When leadership models and competency programmes are taken too seriously and are seen as *the* means for optimizing public organizing (instead of symbolic and political vehicles for linking public organizing to contexts), leadership models will harm instead of help organizations.

From professional managers to professional leaders

Since the 1980s and 1990s, many Western countries experienced the rise and spread of 'professional' public managers. Managers such as police managers, health care executives, educational managers and policy managers became visible, erected (or resurrected) managerial associations, set-up schooling programmes and identified their own managerial competencies. As indicated before (e.g. Noordegraaf 2007; Noordegraaf and Van der Meulen 2008; Noordegraaf and Schinkel 2011), many managerial fields started to rely upon traditional professional mechanisms for improving work. As with classic professions – such as medical and judicial professions – they tried to establish the technical and ethical standards of managerial work. They tried to form so-called technical bases (cf. Wilensky 1964) in order to improve the expert base of managerial action, with management ideas, principles, knowledge and skills. They also tried to agree upon ethical codes, in order to regulate managerial service ethics (cf. Wilensky 1964). These standards were established and regulated by newly formed or reformed managerial association, with boards and committees that defined member profiles, formalized management models, selected competent managers and established educational programmes for improving member behaviour (see Noordegraaf and Schinkel 2011 for more details).

Since the 1990s and the turn of the century, most of these managers have to become public *leaders* (e.g. Terry 1998; Moynihan and Ingraham 2004; Ford 2006). To take a few examples, the European Health Care Management association (EHMA) states that 'A core part of EHMA's mission is our commitment to supporting policy frameworks that enable innovative health management and leadership, both at EU and country level' (www.ehma.org). The International Confederation of School Principals (ICP) speaks about 'school leaders' and wants to 'encourage closer relations among school leaders of all nations through: the exchange of people and ideas, professional publications and resources, and international participation in meetings and conferences' (www.icponline.org). The British Police Superintendants Association has a vision:

> The PSAEW will provide superintendents in England and Wales with a national voice and leadership, support in adversity, and advice regarding conditions of service. We will harness and develop the skills, talents and opportunities of our membership, assisting them to maximize their full potential as leaders of the Police Service.
>
> (www.policesupers.com)

The International City/County Management Association (ICMA) sees itself as the 'premier organization of local government leaders building sustainable communities to improve lives worldwide' (www.icma.org).

More generally, managerial associations have adopted models and pro-grammes that portray managers as leaders, who make strategic choices, inspire and motivate people and add social value. Competent managers have to show leadership skills and programmes for improving managerial action have become leadership competencies programmes. Sometimes, leadership dis-courses become all encompassing. In education, for example, school super-intendants have not merely become school leaders; school management has become part of nation-wide 'leadership agendas' (e.g., Currie and Lockett 2007), which define leadership as the key to better educational futures and have stimulated the rise of leadership models and programmes, as well as various leadership institutes and centers. In the UK, for example, 'Transformational leadership has become a buzzword among education ministers in successive Labour governments as a means by which poorly performing schools can be "turned around"' (Currie and Lockett 2007: 344).

Previously and elsewhere, other leadership models have become well-known as well, for example, distributed leadership (e.g., Hatcher 2005). In other domains, managers have remained 'managers' or they have become 'executives', and leadership discourses are less hegemonic, but, nevertheless, managers are also forced to develop their leadership skills. Police managers or health care executives, for example, participate in leadership programmes and their careers are affected by leadership competency models. One of these competency models is summarized in Table 11.1, the model that is used in The Netherlands to develop, select and appoint police managers (Ministry of Internal Affairs 2002; also spl.politieacademie.nl).

In many ways, the notion of leadership has become the ideational anchor for substantiating management. It is used as a practical idea aimed at developing managers who can get things done, but as a practical and results-oriented idea, it has acquired almost mythical proportions. It is questionable whether and how this mythical idea is actually turned into practical behaviour.

Professionalization as process

From an occupational perspective, (re)constructions of managerial work in public domains are understandable. Managerial work is turned into 'normal' work, managers become part of occupational fields and their occupational behavior is regulated by managerial associations. In this way, occupational principles are established, enabling workers to enact 'professional control' (cf. Freidson 1994) – that is, well-organized self-control. This resembles the structuring of other forms of professional work, for example, in medical and legal domains.

In other words, the formation of managerial professionalism can be seen as a (recent) historical process, among a bundle of (older) historical processes

Table 11.1 Leadership competencies for Dutch police managers

Core competency	Definition
Ethical	Maintaining generally accepted social and ethical values, both verbally and behaviourally
Brave	Making effective decisions in situations that call for direct response, in a transparent and accountable way
Creative	Finding original solutions for problems that relate to functions and organizations
Entrepreneurial	Acknowledging and grasping opportunities
Sociable	Establishing and maintaining contacts in a smooth and effective way
Empathy	Acknowledging feelings and needs of others, and understanding the effects of one's own actions
Societally oriented	Being informed about societal and political developments and other external conditions, and responding to these circumstances
Results oriented	Translating long-term visions into operational targets and realizing these targets by clear and strict direction
Politically sensitive	Anticipating and acknowledging events and situations that affect the positioning of policing in political and executive contexts

Source: Dutch Ministry of Internal Affairs (2002)

that affect the organization of work. One can think of the formation of guilds (e.g. Krause 1996), seventeenth-century 'turf wars' between professionalizing groups such as medics and midwives (Phillips 2007), the rise of nineteenth-century 'status professionalism' such as medicine and law (cf. Larson 1977), the appearance of twentieth-century 'welfare professionalism' such as social work (e.g. Exworthy and Halford 1999) and the rise of 'post-welfare professionalism' such as nurse practitioners and paralegals (Lively 2001). Recent attempts to professionalize fields such as public management (see Kitchener *et al.* 2000; Bolton 2005; Noordegraaf 2006, 2007; Noordegraaf and Van der Meulen 2008), but also management, project management, risk management, quality management and consultancy (e.g. Reed and Anthony 1992; DuGay *et al.* 1996; Hodgson 2005; McKenna 2006) rest upon the same mechanisms that were applied earlier. Managers form professional associations that erect and guard certain 'pillars of professionalization' (see Noordegraaf and Van der Meulen 2008):

- selection and appointment (competencies, procedures);
- training and education (programmes, institutes);

- knowledge development and transfer (books, journals, conferences, research);
- occupational regulation (codes of conduct, ethical guidelines).

Since the 1980s, many managerial groups turned to managerial discourses, in order to (re)invent occupational profiles. This was fuelled by the rise of New Public Management (e.g., Hood 1991). Since the 1990s, most of these groups choose to emphasize leadership vocabularies, programmes, models and systems in order to produce competent public leaders.

Managerial professionalization as ambiguous process

Although this process is understandable, the professionalization of managers is not as clear-cut as the professionalization of workers such as medical professionals. First of all, the professionalization of managers is accompanied by the *de*-professionalization of classic professional work, such as medical work. The rise of neo-liberalism and managerialism, aimed at delivering 'value for money', efficiency, transparency, accountability and consumer choice (e.g. Hood 1991; Pollitt 1993; Pollitt and Bouckaert 2004; Ferlie *et al.* 2005), has restricted professional autonomies and weakened professional standards (Harrison and Pollitt 1994; Clarke and Newman 1997; Farrell and Morris 2003; Kirkpatrick *et al.* 2005; Waring and Currie 2009). Paradoxically, those who are responsible for constraining classic occupational shelters and treating professional workers such as medical doctors as normal employees, namely managers, seek to institutionalize occupational principles of the professional groups they try to manage.

Second, managerial work itself is highly *contingent* (Whitley 1989; 1995) and work settings are *diverse* (Leicht and Fennell 1997), whereas professionalism presupposes certain generic and uniform standards (e.g. Wilensky 1964). Managers work in specific organizational contexts, and are loyal to organizational values, while the work of many other professionals, such as medical doctors who see patients, do not directly depend on organizations. Classic professionals are loyal to occupational fields that transgress organizational borders (also Blau and Scott 1962). In addition, managerial work is *ambiguous*, as it has many intangible, moral and political sides (Currie and Lockett 2007; Noordegraaf 2007; Mintzberg 2009). Although managers wish to act on the basis of 'evidence', technical skills, procedures and results or outcomes are difficult to objectify (e.g. Learmonth and Harding 2006).

This confuses the professionalization of public managers, and it might be the reason why many professional associations turn to subtle vocabularies, including *leadership* vocabularies, in order to enact managerial professionalism. By using words such as 'leadership', they strengthen *their* work and positions, but they also indicate that they inspire and serve *others*, including other professionals. The usage of leadership vocabularies, however, turns out to be ambiguous and does not clarify the nature of managerial work. On the contrary, it clarifies the contingencies and contradictions of managerial leadership (e.g. Hatcher 2005; Grint 2005; Collinson 2005; Ford 2006).

Against this background, we do not see the re-construction of managerial professionalism-as-leadership as a functional improvement, but as a bundle of 'professionalization projects' (cf. Larson 1977; Hodgson 2005; Noordegraaf and Van der Meulen 2008) that position and legitimate managerial work. Instead of seeing professionalism as improving work and work outcomes, we see it as a vehicle for coping with ambiguous circumstances. This means we should adapt mainstream views on public leadership in two ways. First, we should see leadership as a special *construct*, which is used by managers to (re)position themselves. Second, we should link such (re)positioning to changes in wider *arenas* that affect the conditions and consequences of managerial work in public domains.

Beneath, we study two professionalization projects in which two types of highly ambiguous managerial work – policy management – are turned into forms of leadership. We use these projects to analyze how and why managerial work is actually professionalized and turned into a leadership affair. First, we study how secretaries-general in Dutch national administration were turned into competent leaders; next we study how municipal secretaries were transformed into local leaders. The focus on Dutch project constrains generalizations to broader developments, i.e. various projects in various countries. But it enables us to illustrate the theoretical point made, make comparison between closely related projects in one and the same country and search for explanatory factors: what explains the evolution of projects and their differences?

The two observed projects will be seen as social constructs, full of terms and categories, built amidst institutional forces and resources. In this way, we go behind the functional and mythical 'façade' of leadership models and competencies. Before both projects are analyzed, we elaborate our perspective and explain how we studied professionalizing managers.

Perspectives on professionalization processes

Professionalization processes can be understood in different ways (also Freidson 1986; Reed and Anthony 1992; Hodgson 2005; Evetts *et al.* 2009; Noordegraaf and Schinkel 2011). First, they can be seen as *rational* projects, aimed at improving work. By controlling content, skills and competencies are improved, work practices are regulated and clients receive better services. Wilensky (1964) portrays professionalization as a step-by-step process that structures occupational fields; according to Mintzberg (2004), management can never become a profession because it lacks a technical base.

Second, professionalization projects can be seen as *political* processes, aimed at forming autonomous spaces and jurisdictions (Abbott 1988). Professional groups compete over control; distinctive professions are formed within larger 'ecologies of professions' (cf. Abbott 1988); struggles within professions can not be avoided, like struggles between certain groups or 'segments' (Bucher and Strauss 1961; also Phillips 2007); professionals oppose non-professionals, such as managers who try to constrain autonomous spaces (Kitchener *et al.* 2000; Kirkpatrick *et al.* 2005; Ackroyd *et al.* 2007; Waring and Currie 2009).

Third, professionalization projects can be seen as *social* projects that determine how work is defined, reference groups are created, work practices are structured and how members are socialized. By establishing closed-off professional groups, working methods, loyalties and identities are formed. Through professionalization social relations (e.g. Lively 2001; Hodgson 2005), communal and sub-cultural ties (e.g. Krause 1996; Brooks 1999) and identities (e.g. Blakeman 2003) are formed.

These different accounts, however, do not provide clear-cut research perspectives that can be used in empirical research. On the contrary, they can be applied in different ways, and show overlap. They generate different research *perspectives* on professionalization projects, which are not so much about 'what they are' (rational, social, political?), but about 'how they evolve' (amidst rational, social, political outlooks). The rise of associations, technical bases, magazines, work standards, codes of conduct and the like can be interpreted as *objectified* phenomena, representing essential features of work and work standards, or as *social constructs*, fabricating work and work standards. Based upon such general perspectives, specific empirical indications can be selected and interpreted.

In the next few paragraphs, a constructionist perspective will be applied to understand real-life professionalization of managers-with-positions. As these managers often start from the first (objectivist) perspective, and pretend they improve their work, they run into difficulties that can be understood when the second (constructionist) stance is taken. Moreover, because profession-alization projects in the field of management can be thought to be ambiguous, it is logical to use a constructionist perspective that privileges how people make sense of ambiguities (e.g. Weick 1995; DuGay *et al.* 1996). This implies that professionalism can be seen as both 'rhetorical device' as well as 'ideological resource' (cf. Reed and Anthony 1992), invoked and institutionalized to 'legitimate the claims various expert groups and their representatives make on society's material and cultural resource base' (1992: 596). *Leadership* especially can then be seen as a distinctive device; despite its 'soft' and attractive connotations, it disciplines the disciplinary role of managers. Managers are taught how to get a grip on and control equivocal circumstances by expressing that they-as-leaders are not really in control.

Understanding processes as constructions

In order to apply a social constructionist perspective to real life profession-alization projects, it is useful to analyze professionalization processes and their observable pillars – the 'building' of associations, membership, codes of conduct, et cetera – as constructions. Certain images of work and definitions of what it means to be a 'good' worker – for example, managers or leaders – are institutionalized. This mirrors constructionist analyses that see professionalism (Becker 1970; Watson 2002), but also other organizational phenomena such as management (Weick 1995; DuGay *et al.* 1996; Hodgson 2005; Rhodes *et al.* 2007) and governance (Bevir and Rhodes 2004) as the outcomes of interpretative social acts that standardize and regulate work practices. The 'making' of *standards*, which is both cultural and political (also Hodgson and Cicmil 2007), rests upon communicative acts and discursive practices that produce 'professional' occupational realities. For studying the (re-)making of such occupational realities, the continuous interplay between *sense-making* or interpreting work practices and *structuring* or institutionalizing work, will have to be understood, preferably over time (see also Weick *et al.* 2005: 417).

Leadership in public domains, then, is no unavoidable or natural phenomenon; it is a bundle of fabricated ideas and images that (slowly) pervade and programme organizational practices.

From a sense-making perspective, phenomena such as professionalism and leadership are enacted and thus interpreted by establishing distinctive terms and categories that substantiate 'professionalism' and set it apart from 'non-professionalism'. Professional membership is defined, behavior is coded and ethical parameters are set. By using certain *terms*, images are conveyed, 'professional' work is framed, work practices are defined and repertoires are built. By construing certain *categories*, distinctions are made to set 'professional' practices apart from 'non-professional' practices and professional work is coded and classified. Competency lists and profiles, which are used by most professional associations nowadays to define the core elements of leadership, are a good example.

These interpretative acts can not be detached from earlier interpretations that depend on ongoing processes that reproduce earlier meanings of professional work. Terms and categories are shaped by conventions and symbols, or 'webs of rules, routines and rituals' (cf. Rhodes *et al.* 2007) that make up organizational realities (e.g. March and Olsen 1989). In a way, such 'institutional facts' can be used to 'explain' what is happening, especially as professional manager groups will not be isolated from wider social worlds. Indeed, the construction of managerial professionalism will largely depend on what is happening *outside* manager groups. This has been argued before, for instance by Whitley (1995) who showed how institutional features such as 'the power of professional elites in controlling labour markets', 'the legitimacy of lay audiences' and 'the involvement of the state' influence professionalization.

Such institutional features can be captured over time, by tracing forces and resources that channel and structure 'meaning making' (also e.g. Meyer and Rowan 1977; Neal and Morgan 2000; Thelen 2004). More exogenous events, such as exposed incidents in service delivery, electoral changes or economic downturn, and more endogenous impulses, such as new board members, (board) decisions or best-selling leadership books, will alter interpretative courses of action. Such *forces* might trigger meaning-making, or adjust

Table 11.2 Interpreting and institutionalizing professional work

Dimension of construction	Component	Features
Interpretation	Terms	The images and definitions that are used to make projects real
	Categories	The distinctions and codes that are used to make projects workable
Institutionalization	Forces	The events, incidents, acts and impulses that make projects durable
	Resources	The budgets and positions that make projects viable

dominant interpretative frames. Members of professional associations might act defensively to prevent comparable events from happening, or to counter decisions taken elsewhere. Or they might act more offensively to establish new organizational realities that provide perceived advantages. This will be supported by the use of *resources*, budgetary or otherwise, which can be seen as the institutional translation of changing cultural and political positions.

Table 11.2 summarizes these interpretative and institutional sides of our constructionist perspective by listing the conceptual components identified above. These components can be used to study real-life professionalization projects.

Studying professionalization

Our constructionist perspective, summarized in Table 11.2, can be used to understand professionalization projects in different countries, different policy domains and different organizational contexts. Despite commonalities, professionalization projects will differ because interpretative practices will differ, because institutional contexts will differ. As far as leadership is concerned, this implies that different manager groups construct their own leadership realities. Behind observable 'façades', embodied by formal leadership models and programmes and universal leadership lists and tools, groups of managers create *their own* leadership discourse in order to deal with context-specific circumstances.

Beneath, this perspective will be used to analyze the professionalization of policy managers, as these managers perform highly ambiguous types of work, although they are expected to perform and produce results. We compare two Dutch professionalization projects, which have a lot in common, but have evolved in distinctive ways. In both cases, *policy* managers with positions are made more 'professional' *and* they are turned into *leaders*. The work of high-ranking policy managers in central and local government has been framed as leadership and has become part of extensive leadership development programmes. We study the professionalization of senior positions in central government, *secretaries-general*, working in-between political superiors and other high-ranking policy managers. In addition, we study the profession-alization of high-ranking administrators in local government, *municipal secretaries*, who head municipal administrations and act as go-betweens between politics and administration. These Dutch projects resemble projects elsewhere. Civil service managers and city managers have started to 'make' leaders throughout the Western world (cf. Stillman 1974; Reed and Anthony 1992; DuGay *et al.* 1996; Bolton 2005), most specifically through senior executive services (SES) and city manager associations that define managerial work, form identities and govern conduct.

Despite commonalities, both professionalization projects have taken different routes and shapes, and their turns to leadership evolved very differently. Secretaries-general are part of a rather homogeneous administrative system and are working in a limited geographical area, the Dutch administra-tive capital of The Hague. But their occupational profile only became stronger after 1995, when the Dutch Senior Executive Service was established, and still, they are not really seen as a distinctive professional group. Leadership is stressed, but the notion of leadership is multifaceted and contested. Municipal secretaries, on the other hand, are part of a dispersed administrative system. Although they are not forced to become members of professional groups, most are members of the Association of Municipal Secretaries, which has existed since 1947. Since then, a clear occupational community has been developed, and, more recently, a managerial occupational profile was developed, with a clear emphasis on local leadership.

These projects show how *shared* ambitions – 'making professional public leaders' – are enacted and institutionalized in *different* ways. In order to understand the making of leaders, as the interplay between work interpretations and institutional conditions, a four-step research strategy was pursued. First, a *secondary* analysis was undertaken in order to explore how experts described and analyzed the rise and evolution of both associations and their attempts to professionalize members. We selected secondary sources, i.e. academic and practical analyses of secretaries-general and municipal secretaries and their work. Second, a *documentary* analysis was undertaken in order to trace the rise and evolution of terms, categories and (espoused) practices over time. Documentary sources were: organizational documents, reports by members of associations, Parliamentary and local Council proceedings and newspaper reports. Third, *interviews* were held with key players in order to 'get behind' the 'façade' of professionalization, to trace the construction of terms, categories and practices. Key players are, inter alia, representatives of professional associations (members and board members of both professional associations), representatives of sub-groups within associations (such as programme leaders), advisors and academic experts. Finally, construction practices were *observed*, primarily in participatory ways, when the researcher attended (expert) meet-ings, conferences and training sessions.

Below, the outcomes of this research strategy will be described, first by studying the sudden rise and evolution of professional leaders in central government, and then the slower evolution of professional leaders at the municipal level. The evolution and features of both professional constructs will be described. The making of policy leaders will analyzed by understanding both projects as the interplay of interpretation (terms, categories) and institutionalization (forces, resources), in line with Table 11.2.

Permanent secretaries

Secretaries general in central government head government ministries as the highest ranking civil servants. They work just below political executives, who are members of the cabinet, and just above other high-ranking civil servants (*directors-general*). Although they all work in the administrative capital The Hague, and have comparable positions (e.g. Lemstra 1993), they have not evolved into a close-knit occupational group. In 1995, however, the Dutch Senior Executive Service (SES) was established.

Features

The Dutch Senior Executive Service (SES), or in Dutch, ABD ('General Governing Service'), was established as a clear attempt to 'managerialize' the public service (also Van der Meer and Raadschelders 1999). In the words of Dargie and Locke (1999), it was set up as 'a managerialist tool for leading the civil service'. On the one hand, it is a *practical* tool, with tangible instruments. In its most literal sense, the ABD is a Bureau, part of the ministry of Internal Affairs, headed by a Director-General. It keeps stock of vacancies, searches for candidates, selects and appoints new high-ranking managers, coaches and trains people, sends out interim managers and organizes conferences. On the other hand, it is a *virtual* tool, an imaginary occupational group, consisting of around 900 managers, occupying '15+' positions (i.e. specific leadership positions above a certain salary scale).

Practical and virtual sides reinforce each other. Practical HRM and MD instruments are used to strengthen the virtual occupational community of high-ranking public managers. The virtual occupational community strengthens the use of HRM tools that increasingly focused on leadership development. Several practical instruments have become crucial for giving the ABD its distinctive meaning. ABD members can occupy positions for five years; the 70 highest ranking members, including secretaries-general, belonging to the so-called Top Management Group, can occupy positions for seven years. The ABD works with competency tools; a comprehensive competency profile has been developed, with is used to match people and jobs. Furthermore, ABD managers can profit from certain services, in order to improve their work: coaching trajectories, conferences, magazines and booklets, training modules. Future candidates for ABD positions can be selected for the so-called ABD

Candidates Programme, which trains (and socializes) lower-level managers. Finally, the ABD has links with outside parties, such as Dutch cities and the European Union.

Evolution

After a decade of businesslike organizational change, with so-called 'no-nonsense' policies, managerial behaviour and competencies moved upwards on change agendas in the early 1990s. In order to change, adapt, reinvent and restructure central government, public managers had to change, it was felt by many (including politicians), and a 'civil service' type of government had to be established. Interestingly, politicians and others turned to the UK and its 'civil service' for inspiration, whereas the UK government tried to curb civil service powers and to 'de-Sir Humphreyfy' Whitehall (Hood 1990). The emphasis on better civil service explains why the Personnel Management unit of the ministry of Internal Affairs became the institutional centre for coordinating improvements. This was framed in 'management development' terms, for example, by the units director (Welling 1995: 216):

> The way in which shrinking central government works as an 'internal labor market', combined with demographic change and with labor conditions that are lagging behind when government is compared to private companies, causes 'rigidity' and 'pillarization'. As a result government will lack qualities that are necessary to respond flexibly to a society that is increasingly complex. The sketched bleak image must not become reality.

The ABD was presented as a 'next step'. In 1993 the 'contours' of the ABD were presented. In 1994 the minister for Internal Affairs described the 'new' public manager (ABD 1994; also Welling 1995: 227–228), who would be 'outward looking' and 'network-oriented', and 'output' and 'customer oriented', who would possess '(international) negotiation skills', would have a 'feeling for policy and implementation', as well as 'integral management qualities' and '*leadership* qualities'. As indicated, this was supported by politicians, also in Parliament.

The ABD's reach had to be determined: which high-ranking managers had to be included? Although early on several key players envisioned an ABD that would include 10,000 officials, the cabinet decided to include a limited group, around 300 managers (based upon salary scales), for 'practical reasons'. Later on, in 2000, scale 16 positions were included, which provided an additional 400 managers. In 2001, scale 15 jobs were also added, which added 200 extra jobs. In political debates that were held during those years, members of Parliament stimulated the minister to introduce more ABD-managers. After the turn of the century growth was halted, however, because the ABD had to remain 'manageable', and because an 'esprit de corps' had to be developed.

The ABD had to define the occupational profile of ABD managers: how to describe and develop ABD managers? Although it was clear that ABD managers had to be mobile, flexible and 'on the move', questions were raised. In a general sense, critics started to wonder whether high-paced mobility would harm the quality of public administration (e.g. Niessen 2001). Incidents, caused by mobility moves, turned mobility into an even more contested issue. Slowly, the ABD started to broaden its horizon; it turned from *mobility* to *competency*. It developed the so-called 'Magnificent Seven' competency profile (ABD 2002). Later on, a very detailed competency profile was presented, with seven core competencies and 35 sub-competencies (ABD 2003).

After the turn of the century, the ABD entered a new 'phase' (ABD 2002), with an emphasis on *leadership* and 'personal development'. This was influenced by developments that legitimated 'soft' concepts such as 'culture' and 'quality' and ultimately 'spirit', 'talent' and 'personal growth'. In order to improve labour market conditions in government, 'cultural transformations' were needed, as argued by the so-called Van Rijn Committee (2001). Policy incidents, moreover, especially in implementation and service delivery (such as a dramatic fireworks explosion in the east of The Netherlands) fuelled calls for a 'cultural revolution', so that administrative organizations would cooperate, coordinate and integrate. This fitted wider social change, in the post-9/11 era, which called for more decisive and problem-solving governmental performance. Politically this was reflected in Dutch politics – after a political killing and confusing elections – in drastic changes in political landscapes. In a populist political climate, repeated calls for drastic change could be heard. The 'citizen' became a focal point for political action, 'society' had to be served, and 'leaders' were necessary. The ABD turned towards a managerial *leadership* discourse. In 2004 the minister for Internal Affairs wrote to Parliament:

> I want to develop administrative leadership, which is anchored in personality and which combines self-insight with expertise and commitment. Studies in the USA and The Netherlands, both in public and private sectors, have shown that experiencing things, meeting challenges, and the ability to reflect on personal functioning are universal characteristics for successful leadership.

Municipal secretaries

Although the Dutch Association of Municipal Secretaries (VGS) has been in existence since 1947, its 'existence' is ambiguous. In many ways it has real features. It has members, the highest-ranking local administrators who head the administrative machinery and act as the liaison or 'go-between' between politics and administration. Compared with the possible number of members, the VGS has managed to establish high levels of coverage. Out of a possible pool of around 540 local, regional and sub-local municipal secretaries, almost 500 are members. Furthermore, the VGS has a Board and committees and publishes a magazine, organizes big and small conferences, acts as lobbyist and takes a stance on issues.

Features

The strength of the VGS must not be exaggerated. Members – as they argue themselves – are not really experiencing VGS membership if they are not eagerly seeking contacts with other VGS members. They receive a magazine, invitations to conferences and information on events and publications, but other than that, they choose to see and structure their work in their own way. Furthermore, members might choose to participate in clubs and associations *outside* the VGS, because they have other institutional or political loyalties. In addition, local and regional clubs or associations of municipal secretaries, so-called 'circles', are what 'really' forms the municipal secretaries community. They are small-scale gatherings of municipal secretaries, which often exist for quite some time, and have arisen for different reasons.

Loyalties are not only institutional 'givens'; they also embody contradictory images of municipal secretaries and influence searches for occupational principles. Especially in the 1980s and 1990s, this proved to be important. First, local administrations were confronted with increasing expectations, as municipalities had to 'perform', and administrators such as municipal secretaries had to re-interpret their roles. Not only because of general performance cultures, but also because of specific trends, such as the growing importance of information and communication technologies (ICT), new service concepts and new models for organizing administrations. These developments increasingly called for 'professional management'. As one of the former chairmen of the VGS argued (Buytels 2007):

> Until the 1980s, craftsmanship, legal knowledge, knowledge of policy sectors, and experiences were crucial. In the 1980s and 1990s technical and operational management, reorganizations, cutbacks, core tasks were emphasized.

This is emphasized in a number of attempts to assess the occupational state of affairs (e.g. Renou and Lutters 1993; Cox *et al.* 1997; Berveling *et al.* 1997), stressing the growing importance of 'management' and 'management teams', chaired by municipal secretaries.

Second, and related, the population of municipal secretaries has changed. Whereas the field of municipal secretaries was historically dominated by older male secretaries, with longstanding careers in (local) government, the current field is much more varied: more women, more from younger generations, more people from outside government, varying from consultants to school managers. More importantly, educational backgrounds shifted; less municipal secretaries have been trained as lawyers (e.g. Berveling *et al.* 1997). This has affected taken-for-granted features of municipal secretary work, and strengthened ambitions to 'modernize' the job.

Third, local administrations have been facing distinctive *outside* pressures. Early in the 1990s, the VGS's so-called Professionalization Committee called for change because of 'fundamental trends' such as declining trust, demanding citizens and risk-prone service delivery. Around the turn of the century, the need for more professional management and most specifically 'leadership' was emphasized. This was also caused by more administrative (systems) changes. The Dutch system of local administration was changed (in 2002) when relations between city councils (with chosen political representatives) and executive councils (with mayors and aldermen) were turned into more political relations. Furthermore, plans to introduce elected, instead of appointed, mayors seemed to become reality. Although these plans were rejected just before they were to be implemented in 2003/2004, the cabinet tried to establish more direct links between mayors and citizens. This would affect working relations between mayors and their municipal secretaries. As one former VGS chairmen argued, and others confirm: 'The elected Mayor was a major driving force; it was a crucial vehicle for seeking new municipal secretary profiles.'

Evolution

The increasing 'complexity' of municipal secretary contexts, as VGS members themselves tend to stress, also provided strategic leeway. VGS Board members consciously 'used' developments as 'vehicles' for adapting municipal secretaries' positions and work. Just before the turn of the century the VGS Board was busy with changing the VGS from a 'traditional occupational organization' into a 'professional interests organization', as one respondent argued (also Renou and Lutters 1993). Distinctive 'occupational roles' were identified: 'administrative support, management, substantive affairs, representation and external contacts'. Later, Cox *et al.* (1997) defined three major roles: 'administrative/judicial, managerial, and generalist'.

Just after the turn of the century – especially after 2002 – the new VGS Board moved towards a 'professional expert organization', as respondents observe, trying to 'bind people' by focusing less on 'direct interests', and more on 'items' that would affect municipal secretary work. Together with 'stakeholders' and academics they not only took stances, but also tried to model municipal secretaries' work in order to strengthen 'roles' and 'competencies'. As one respondent argued, and others clearly echoed: 'In a much rawer political climate, the municipal secretary can easily become a scapegoat.'

As a result of these modelling activities, VGS (Board) members came up with distinctive competencies, such as: 'administrative and political sensitivity, communicative skills, initiative and decisiveness, problem-solving capacities, personal conduct, self reflection' (Buytels 2007). In 2005 a 'role model' was formalized.

1   Municipal secretaries are *advisors*, who support mayor and aldermen.
2   Municipal secretaries are *employers*, who manage human resources.
3   Municipal secretaries are *service providers*, who improve service delivery.

This model was used to (re)design educational programmes for municipal secretaries; together with an interuniversity institute (SIOO), a 'Local Leadership' course was developed. This course still exists. The role model was also used to frame advertisements for job vacancies, to structure interactions with 'outside' agents, such as mayors, in order to guard professional practice, and for outside PR purposes.

Leadership as strategic response

As argued, the Dutch ABD and VGS have much in common, but differ in many ways too. Both are about the making of managers-with-positions, close to politics; both institutionalize their professionalism by (re)forming associations and establishing mechanisms of control; both groups of managers stress the importance of leadership; in both cases words such as 'professional', 'competencies', 'codes of conduct', 'training', 'expertise' are used. This is part of broader strategies to organize occupational control in changing circumstances. Both groups have managed to create institutional *spaces* that surround managerial work and influence managerial careers.

This happens in different ways, however. Most importantly, the making of professional secretaries-general, who can be expected to be part of a rather close-knit occupational group, is fraught with fragmentary forces. Although early occupational developments would have been expected, it was only at the end of the twentieth century that occupational connections were strengthened. And even then, secretaries-general are part of a broader occupational domain, loosely structured by the Dutch Senior Executive Service. The VGS, on the other hand, is expected to be rather loose and weak, and yet occupational ties between members are rather strong. Despite diversity, the VGS managed to define municipal secretary work, and to institutionalize an occupational profile.

The cases also show that these differences can *not* be explained by the professionalization projects themselves. Both the ABD and the VGS depend on the interplay between *outside conditions* and *internal dynamics* that influence whether and how institutional 'spaces' are created. The Dutch Senior Executive Service depended on outside support, most importantly political support, from the cabinet and Parliament. An existing occupational system could be re-framed rather smoothly, and managerial work and careers could be reshaped. The VGS depended on outside events, rather threatening events, such as legal changes in municipal administration and the 'threat' of elected mayors. This could be countered by an historical grass-roots structuring of its rank and file. Because of outside threats, the VGS could overcome its fragmentary forces. This general account of how projects-in-context evolve can be refined by applying the constructionist perspective that was introduced before.

Interpretative acts

In terms of interpretation (terms, categories) both cases show convergent and divergent patterns. In terms of *terms* that are used, both cases show how members are defined and portrayed 'managerially'. The ABD did so right from the start, influenced by a managerial, performance-oriented climate that surrounded its establishment in 1995. Indeed, managerial discourses were constitutive: the establishment of the ABD was caused by pressures to 'perform'. The VGS also turned to managerial terms and 'professional' management in the 1990s, when performances started to count for municipal secretaries, but the VGS itself did not depend on the rise of 'management'. The ABD and VGS, moreover, differ in their use of managerial terms.

The VGS is more reluctant when it comes to seeing members-as-'managers', although links to European and American municipal secretary associations (UDITE, ICMA) have stimulated moves towards defining municipal secretaries as 'city managers'. Many VGS members, moreover, such as one of the former Chairmen, are attracted to terms such as *leadership*. The latter term has acquired institutional status because of Local Leadership courses. In the meantime, the managerial status of municipal secretaries is symbolized by the use of the term 'director' in job vacancies, who has to show leadership skills in managing municipal administrations. In case of the ABD, however, the use of leadership terms is not so much about *work*, but about the *workers* themselves; ABD members must become leaders. This is reinforced by alliances that were established, most importantly, with a small training bureau that offers an educational programme for ABD Candidates aimed at personal development.

Both cases also share terms such as 'competencies' and they fabricate *categories* in order to make such terms tangible, such as competency categories. These categories differ between cases. In case of the ABD, there is a strong emphasis on competencies: a competency framework with highly specified competencies is used for selecting, appointing and moving managers. Institutionally, this can be explained by the ABD's personnel management origins, inside the ministry of Internal Affairs. This does not mean that competency framing is strict and consistent. Over time, competency framing became more refined, and its usage shifted. Whereas early on, mobility was emphasized from an organizational angle, lately 'leadership' is emphasized from a more personal angle. This implies that linkages between competency lists and other categorizations shift as well. Whereas early on, mobility categories were stressed, lately, biographical categories are stressed – building 'personal leadership' became increasingly important.

In case of the VGS, there is an emphasis on competencies as well, and there is a shift from management to leadership, but other than that, the VGS story differs. Much more than the ABD, competencies are tied to organizational *roles* ('advisor', 'employer', and 'service provider'). These roles were formalized after extensive discussions about municipal secretary work, although they resemble earlier role distinctions and match role summaries by individual municipal secretaries. The 'new' roles are used to structure VGS programmes, aimed at improving municipal secretary work.

Institutional realities

Professionalization projects are situated in different institutional environments, with forces and resources, providing different institutional facts that shape professionalization projects. The foregoing case descriptions show different *forces* at work. Many of these forces influence occupational developments rather *indirectly*. The build-up of performance climates in the 1980s and 1990s, and the increasing necessity to *perform* produce evident but equivocal pressures on public organizations and people inside those organizations. At the same time, professionalization projects at national and municipal levels are influenced by more direct, albeit *incidental* forces, such as terrorist attacks and the assassination of a Dutch political leader. They reinforce, but also readjust performance-based ambitions.

In case of the ABD, its short historical evolution clearly depended on strong political support. Because politicians wanted a stronger, more effective national government, with a more homogenous top-managerial group, the ABD and its members became facts of life. Such political support came from almost all Parliamentary parties, and did not depend on coalition relations in the Cabinet. Because of *outside* political support, an autonomous space was created, which could be filled by the Bureau ABD, also by stressing the importance of 'competencies' and 'leadership'. Backing by both Parliament and the cabinet can not easily be set aside. Because of political support, ABD members-as-managers had to take the ABD into account, even when the ABD offers things and provides services that members do not value. Political backing turned the ABD into a fact of life.

The ABD builds upon a clear administrative *system*, with well-known positions, administrative hierarchies and legally defined parameters, such as salary scales, which means occupational control is already *pre-structured*. Because political agents, such as cabinet members, are able to influence administrative systems, ABD members can be controlled, albeit indirectly. The administrative machinery offers resources, but also restrains coordinated action. Institutionally, government ministries still have a lot of autonomy (e.g. De Vries 2001), resulting in departmental strategies, projects and reorganizations that have little to do with ABD ambitions and acts.

In case of the VGS a different story developed and different resources were deployed. The association of municipal secretaries developed *without* political support, but did use political circumstances to strengthen their position. Changing circumstances, flowing from decisions about the restructuring of the Dutch mayoral system, were used as *vehicles* for initiating occupational change. Without direct political support, however, the VGS had to involve their members much more consciously, and it had to offer things members valued.

Leadership development was part of this. Because the association pursued a 'grass roots' strategy, supported by long-standing grass roots 'circles', this became possible.

Conclusions

Attempts to isolate and standardize managerial work-as-occupation and develop professional managers-as-leaders must be put into perspective. First and foremost, these projects are *no* mere formal and functional attempts to improve work, despite rhetorical emphases on 'improving work'. On the grounds of a constructionist perspective, professionalization projects can be understood as attempts to build institutional spaces that enable workers such as high-ranking policy managers to be 'in control'. They do so by setting-up informal networks and by sharing terms and categories, which provide strategic means to counter outside pressures and events. In addition, by sharing certain resources, outside support can be enhanced.

This double-edged link with outside worlds implies that professionalization projects *do* isolate work, but it also implies that such isolation can never be complete. Professionalization projects do not secure, but seek and *suggest* control. 'Leadership' must not be taken literally – it does not represent clear work forms, but symbolizes changing links between managerial work and environments. It suggests control, without really being in control.

The professionalization of secretaries-general and municipal secretaries shows how professionalization projects can be set up and how results can be realized, not despite but *due to* outside influences. It is *not* so much distinctive competencies (i.e. leadership competencies) that count, but certain *distinctive contingencies* that affect the substance and form of professionalization. External circumstances and how they are experienced and used determine how managers are perceived, when leadership terms are introduced and what leadership models are applied. Political support and stakeholder influences, mediated by events and perceived outside changes, are crucial. Without clear political support, for instance, the rather homogenous group of secretaries-general remained weak for a long period of time, whereas an institutionally fragmented field of municipal secretary work was held together by strong occupational grass-roots connections. Secretaries-general needed positional resources, offered by politicians, to close the ranks and leadership discourses provided a politically innocent way to accomplish this. Municipal secretaries needed programmatic resources, offered by sub-groups, to fuel occupational development, to 'break through' traditional occupational images and 'managerialize' the field, without merely becoming instrumental managers – but 'local leaders' instead.

In terms of the promises and pitfalls of leadership, this means that leadership as such has no definitive promises or pitfalls. Leadership discourses construct appealing promises, not so much because they define the technical base of managerial work, but because they suggest that managers can be in control in rather uncontrollable circumstances. They promise the rise of competent leaders who are able to produce results in a world that complicates the production of clear and uncontested results. This, in turn, clarifies the pitfalls of leadership. When leadership vocabularies and models are taken too seriously, there will be serious problems. Leadership is a fabricated myth, which is useful to position managerial work *vis-à-vis* other types of work and establish occupational spaces, also practically, but it says little about the real and practical nature of managerial work. In order to understand the real work of secretaries-general and municipal secretaries, other vocabularies and models are required.

Acknowledgements

Earlier versions of this paper were presented at the Critical Management Studies Conference, Manchester, July 2007, and the EGOS Colloquium, Amsterdam, July 2008. The author thanks discussants and participants for their valuable comments.

References

Abbott, A. (1988) *The Systems of Professions: An Essay on the Division of Expert Labor*. Chicago: The University of Chicago Press.

ABD (1994) *Koers naar de ABD [Course Towards ABD]*. The Hague: ABD.

—— (2002) *Streefprofiel ABD manager [ABD Manager Profile]*. The Hague: ABD.

—— (2003) *Competentie management [Competency Management]*. The Hague: ABD.

Ackroyd, S., I. Kirkpatrick and R.M. Walker (2007) Public Management Reform in the UK and its Consequences for Professional Organization: A Comparative Analysis. *Public Administration*, 85 (1): 9–26.

Becker, H. (1970) The Nature of a Profession. In: H. Becker (ed.) *Sociological Work*. Chicago: Aldine.

Berveling, J., M.J.E.M. van Dam and G. Neelen (1997) *De deugd in het midden [The position of municipal secretaries]*. Delft: Eburon.

Bevir, M. and R.A.W. Rhodes (2004) *Interpreting British Governance*. London: Routledge.

Blakeman, P.D. (2003) Management Styles and Professional Identities among UK Podiatrists. *International Journal of Public Sector Management*, 16 (2): 131–140.

Blau, P.M. and W.R. Scott (1962) *Formal Organizations: A Comparative Approach*. San Francisco: Chandler.

Bolton, S.C. (2005) 'Making up' Managers. The Case of NHS Nurses. *Work, Employment and Society*, 19 (1): 5–23.

Brooks, I. (1999) Managerialist Professionalism: The Destruction of a Non-conforming Subculture. *British Journal of Management*, 10 (1): 41–52.

Bucher, R., and A. Strauss (1961) Professions in Process. *The American Journal of Sociology*, 66 (4): 325–334.

Buytels, P. (2007) *Meebewegen en richting geven [Moving Along and Providing Direction]*. 's-Gravenhage, the Netherlands: VGS.

Clarke, J. and J. Newman (1997) *The Managerial State*. London: Sage.

Collinson, D. (2005) Dialects of Leadership. *Human Relations*, 58 (11): 1419–1442.

Cox, J., J. van den Bosch and E. Figee (1997) *En bracht de schare tot kalmte* [*Reflections on municipal secretaries*]. The Hague: Sdu.

Currie, G. and A. Lockett (2007) A Critique of Transformational Leadership Moral, Professional and Contingent Dimensions of Leadership within Public Services Organizations. *Human Relations*, 60 (2): 341–370.

Dargie, C. and R. Locke (1999) The British Senior Civil Service. In: E.C. Page and V. Wright (eds) *Bureaucratic Elites in Western European States*. Oxford: Oxford University Press: 178–204.

De Vries, J. (2001) The Netherlands: 'Fragmenting Pillars, Fading Colours'. In: R.A.W. Rhodes and P. Weller (eds) *The Changing World of Top Officials*. Buckingham: Open University Press.

Du Gay, P., G. Salaman and B. Rees (1996) The Conduct of Management and the Management of Conduct: Contemporary Managerial Discourse and the Constitution of the 'Competent' Manager. *Journal of Management Studies*, 33 (3): 263–282.

Evetts, J., C. Gadea, M. Sánchez and J. Saez (2009) Sociological Theories of Professions: Conflict, Competition and Cooperation. In: A.B. Denis and D. Kalekin-Fishman (eds) *The ISA Handbook in Contemporary Sociology*. Los Angeles: Sage.

Exworthy, M. and S. Halford (eds) (1999) *Professionals and the New Managerialism in the Public Sector*. Buckingham: Open University Press.

Farrell, C. and J. Morris (2003) The 'Neo Bureaucratic' State: Professionals, Managers and Professional Managers in Schools, General Practices and Social Work. *Organization*, 10 (1): 129–156.

Ferlie, E., L.E. Lynn and C. Pollitt (2005) *The Oxford Handbook of Public Management*. Oxford: Oxford University Press.

Ford, J. (2006) Discourses of Leadership: Gender, Identity and Contradiction in a UK Public Sector Organization. *Leadership*, 2 (1): 77–99.

Freidson, E. (1986) *Professional Powers: A Study of the Institutionalization of Formal Knowledge*. Chicago: University of Chicago Press.

—— (1994) *Professionalism Reborn*. Cambridge: Polity.

Grint, K. (2005) Problems, Problems, Problems: The Social Construction of 'Leadership'. *Human Relations*, 58 (11): 1467–1494.

Harrison, S., and C. Pollitt (1994) *Controlling Health Professionals*. Buckingham: Open University Press.

Hatcher, R. (2005) The Distribution of Leadership and Power in Schools. *British Journal of Sociology of Education*, 26 (2): 253–267.

Hodgson, D. (2005) Putting on a Professional Performance: Performativity, Subversion and Project Management. *Organization*, 12 (1): 51–68.

Hodgson, D. and S. Cicmil (2007) The Politics of Standards in Modern Management; Making the Project a Reality. *Journal of Management Studies*, 44 (3): 431–450.

Hood, C. (1990) De-Sir Humphreyfying the Westminster Model of Bureaucracy: A New Style of Governance. *Governance*, 3 (2): 205–214.

—— (1991) A Public Management for all Seasons? *Public Administration*, 69 (1): 3–19.

Kirkpatrick, I., S. Ackroyd and R. Walker (2005) *The New Managerialism and Public Service Professions: Change in Health, Social Services and Housing*. Basingstoke: Palgrave Macmillan.

Kitchener, M., I. Kirkpatrick and R. Whipp (2000) Supervising Professional Work under New Public Management: Evidence from an 'Invisible Trade'. *British Journal of Management*, 11 (3): 213–226.

Krause, E.A. (1996) *Death of the Guilds*. New Haven: Yale University Press.

Larson, M.S. (1977) *The Rise of Professionalism*. Berkeley: University of California Press.

Learmonth, M. and N. Harding (2006) Evidence-based Management: The Very Idea. *Public Administration*, 84 (2): 245–266.

Leicht, K.T. and M.L. Fennell (1997) The Changing Context of Professional Work. *Annual Review of Sociology*, 23: 215–231.

Lemstra, W. (1993) *De secretaris-generaal [Secretaries-General]*. Alphen aan den Rijn, the Netherlands: Samsom H.D. Tjeenk Willink.

Lively, K.J. (2001) Occupational Claims to Professionalism: The Case of Paralegals. *Symbolic Interaction*, 24 (3): 343–366.

March, J.G. and J.P. Olsen (1989) *Rediscovering Institutions*. New York: Free Press.

McKenna, C. (2006) *The World's Newest Profession*. Cambridge: Cambridge University Press.

Meyer, J. and B. Rowan (1977) Institutionalized Organizations: Formal Structure as Myth and Ceremony. *American Journal of Sociology*, 83 (2): 340–363.

Ministry of Internal Affairs (2002) *Kerncompetencies politie [Core Competencies Police]*. The Hague: Bureau LMD.

Mintzberg, H. (2004) *Managers not MBAs*. London: Financial Times Prentice Hall.

—— (2009) *Managing*. Essex: Pearson Education.

Moynihan, D.P. and P.W. Ingraham (2004) Integrative Leadership in the Public Sector. *Administration and Society*, 36 (4): 427–453.

Neal, M. and J. Morgan (2000) The Professionalization of Everyone? A Comparative Study of the Development of the Professions in the United Kingdom and Germany. *European Sociological Review*, 16 (1): 9–26.

Niessen, C.R. (2001) *Vluchten kan niet meer [Impossible to Escape]*. Inaugural address, University of Amsterdam.

Noordegraaf, M. (2006) Professional Management of Professionals: Hybrid Organisations and Professional Management in Care and Welfare. In: J.W. Duyvendak, T. Knijn and M. Kremer (eds) *Policy, People, and the New Professional*. Amsterdam: Amsterdam University Press: 181–193.

—— (2007) From Pure to Hybrid Professionalism. Present-day Professionalism in Ambiguous Public Domains. *Administration and Society*, 39 (6): 761–785.

Noordegraaf, M., and M. Van der Meulen (2008) Professional Power Play: Organizing Management in Health Care. *Public Administration*, 86 (4): 1055–1069.

Noordegraaf, M. and W. Schinkel (2011) Professional Capital Contested: A Bour-dieusian Analysis of Conflicts between Professionals and Managers. *Comparative Sociology*, 10 (1): 1–29.

Phillips, M. (2007) Midwives versus Medics. A 17th-century Professional Turf War. *Management and Organizational History*, 2 (1): 27–44.

Pollitt, C. (1993) *Managerialism and the Public Services: Cuts or Cultural Change in the 1990s?* Oxford: Blackwell.

Pollitt, C. and G. Bouckaert (2004) *Public Management Reform* (2nd edn). Oxford: Oxford University Press.

Reed, M. and P. Anthony (1992) Professionalizing Management and Managing Professionalization: British Management in the 1980s. *Journal of Management Studies*, 29 (5): 591–613.

Renou, P.M. and A.H.A. Lutters (1993) *De verander(en)de gemeentesecretaris [Changing Municipal Secretaries]*. 's-Gravenhage, the Netherlands: VGS.

Rhodes, R.A.W., P. 't Hart and M. Noordegraaf (2007) *Observing Government Elites: Up Close and Personal*. Basingstoke: Palgrave Macmillan.

Stillman, R.J. (1974) *The Rise of the City Manager*. Albuquerque, NM: University of New Mexico Press.

Terry, L.D. (1998) Administrative Leadership, Neo-Managerialism and the Public Management Movement. *Public Administration Review*, 58 (3), 194–200.

Thelen, K.A. (2004) *How Institutions Evolve*. Cambridge: Cambridge University Press.

Van der Meer, F.M. and J.C.N. Raadschelders (1999) The Senior Civil Service in The Netherlands: A Quest for Unity. In: E.C. Page and V. Wright (eds) *Bureaucratic Elites in Western European States*. Oxford: Oxford University Press: 205–228.

Van Rijn Committee (2001) *De arbeidsmarkt in de collectieve sector* [*The Labour Market in the Collective Sector*]. The Hague: Ministry of Internal Affairs.

Waring, J. and G. Currie (2009) Managing Expert Knowledge: Organizational Challenges and Managerial Futures for the UK Medical Profession. *Organization Studies*, 30 (7): 755–778.

Watson, T.J. (2002) Professions and Professionalism. *International Studies of Management and Organization*, 32 (2): 93–105.

Weick, K.E. (1995) *Sensemaking in Organizations*. Thousand Oaks, CA: Sage.

Weick, K.E., K.M. Sutcliffe and D. Obstfeld (2005) Organizing and the Process of Sensemaking. *Organization Science*, 16 (4): 409–421.

Welling, P.J. (1995) De Algemene Bestuursdienst en de moderne ambtenaar [The ABD and modern administrators]. In: M. Noordegraaf, A.B. Ringeling and F.J.M. Zwetsloot (eds) *De ambtenaar als publiek ondernemer* [*Civil servants as public entrepreneurs*]. Bussum, the Netherlands: Coutinho: 216–229.

Whitley, R. (1989) On the Nature of Managerial Tasks and Skills: Their Distinguishing Characteristics and Organization. *Journal of Management Studies*, 26 (3): 209–224.

—— (1995) Academic Knowledge and Work Jurisdiction in Management. *Organization Studies*, 16 (1): 81–105.

Wilensky, H.L. (1964) The Professionalization of Everyone? *American Journal of Sociology*, 70 (2): 137–158.

12 Concluding discussion

Paradigms and instruments of public management reform – the question of agency

Ewan Ferlie

Introduction

We will here frame the leadership debate within the broader context of narratives of higher level public services 'reforming'. This concluding chapter therefore presents a broad public management-based analysis of the current leadership wave within public services reform rather than one solely located in the growing leadership literature on public services settings which typically focuses on the nature of leadership offered, and the extent to which it can be seen as individualized or collective (e.g. Currie and Locket, 2011). By contrast, our wider focus is on the role of leadership-based approaches to public services reforming within the context of broader reform ideas. We will use this broader perspective to take an overview of the chapters contained in the book.

We will firstly recapitulate two important narratives of public sector management – the New Public Management (NPM) and the New Public Governance (NPG) paradigms – already introduced in the introduction and then pull out specific implications for agency in reforming, particularly their accounts of management and leadership activity. There have been previous attempts to compare and contrast these two reform paradigms (Paradeise *et al.*, 2009), but their implications for leadership and agency have not so far been explicitly explored. As often in social science-based analysis, there is a tension between structure- and agency-based explanations that we need to explore: what is the realistic role of agency (leadership) in public services reform, given such settings are highly institutionalized and therefore might be thought difficult to change or lead?

From the broader perspective adopted here, leadership-based approaches are but one policy instrument that may be adopted in strategies of public services reform. Governments in various countries have experimented with a number of different approaches in trying to achieve ambitious restructuring of the public services. Sometimes, that dangerous phrase 'transformational change' (as opposed to the more modest 'transactional change') has been used, at least rhetorically, by politicians and senior public sector managers, raising high expectations of reform that then need to be satisfied. The declared content of public sector reform programmes varies across countries but stated objectives often include a mix of cost containment, performance and quality improvement and greater openness to consumer influence. Besides leadership-based approaches, other available policy instruments include non-agency-centred approaches such as quasi markets and incentives, new regulatory regimes or imposing central targets. Of course, public services reform discourse may also have an undeclared, rhetorical and symbolic purpose in presenting an impression of action by government to voters, irrespective of content or stated objectives (thus successive cycles of reform by New Labour in the UK moved from market to network and then back to market; few observers noticed such contradictions and an impression of purposeful activity was produced throughout). So leadership discourse may have a rhetorical as well as a substantive function that we need to consider.

Often governments have engaged in repeated structural reorganization or 'hyper innovation' as in the UK (Moran, 2003) or Canadian health care (Denis *et al.*, 2011) as part of their reform strategy. Such approaches risk having little long-term impact: the effects of the last reorganization merely cancel out those of the penultimate one and lead to 'reorganization fatigue' and staff cynicism. Other reform strategies have had greater long-term effects, given their persistent use. Influential ideas from the NPM reform wave of the 1980s and 1990s (Hood, 1991; Ferlie *et al.*, 1996) contributed to the use of privatization, quasi markets, performance management information, incentives and strong contracts between principals and agents as core reform levers. The State downsized, but still wished to 'steer but not row' through strong contracts with providers (although whether contracts were a robust enough instrument of coordination to enable the State to retain a strategic steering role in privatized arenas is explored in the chapter by van Gestel). The instruments listed above all reinforced impersonal market-like or performance management systems forces rather than used agency-based approaches. In the UK, NPM ideas were strongly influential in the period of Conservative political control (1979–1997) and retained some remaining influence afterwards.

What are the implications of the NPM paradigm for the specific question of agency (we will consider the NPG paradigm later)? On the demand side, historically passive users of public services (and their proxies) are recast as active and choosing consumers within new quasi markets. On the supply side, NPM sought to strengthen senior managerial agency within public services organizations through its doctrine that 'management must manage'. In particular, senior general managers and non-executive members of stronger Boards were encouraging to develop directing roles, behaving more like principals (Ferlie *et al.*, 1996). This emphasis on managerial agency within NPM accounts may be because the quasi market forces developing were still too weak or contested to exert major or automatic effects on their own: these managed markets could be too managed and not market-like enough (Le Grand *et al.*, 2004) from the point of view of those who wished to see strong market effects.

The political economy of the NPM redistributed power from rank and file staff and public sector trade unions to an empowered management function recast as a modernizing elite. These senior managers were expected to implement top-down organizational restructuring, often designed to achieve major cost savings. NPM's account of managerial agency tends to be functionalist and narrowly defined in terms of using senior managerial role power to implement planned top-down restructuring. Alongside tales of heroic turnarounds led by individual managers following privatization, however, some independent studies (e.g. Pettigrew *et al.*, 1992, on the UK NHS) were already pointing to the paucity of heroic or individualized leadership and the dominance of small mixed team approaches, including professionals as well as general managers, in managing large scale change in public services organizations.

Within this broader context and perspective, various chapters can be seen as exploring the nature and impact of NPM-based reform instruments. Enders examines the specific case of the higher education, exploring the process of organizational transformation through which the traditionally 'public-ness' of universities is privatized. Typically NPM orthodox policy instruments of competition, the increased role of private financing, and new inter-sectoral organizational networks and partnerships drive this process. NPM-style changes to governance and management are an important part of this policy mix: there has been a strengthening of the corporate core of the University and an importing of techniques of strategic management from the private sector. As Enders notes:

> Academic leaders have been encouraged to become managers and to develop strategic management for their organisations. The introduction of new management tools and devices as well as the recruitment and training of more qualified management are supposed to further develop their capacity for internal governance.

But these agency-based changes sit alongside wider public management reforms, including to non-agency-based domains of financing, ownership and organizational form.

Van Gestel's chapter on the management of privatized employment services in the Netherlands also highlights NPM-based steering instruments: (i) contracts that specify performance criteria and/or process criteria, (ii) monitoring through the collection of performance-based and benchmarking information, and (iii) financial incentives, clearly related to performance. The market creation process created distinctive dynamics, notably elaborating a set of central standards to guide contract letting, which inhibited the service innovation originally desired. The market became over managed, stifling innovation and flexibility, and also threatened to erode the pursuit of public values that the State wished to retain. While there was an attempt to exercise public leadership in these privatized spaces, it was not strong enough to move private firms back from the pursuit of short-term performance gains as measured in the contract to core public values of equity and social justice. As van Gestel concludes: 'public leaders were not able to reconcile competing values within contractor relationships'.

The State no longer rowed; but it did not steer either.

Critique of the NPM and the challenge from the NPG

Major and cogent criticisms of NPM-based reforms soon emerged (Hood and Dunleavy, 1994). NPM values promoted efficiency and value for money; but eroded political accountability and led to a 'democratic deficit' as operational service delivery functions were shifted from direct political control to stand alone agencies. Core public values (such as equity and social justice) could be undermined, as van Gestel suggests. The fragmentation of the public sector into a cat's cradle of separate organizations, weakly linked by contracts, led to an erosion of systemic capacity and the centre's ability to steer. NPM reporting lines were vertical in nature so that lateral working between agencies remained weak. The challenging NPG reform narrative (Newman, 2001; Osborne, 2006, 2010) opened the door to a post-NPM shift towards: use of networks as a newly favoured governance mode, the development of high trust collaboration and social capital across organizational boundaries, the lateral rebuilding of systemic capacity in the 'fragmented state' and greater use of relational forms of contracting. Some of these ideas were adopted by UK New Labour governments (1997–2010), although ambiguously so as some core NPM ideas (such as transparency, active performance measurement and management, and greater use of private capital) proved embedded and resilient.

What are the implications of the NPG paradigm for the question of agency in public services reform? Compared to the NPM, the NPG places less emphasis on impersonal and economic modes of coordination such as quasi markets, incentives and strong contracts, and is more sociological and relational in orientation. It is less preoccupied with increasing levels of efficiency and productivity within an agency and more concerned to rebuild systemic capacity across a fragmented service delivery system. It promotes quality-led approaches to service redesign, especially on a systemic or whole patient pathway basis (such as service improvement initiatives in the UK NHS) to rebalance NPM's concern with crude input/output measures of productivity.

Newman (2001: 24) proposes that government typically here moves to an indirect, system building role: 'providing leadership, building partnerships, steering and coordinating, and providing system wide integration and regulation'. The use of the word 'leadership' is significant: there is a shift of focus from 'hard' internal management to 'soft' and broader leadership. Such leadership is concerned with the crossing of organizational and professional boundaries within polycentric network settings, so requires diplomatic and brokering skills. It may take the form of a multi disciplinary team rather than being individualized in nature. Leaders operating outside their own organization have little direct role power (unlike the NPM-style empowered CEO) but depend on the winning of influence, through reciprocity, trading and high trust behaviour or expert knowledge. Lacking pressure from quasi markets, they may instead steer change by seeking to raise organizational energy levels through providing visionary and inspirational and motivational behaviours that have the possibility to break through fixed behaviours.

Crosby *et al.*'s (2010) discussion of leadership within complex public policy arenas addresses these themes, seeing it as an important integrative resource. Using a case study of an American collaborative transportation initiative, they argue that visionary (rather than purely transactional) leaders can act to integrate diverse and fragmented public policy settings to work out sustainable solutions. Visionary leadership practices include projecting a macro energizing vision but also paying attention to political and ethical dimensions. These committed and tireless champions are seen as vital in encouraging shared sensemaking and meaning that is helping diverse stakeholders develop a shared understanding and commit to a joint solution. While they are complemented by boundary objects, boundary experiences and boundary groups in facilitating multi-stakeholder and cross-boundary collaborations, perhaps facilitated by new ICTs; the visionary model of leadership is held up as a major integrative instrument.

Both Newman (2005) and Osborne's (2006) account of the NPG suggest the State should be seen as becoming both more plural and pluralist. Significant non-state actors (such as civil society, NGOs and private firms) inhabit complex public policy networks as well as the State. Such non-state actors and polycentric networks may develop a self steering capacity and certainly it should no longer be assumed that the State retains a monopoly over steering. Indeed, from a point of view that is aligned with the value of subsidiarity or the movement of functions down to the lowest possible level, the growing capacity for non-state agents to contribute to steering may be an advantage. We will later suggest the professions also need to be conceived as important quasi autonomous social actors: at least in knowledge-based sectors, they may seek to steer the State as well as vice versa.

The major differences between the two paradigms in their treatment of agency in prescriptions for public policy reform have implications for the way in which we read the chapters in the book. Some of the chapters are clearly embedded in either of the two paradigms: for example, Contandriopoulos and Denis' analysis of political reform systems in a loosely integrated and pluralistic heath system is closely aligned to NPG categories; while van Gestel (albeit critically) works with NPM categories.

We now make some remarks about the strengths and limitations of the chapters from this broader perspective. First, what can we say about their geographical coverage? One strength is that many of the countries discussed appear to be strongly NPM influenced and have launched major public policy reform efforts: the UK has notably been influenced by both NPM and NPG ideas. This makes it easier to tie a discussion of leadership with a wider awareness of public policy reforming. Our countries are for the most part located in Northern Europe but there is also a chapter from Francophone Canada. The UK is best represented, perhaps reflecting its position as a high reform country but there is also a cluster of chapters from various Scandinavian countries and the Netherlands. Dent *et al.*'s comparative study includes Kaiser Permanente (otherwise we have little from the USA) as well as European countries. Teelken presents comparative data from Dutch, Swedish and British higher education systems. The absence of Neo Weberian States such as France and Germany is a gap (Pollitt and Bouckaert, 2004) in our comparative coverage, as is the lack of coverage of developing countries, but helps us set up a clear NPM/NPG binary to discuss.

What are the limitations of the edition? Where would we want to see more work in the future? With the exception of the chapter by Contandriopoulos and Denis on the design of the whole system of health care reform, the nature of political (as opposed to managerial or professional) leadership is an important topic which has not been fully explored here. What makes for an effective whole systems reform leader – in terms of personal skills and also the underlying system – at ministerial level? Research from regional government settings where elected representatives often take a political leadership role would be likely to explore this question more.

Secondly and methodologically, the chapters reflect their origins in the discipline of organizational studies rather than (say) social psychology or organizational economics. In terms of methods, they are typically based on personal overviews of literatures and policy texts, documentary analysis or qualitative studies, often using case study approaches, and there are no highly quantitative chapters. The underlying paradigm is more interpretative and social constructionist than positivistic.

Third, what theoretical framings are apparent in the chapters? How are the authors seeking to conceptualize their empirical analyses? The NPM vs NPG debate is influential (with a strong continuing interest in the NPM) across the edition. Other theoretical framings apparent include concepts of organizational change and inertia, including the use of an institutionalist framing to analyze resistance to management driven change. Other chapters (such as that by Jespersen) draw on the sociology of the professions' literature, drawing attention to professionalization projects and roles of and relationships between professionals (so important in many public services settings) and managers. These theoretical framings usefully connect the classic NPM literature with wider theories of organizational change and inertia and also processes of professional autonomy, dominance and now perhaps managerialization.

Fourth, the unit of analysis ranges across the chapters from the macro or system level (Contandriopoulos and Denis; Enders) where there is a strong political perspective; or even the comparative analysis of health care systems (Dent; Jespersen), down through the meso, site or locality level (Fitzgerald *et al.*) to the micro level of the individual 'leader' (Deem; Teelken). Clearly explanations, literatures and concepts vary according to which level of analysis is employed.

The substantive fields discussed include health care and higher education (each with a cluster of chapters) which are both highly professional and knowledge-based settings. We also have coverage of privatized employment services, the higher civil service and local government. There is less material on schools, social services or social work.

We now move on to consider the main thematic analyses to come out of the chapters and make some general observations.

Understanding leadership doctrines in their ideological, political and institutional contexts

As already suggested, the NPM and NPG paradigms of public services reform have distinctive implications for their treatment of agency. These two paradigms contain strong ideological elements, as would be entirely expected in normative forms of political argumentation. However, these reform narratives do not exist solely in the ideological sphere but move 'downstream', producing practical reform doctrines and tools that can be adopted by political parties and governments ideologically receptive to them. For instance, the UK New Labour governments were influenced (admittedly to an ambiguous and partial degree) by the NPG paradigm and vigorously promoted leadership development as a post-NPM policy instrument to achieve its goals of service modernization, strategic change and rebuilding systemic capacity. The UK can be seen here as an exemplar care where leadership doctrines 'fitted' with underlying post-NPM ideological and political contexts, supplying politicians with a set of practical tools.

O'Reilly and Reed explicitly link UK New Labour regimes with the promotion of 'leaderism' as a reform instrument. Their use of the term 'leaderism' suggests that the discourse should rightly be seen as containing ideological as well as technical components, They note: 'Ideologically, leadership is equated to the narratives that change is endemic; that leaders are change agents and that everyone has the potential to be a leader.' They see 'leaderism' as an evolution of NPM-style 'managerialism', mixing elements of both continuity and change. They suggest that the root difference between 'managerialism' and 'leaderism' lies in how the two concepts conceive of social coordination: for the NPM coordination is achieved through a principal agent relationship involving performance management and accountability regimes; whereas leaderism assumes a (at least potential and achievable) commonality between different agents. They note the use of leaderism as a social technology for public services reform under New Labour linked to new institutional sites (the creation of national leadership development bodies in various sectors).

Their discursive analysis of recent UK public policy texts highlights recurrent phrases (such as freedom, personalization, diversity and devolution), associated with attempts to construct 'post-bureaucratic' forms of public services. The bureaucracy–post-bureaucracy debate is a major theme in the organizational studies literature and has been well rehearsed elsewhere (Clegg *et al.*, 2011), but here the connections between the NPG narrative and post-bureaucratic ideas can be highlighted.

Picking up these general themes of the discursive and ideological role of 'leaderism', Deem's chapter specifically examines the UK higher education sector, exploring service modernization and senior team leadership development strategies under New Labour. The policy discourse in higher education similarly indicated a shift of emphasis from 'management', including promoting inspirational forms of 'leadership'. The chapter considers the role of the UK Leadership Foundation for Higher Education (LFHE, founded 2004) which ran an influential Top Management Programme (TMP) to develop aspiring university leaders and the relationship of this agency with government policy. Similar agencies were set up in other sectors such as health care and secondary education so the LFHE was part of broader policy to promote leadership development across core public services, as O'Reilly and Reed suggested. While the HE senior respondents interviewed clearly indicated they did not feel that this course was promoting government policy directly, Deem notes, 'nevertheless, there was no evidence that alternatives to the status quo were actively considered in LFHE courses'.

By way of comment on Deem's chapter, some intriguing questions arise: what was on the TMP curriculum and what was not? Which books and articles were cited and which were not? Were certain forms of 'inspirational leadership' privileged and literature on forces that 'resist strategic change', such as a highly institutionalized sector and strong professions, marginalized? Was the 'hidden curriculum' of the TMP in fact to subjectivate and skill up future senior level change agents across the sector? Did this succeed or was it resisted by course attenders? If elite production was indeed an objective of the curriculum, then perhaps policy makers were too optimistic in the effect of leadership capacity (at least in the short term) to change what remains a highly institutionalized and professionalized higher education sector – in the absence of reinforcing pressures such as an opening up to greater market forces (which only now may be happening).

Leadership patterns found in practice are often mixed, messy and mundane rather than heroic or inspirational

Contandriopoulos and Denis remind us that much existing literature on organizational reforming within the public services suggests distributed rather individualized forms of leadership operating within 'leadership constellations' (reinforced by Currie and Lockett, 2011). Fitzgerald *et al.*'s chapter on the leadership of service improvement processes in the UK NHS develops the suggestion that distributed leadership patterns are 'mixed and messy'. There are few explicit project management roles but rather a broader and looser cast of characters, including (importantly) health care professionals who may take on part time leadership roles and who represent an important source of change capacity. Boundary spanning activity in loose multi agency settings is an important capability. The chapter by Dent *et al.* reinforces the observation that distributed leadership is more likely in the health care settings studied than individualistic forms. It was a notable finding that there was little evident presence of NPM style and highly directive top managers within the set of chapters, nor of heroic or inspirational forms of leadership.

Leadership patterns are sensitive to (multiple) contexts

We now move on to consider how context(s) affect leadership profiles. McGivern *et al.* (2011) argue that conventional leadership theory neglects the extent to which organizational context affects the nature of appropriate leadership. In particular, public service settings may provide severe constraints on agency as they are strongly institutionalized fields with high levels of politicization and professionalization (we will explore the effects of this condition later): as a field, it may tend to inertia more easily than radical change. The developing literature on leadership in public services settings already explores such contextual effects (Contandriopoulos and Denis).

Several chapters suggest that leadership capacity and style is strongly context dependent. But how do they define that slippery word 'context'? Local contexts may vary even within the same overall field: Fitzgerald *et al.*'s chapter on the UK NHS found that local sites (even where they consisted of the same organizational forms such as Primary Care Trusts) strongly varied in their ability to progress mandated service improvement changes.

Sectoral contexts are a second dimension, but it should be recalled that the traditional public sector form that is important here may be undergoing evolution. The NPM movement changed this macro context with its privatization and outsourcing of services traditionally provided by the public sector. The question arises as to the effects on management and leadership capacity and style of this change in ownership mode (if indeed there are any consistent effects). Van Gestel's chapter is not optimistic concerning the influence of leadership activity in the privatized employment services in the Netherlands, noting the failed attempt by government to assert core public values (such as justice, equal treatment and general access) in these privatized arenas: 'this calls upon an active rather than a passive mode of public management'. However, government no longer had control or even effective indirect influence to exert after this NPM-style reform as the new private provider (rationally) worked to the incentives contained in the contract.

Finally, structural and historical contexts at a national level including national welfare state types, political regimes, path dependencies and long-term reform trajectories may all exert an important impact on empirically evident leadership patterns, as Dent *et al.* argue in the case of clinical leadership profiles. Such macro contextual factors broadly explained, for instance, why

Danish doctors have been less resistant to becoming involved in management roles than their UK counterparts: Danish reforms were not seen as part of an aggressive NPM-led reform wave. In terms of the incorporation of professionals within management, there was a clear spectrum found in their cases ranging from Kaiser Permanente as the most integrated to the Netherlands as the most differentiated.

Nevertheless, there may be some scope for effective action even in these institutionalized and path dependent fields, notably when action it fits well with and reinforces the underlying context (Pettigrew *et al.*, 1992; McGivern *et al.*, 2011). Some studies of public sector leaders have found empirically that they are both affected by and able to manipulate their context (Wallace and Tomlinson, 2010). For example, Newman (2005) describes how UK local government leaders packaged local initiatives to fit with national policy and their own underlying values, acting as both agents and objects of change. Currie *et al.* (2009) also suggest UK school leaders were able to creatively play with contradictory national policy pressures to enact leadership based upon their own visions, values and ethics. We need to understand more about how leaders enact contexts in practice (Pawar and Eastman, 1997; Bryman, 1992).

The distinctive nature of leadership in professionalized public services organizations

Both health care and higher education settings are highly professionalized or even characterized by the presence of multiple professions, notably in health care. They can be seen as reflecting another important dimension of context, which we explore in more detail here. What observations can be made about the nature of agency and 'leadership' in such professionalized fields? Surely there will be sharp constraints and limitations. Professionals are likely to contest the authority of general managers to impose direction and prefer to accept the authority of senior professionals or professional colleges, if they accept any authority at all. They are likely to look inwards to their own profession and may find it difficult to cross professional boundaries even into neighbouring professions. Professional colleges (such as the Royal Colleges in UK health care) can act as 'boundary police' and protect traditional professional jurisdictions. The presence of a well developed 'power/knowledge' nexus linked to a basic science base and a legitimated ability to define authoritative knowledge is another important feature of these professionalized arenas (notably medicine) so that sapiential influence from leading professionals may become as important as formal managerial role power.

One important possible implication of this analysis is that managerialization is not by itself enough to provide effective capacity for managing change in professionalized public services. Fitzgerald *et al.* emphasize the importance of drawing clinical professionals into part time managerial roles as a core component of a multi disciplinary team (which might also include a general manager). Such hybrids also need to continue to practice clinically to retain peer credibility. Leadership may come from such hybrids as least as much as from 'lay' general managers.

These highly institutionalized and professionalized fields may make agency centric approaches to public policy reform highly problematic. Jespersen's chapter explores the relationship between NPM related quality management programmes and professional autonomy and adaptation within health care fields in Denmark and Norway, drawing on the sociology of the professions literature. A classic professional closure project includes the ability to define the content and definitions of the quality of professional work. His portrait of these two health systems draws attention to their highly institutionalized nature historically, as they were highly dominated by professional bodies. Government has more recently brought in rafts of NPM reforms to act as a countervailing power; but elite segments of the medical profession retain the capacity to adapt and recapture the policy agenda.

While traditional accounts of manager/professional conflict suggest professionals would resist managerially led change and defend old working practices; newer work highlights the possibility of more nuanced dialogue, engagement and also adaptation or even the reverse colonization of originally managerial arenas. Jespersen suggests that elements of the medical scientific elite actively move into the emergent quality health policy arena through the exercise of professionally orientated leadership, helping to define the new quality standards, arguing, 'the medical professions seem to engage in policy formation and the construction of standards and quality development schemes'. The success of this reverse colonization strategy is linked to a novel 'neo-bureaucratic' governance structure in such policy arenas as quality management in health care where line management is weak and the medical power/knowledge nexus is strong.

This process of reverse colonization opens up intriguing questions about a possible two way flow of leadership. In an NPG-style system where the State is plural and pluralist, it may no longer be the only directing actor or source of leadership. External agency and leadership may be exerted from outside into public policy arenas. The question is which groups have the capacity to exert such influence: they would appear to need to be powerful, well organized and well placed to colonize public policy arenas. Here an elite subgroup (leading medical academics) drawn from the powerful profession of medicine appears to be exerting leadership upon state agencies; the question is whether a broader range of actors can succeed in such external influencing of State arenas.

The rhetorical (over) promise of leadership: more mundane and less inspirational?

O'Reilly and Reed's discussion of 'leaderism' as a managerial ideology critically traces the origins and political purpose of leadership discourse. But does it over promise when it talks of visionary-based leadership? Do actors rather use such influential discourse as a rhetorical device to claim a strategic role for themselves? Noordegraaf observes:

> The promises of leadership do not come from the competencies and skills of public leaders, but from the fact that leadership models and programmes construct an appealing, almost mythical promise. Leadership models promise the rise of competent leaders, who are able to produce results in complex circumstances. The pitfalls of leadership relate to the fact that these promises are taken too literally.

Teelken's discussion of higher education suggests that leadership rhetoric may have indeed over promised in that sector: respondents interviewed spoke of newly appointed research managers operating as transactional NPM-style managers (for example, recording indicators of research productivity including number of articles published in externally ranked journals). Such managers were in practice managing 'downwards' to survey and record academic activity rather than acting as the inspirational leaders who had been rhetorically promised and who might have been more acceptable to some respondents. She notes: 'It seems that a research manager is much more an administrator, who keeps track of the publication records, than an actual leader. However, some state that more "leadership" would be very welcome but not in its current status.'

There were some reservations about academic managers' attempts to control the primary content of the research process. Some respondents regretted the decline of the old 'upwards facing' research group leader who was skilled in building and preserving research teams over time, protecting them from negative top-down demands and external pressures. In other words, the historic – if invisible – pattern of 'real' research leadership at local level had been displaced by NPM-style performance management. Van Gestel's chapter on post-privatized employment services in the Netherlands reminds us that mundane aspects of public management – such as the renegotiation of daily working practices and inter-organizational relationships – remain as important in organizational functioning as the more heralded leadership of strategic change.

These chapters suggest the nature of agency in public services organizations may in practice be more mixed, mundane and long term than assumed in the visionary model of leadership that has been influential in the policy domain. Does agency and leadership have any substantive role at all empirically in the set of chapters? It may be taking an exaggerated position to dismiss the role of agency entirely, as Fitzgerald *et al.*'s chapter clearly found local contexts and histories important but also specified certain leadership traits, skills and knowledges, which – apparent in faster moving UK NHS sites – were found to be progressing service improvement activity: notably, personal credibility (by continuing to practice clinically in the case of professional managerial hybrids); influencing skills, persuasiveness, ability to use data, strategic and political awareness; contextual sensitivity; a formal knowledge of management and Organizational Development but combined with tacit knowledge of local organizations.

Bringing individual leaders back in: becoming a leader

The leadership discourse implies the presence of individuals willing and able to act as 'leaders'. What processes are happening at this level of the person? Both the Teelken and Deem chapters examine how leaders are constructed and construct themselves within university settings (the traditionally higher levels of autonomy enjoyed by the higher education sector may make this discussion of a particular nature). Deem's interviews with senior respondents suggested that most favoured notions of quiet distributed leadership rather than individual charismatic leadership. While many of them were engaged in major change exercises, they tended to reject the role of 'change agents' being assigned to them, seeing it as over aligned with a government agenda about which they retained some scepticism.

Teelken examines the importation of more clearly defined leadership roles into the higher education sector within a comparative European study. She examined respondents' changing perceptions of themselves and their more powerful managers as these roles changed. In practice, it appeared that these stronger hierarchical roles were being enacted in a narrowly managerial way rather than a leadership-based manner. While there was resentment about greater management scrutiny (for example, attempts to assess research productivity or teaching quality explicitly), there was also a sense that there was little that management could do to force changes in academic behaviour, at least in relation to tenured academic staff. In neither chapter, significantly, was the notion of a transformational academic change agent embraced.

Concluding discussion

Overall, the chapters tell against the widespread application of transformational models of individualized and heroic leadership that have appeared so influential in the public policy domain. Such models in our view contain more pitfalls than promise. They also need to be seen in their political and ideological context, as O'Reilly and Reed rightly remind us, and so are not purely neutral techniques. The chapters rather confirm a pattern of team-based and distributed leadership, especially in such multi professionalized settings as health care. The underlying patterning of professionals' and managers' roles and relationships comes up consistently as a key factor: so the internal dynamics of the public services professions themselves have to be accorded attention. Drawing professionals into leadership roles may be seen as an important process in its own right. So our overall interpretation is one of caution in relation to the visionary models of transformational leadership. Public services fields remain highly institutionalized and as such are highly resistant to the short-term exercise of attempted transformational leadership.

Nevertheless, there is (more positively) evidence from this collection that more subtle and enduring forms of collective agency can help ensure organizational change/reforms are implemented, become embedded and institutionalized. This form of leadership is mixed, messy and at times mundane, also reflecting local context and histories (Contandriopoulos and Denis, Dent *et al.*). A local receptive context (Fitzgerald *et al.*) – which displays a pre-existing pattern of sound inter-relationships – lays structural foundations that fit with and reinforce these lower key approaches to leadership so that structure and agency mesh. Leadership here is grounded in networks/sets of distributed relationships that cross agency and professional boundaries.

We conclude that leadership-based approaches to public policy reform are just one policy instrument among many and that influential but highly subjectivist notions of visionary 'leadership' may not be strong enough to overcome the operation of objective interests, strong professions and institutionalized fields. One implication for policy reformers is that if leadership-based approaches are to have major effects, they may need to be reinforced by other policies that act to deinstitutionalize highly institutionalized fields by, for example, providing for more ready market entry and exit. Nevertheless as one element of agency within the NPM and especially the NPG paradigm, leadership-based approaches should not be entirely overlooked or dismissed. The NPG's emphasis on collaboration and networks, for instance, suggests that the presence of lateral, boundary spanning forms of influence-based leadership may be an important underpinning process that enables these new organizational forms to consolidate.

Much of the literature to date has romantically emphasized the heroic qualities of transformational leadership, but this collection demonstrates that bringing about sustainable change in public sector organizations requires much more than the presence of a rhetorical champion. This is because these remain highly institutionalized fields with objectively existing, entrenched and influential interest groups and lobbies that tend to resist (perhaps rather successfully) radical and externally driven change. We conclude that leadership-based approaches may be one helpful approach to public sector organizational change but need to be used in conjunction with other policy levers and are unlikely to have short-term or dramatic effects. Their effects appear to be messier, more mundane and longer term in nature than the inspirational and heroic rhetoric that is both too apparent and too influential.

References

Bryman, A. (1992) *Charisma and Leadership in Organizations*, London: Sage.

Clegg, S., Harris, M. and Hopfl, H. (2011) *Managing Modernity: Beyond Bureaucracy?*, Oxford: Oxford University Press.

Crosby, B., Bryson, J.M. and Stone, M.M. (2010) Leading Across Frontiers: How Visionary Leaders Integrate People, Processes, Structures and Resources, in Osborne, S. (ed.) *The New Public Governance?*, London: Routledge: 200–222.

Currie, G. and Lockett, A. (2011) Distributing Leadership in Health and Social Care: Concertive, Conjoint or Collective?, *International Journal of Management Reviews*, 13(3): 286–300.

Currie, G., Lockett, A. and Suhomlinova, O. (2009) Leadership and Institutional Change in the Public Sector: The Case of Secondary Schools in England, *Leadership Quarterly*, 20: 604–616.

Denis, J.-L., Davies, H., Ferlie, E. and Fitzgerald, L. (2011) *Assessing Initiatives to Transform Healthcare Systems: Lessons for the Canadian Healthcare System*, CHSRF Series on Healthcare Transformation, Paper 1, Ottowa, ON: Canadian Health Services Research Foundation. Available at www.chsrf.ca/Libraries/Commissioned_Research_Reports/JLD_REPORT.sflb.ashx (accessed 20 January 2012).

Ferlie, E., Ashburner, L., Fitzgerald, L. and Pettigrew, A. (1996) *The New Public Management in Action*, Oxford: Oxford University Press.

Hood, C. (1991) A Public Management for All Seasons?, *Public Administration*, 69 (Spring): 3–19.

Hood, C. and Dunleavy, P.J. (1994) From Old Public Administration to New Public Management?, *Public Money and Management*, 14(3): 9–16.

Le Grand, J., Mays, N. and Dixon, J. (2004) The Reforms: Success or Failure or Neither?, in Clarke, A., Allen, P., Anderson, S., Black, N. and Fulop, N. (eds) *Studying the Organisation and Delivery of Health Services: A Reader*, London: Routledge: 286–294.

McGivern, G., Ferlie, E. and Fitzgerald, L. (2011) Leadership in Health Care Networks: (Re)Framing Context Through a Governmentality Project, working paper given at the Organizational Studies Summer Workshop, 'Bringing Public Organizations and Organizing Back In', 25–28 May, Abbaye des Vaux de Cernay, Paris, France.

Moran, M. (2003) *The British Regulatory State: High Modernism and Hyper Innovation*, Oxford: Oxford University Press.

Newman, J. (2001) *Modernising Governance*, London: Sage.

—— (2005) Enter the Transformational Leader: Network Governance and the Micro Politics of Modernisation, *Sociology*, 39(4): 717–734.

Osborne, S. (2006) The New Public Governance, *Public Management Review*, 8(3): 377–387.

—— (ed.) (2010) *The New Public Governance?* London: Routledge.

Paradeise, C., Reale, E., Blieklie, I. and Ferlie, E. (eds) (2009) *University Governance: Western European Comparative Perspectives*, Dordrecht, the Netherlands: Springer.

Pawar, S. and Eastman, K. (1997) The Nature and Implications of Contextual Influences on Transformational Leadership: A Conceptual Examination, *Academy of Management Review*, 12: 80–109.

Pettigrew, A., Ferlie, E. and McKee, L. (1992) *Shaping Strategic Change*, London: Sage.

Pollitt, C. and Bouckaert, G. (2004) *Public Management Reform: A Comparative Analysis* (2nd edn), Oxford: Oxford University Press.

Wallace, M. and Tomlinson, M. (2010) Contextualising Leader Dynamics, *Leadership*, 6: 21–45.

Index